IDEALS
AND
IDOLS

E. H. Gombrich

IDEALS
AND
IDOLS

Essays on values in history and in art

Phaidon · Oxford

Phaidon Press Limited, Littlegate House, St Ebbe's Street, Oxford
Published in the United States of America by E. P. Dutton, New York
First published in volume form 1979
This edition © 1979 by Phaidon Press Limited

British Library Cataloguing in Publication Data

Gombrich, *Sir* Ernst Hans
    Ideals and idols.
    1. Arts   2. Values
    I. Title
    700'.1   NX65

    ISBN 0–7148–2009–1

Printed in Great Britain by Butler & Tanner Limited, Frome and London

CONTENTS

Preface   7

VALUES IN HISTORY

The Tradition of General Knowledge   9

In Search of Cultural History   24

The Logic of Vanity Fair: Alternatives to Historicism
  in the Study of Fashions, Style and Taste   60

Myth and Reality in German Wartime Broadcasts   93

Research in the Humanities: Ideals and Idols   112

VALUES IN ART

Art and Self-Transcendence   123

Art History and the Social Sciences   131

Canons and Values in the Visual Arts: A Correspondence
  with Quentin Bell   167

A Plea for Pluralism   184

The Museum: Past, Present and Future   189

Reason and Feeling in the Study of Art   205

Notes   209

Bibliographical Note   219

Sources of Photographs   220

Index   221

PREFACE

The titles of the four previous volumes of my collected essays published by the Phaidon Press—*Meditations on a Hobby Horse* (1963), *Norm and Form* (1966), *Symbolic Images* (1972), and *The Heritage of Apelles* (1976)—were derived from the title of one of the papers included. For this collection I have chosen the subtitle of an article on *Research in the Humanities*. I there alluded to the opinion of Francis Bacon that the growth of knowledge was impeded by the worship of false gods, the cult of certain idols. In the eyes of Bacon even ideals were such idols, for they compromised the necessary neutrality of the enquiring mind. The essays in this volume present a different point of view, but I would not want it to be confused with the fashionable demand for 'commitment' and the call for 'relevance'. Ideals can indeed be perverted into idols if they are elevated out of reach of critical debate. But if dogmatic rigidity will paralyse the search for truth, so will the absence of any scale of values. It is a question of tact rather than of principle that we often prefer these values to remain implicit in our choice of topic, our method and our presentation, instead of being spelt out. We want the critic to ask 'what has he found out?' rather than 'where does he stand?'

And yet there are moments in the life of an academic when he feels prompted to get up from his University Chair and mount the pulpit. This happens when he is honoured by the daunting invitation to succeed a number of eminent speakers in giving a lecture which has been founded for the discussion of wider issues. Thus I stepped out of my customary field in the Creighton Lecture of the University of London on *Myth and Reality in German Wartime Broadcasts*. I mention it first because this choice may offer a key to the other lectures and essays. Having witnessed such evil creeds and horrible deeds (and not only in the comparatively distant past), I cannot understand how values can so often be regarded as impurities of which our research should be purged. In my Deneke Lecture at Lady Margaret Hall, Oxford, *In Search of Cultural History* (given earlier), I attempted to explain why my rejection of Hegel's philosophy of history and its false values need not cripple our interpretation of culture; in the Romanes Lecture at Oxford, *Art History and the Social Sciences*, I argued that the all too popular philosophy of cultural relativism could only lead to the demise of the humanities.

There were earlier and later assignments which offered the temptation to elaborate other facets of these convictions. The 'Oration' to the London

School of Economics and Political Science on *The Idea of General Knowledge* explores the link between shared knowledge and shared values, the 'Address' I was asked to deliver to a distinguished assembly of Museum people at Ditchley Park on *The Museum: Past, Present and Future* questions a purely didactic orientation, and when I had the great good fortune of receiving the Erasmus Prize in Holland, temptation turned into duty, for tradition required me to respond with a brief 'profession of faith', which turns on the mutual share of *Reason and Feeling in the Study of Art*.

To the words spoken on these occasions I have added in this volume contributions to philosophical debates on fundamental questions of value. These were at stake, explicitly, in a symposium on *The Place of Value in a World of Fact* organized by the Nobel Foundation in Stockholm, where I spoke on *Art and Self-Transcendence*, and implicitly in the two volumes of the Library of Living Philosophers dedicated to *The Philosophy of Karl Popper*, who has done so much to elucidate these problems and for which I wrote *The Logic of Vanity Fair: Alternatives to Historicism in the Study of Fashions, Style and Taste*.

I have also included my answers to slightly more parochial enquiries about topical academic issues. The paper on *Research in the Humanities*, mentioned above, was a contribution to a number of *Daedalus*, the Journal of the American Academy of Arts and Sciences, devoted to *The Search for Knowledge*, and *A Plea for Pluralism* was written in reply to a question on the state of art history put by the *American Art Journal* to a number of art historians. My correspondence with Professor Quentin Bell on *Canons and Values* was prompted by his reaction to my Romanes Lecture. I am immensely grateful to him for allowing me to reprint it here, for, in a sense, its theme is the theme of the whole volume.

London, May 1979   E. H. G.

VALUES IN HISTORY

The Tradition of General Knowledge

IN ONE OF Agatha Christie's detective stories the murderess turns up at a fashionable luncheon party at Claridge's, dressed up as her victim, whose death, of course, she wants to conceal as long as possible. At first, all goes well for her wicked plans, for she is an accomplished impersonator; but she has neglected one thing which is apparently needed for success at Claridge's, her classical education. Somebody of that select company mentions the Judgement of Paris, the sadly unsuccessful attempt at arbitration that led to the Trojan War. 'The Judgement of Paris?' asks the murderess in her melodious voice. 'Why, Paris does not cut any ice nowadays. It is London and New York that count.'

'It was an awkward moment,' says the narrator. The neighbour on the right drew in his breath sharply, while another guest began to talk violently about Russian opera. But listen to the Duke's reaction. 'His lips were drawn tightly together, he had flushed and it seemed he drew slightly away from the speaker ...' You will not be surprised that this dreadful *gaffe* ultimately leads to the detection of the crime and the undoing of the criminal. She had given herself away.

The episode stuck in my mind, because my years at the Warburg Institute have alerted me to the changing context of the classical tradition. If our librarian had sufficient funds left at the end of this quinquennium to buy a Penguin book, he would certainly put 'Lord Edgeware Dies' on our shelves. I trust the little story exempts me from the awkward need to define what I mean by general knowledge. It is quite clear even from Agatha Christie's brief account, is it not, that general knowledge is knowledge that is not general? It is only supposed to be general among a certain class of people.

You see, like Mark Antony, I have come to bury Caesar, not to praise him; and like Mark Antony, I have ulterior motives. I believe that this tradition of general knowledge is fading away. I don't think that there are many luncheon parties where the Judgement of Paris is mentioned across the table,

Oration delivered at the London School of Economics and Political Science on 8 December 1961.

and fewer still where admission of ignorance of that old story would cause
ladies to talk of Russian opera and dukes to frown. This is a good riddance.
For there were two characteristics of this social convention which nobody
would like to call back. One is the obvious temptation to snobbish intolerance
towards those who do not share a particular piece of information and, as a
corollary, the resentment of those who feel themselves snubbed. The situation
at Claridge's would probably be described by an anthropologist as a clash
between in-groups and out-groups. Not to know about that classical myth
excluded you from a self-appointed élite. Unfortunately, it is likely that even
with this dubious touchstone gone, society will keep inventing new signs and
symbols with which to maintain the barriers of snobbishness. And the possession of knowledge is not, after all, a worse touchstone than the possession
of more tangible status symbols such as cars, yachts, or Impressionist paintings. Indeed, if we must have social hierarchies and a pecking order, the test
of general knowledge as a passport to the upper strata is surely preferable
to the test of birth, wealth, or an 'Oxford accent'.

What is more worrying in the idea of general knowledge is its temptation
to hypocrisy and superficiality. Those who used to be afraid of frowning dukes
were led to countless degrading little lies whenever an item came up which
they feared they ought to know. If the admission of ignorance leads to loss
of caste and loss of face, people are afraid of asking. Yet how refreshing would
it be to hear a person ask 'But what is the Judgement of Paris?' It is at such
moments of truth, alas, still all too rare on this ancient continent, that one
discovers that so-called general knowledge is not only not general but also
not really knowledge. In which of the Greek poets do we read the full story?
Actually in none, at least none of the classical age which are extant. This
fact I did not know before I looked it up. My knowledge about the Judgement
of Paris comes mainly from hearsay. I must have read some potted version
of Greek legends as a boy, but I would not regard it as general knowledge
had I not picked it up again from stray references and from the works of
many artists who enjoyed the opportunity of rendering a beauty contest
among three Goddesses, as Rubens did in his marvellous canvas in the
National Gallery. I think we should admit that most general knowledge is
hearsay knowledge of this kind. There would be nothing reprehensible in
this if it did not tend to give outsiders a totally different impression. We all
know the visitors to our libraries who ask in an awestruck tone: have you
read all these books? and we have to confess that we bought some not to
read but to use, and the others in the fond hope that the time would come
when we could read them at last. But those who are used to libraries do not
have to have this explained, and those who are used to the tradition of general

knowledge take it for what it is, a cloud of rumours about a miscellany of things. Nobody who calls an act quixotic or compares a scene with Dante's Inferno wants to imply that he has read Cervantes or studied the *Divine Comedy*. He simply uses a common coin which he knows to be current. I think we can now see why His Grace the Duke suffered so severely when his luncheon companion failed to recognize the reference. I suggest that his sufferings were due less to snobbery than to a breakdown of communications. You do not have to be a Duke to feel embarrassed if your partner responds, let us say, to a reference to 'sour grapes' with a lecture on the glucose content of fruit. Aesop's little fable of the fox provides such a convenient shorthand formula to characterize a human situation. What a bore it would be to have to explain it all. I venture to think that unnecessary heat has been generated by the simple fact that all cultures rest on some common stock of knowledge, which those who share it can draw upon at will. If you say 'that girl with the Mona Lisa smile' you are scarcely out to impress anyone. You just hope that your partner will know the kind of smile and spot the girl. And if you call somebody a catalyst you equally hope that even non-chemists will understand that you mean a kind of person who brings people together without appearing to be active himself. Clearly all living language is shot through with innumerable such references, hidden or overt, which pre-suppose some sharing of knowledge, some hearsay in the literal sense of the word.

Perhaps it is only those of us who have had to change from one language to another who fully realize the relevance of such shared knowledge. Who could hope to understand a parliamentary debate in this country if he has no inkling of *Alice in Wonderland* or fails to catch references to 'jam tomorrow', to Humpty Dumpty's way with words or to the Red Queen? And how can we fail to feel outsiders when our friends and colleagues talk in cricket terms, of sticky wickets, innings, and hitting for six? If you will allow me to introduce one innocuous technical term, I'd describe such fields of common knowledge as 'sources of metaphor'.

Every culture, of course, has these favoured sources of metaphor which facilitate communication among its members and which, by the way, present such a headache to the translator. Common customs, trades, and, of course, the legends and beliefs of the tribe are fused with the language and modes of thought of any civilization. How can we understand the metaphors of Indian poetry and literature without knowing what the cow means to the Indian villager in his life and in his worship? Or how can we understand Islamic culture without sharing some knowledge of the Koran? For religion provides most cultures with a central area of metaphor. The Olympus or heaven of any nation will offer symbols of power and of compassion, of good and of evil, of menace and consolation, and such is the vitality of these symbols that they will survive the decline of faith. Where would European poetry be without Venus and Mars, Cupid's dart and Jove's thunderbolt and even, occasionally, the Judgement of Paris?

> When Priam's sonne in midst of Ida plaine
> Gave one the price, and other two the foile,
> If she for whom I still abide in paine
> Had lived then within the Troyan soile,
> No doubt but hers had bene the golden ball,
> Helen had scaped rape, and Troy his fall ...
>
> Thomas Watson, *Hekatompathia*, XXXIII.
> London, 1582.

Not all our poetry is as studded with such references as that of the Elizabethan sonneteers. But I still wonder whether we ever can give sufficient credit to those members of other cultures who decide to master our traditions. It must be as hard for a Chinese student to sort out these vanished divinities as it is for us to catch the references to good and bad Emperors that are woven into the fabric of Chinese literature. Of course I do not claim that these obstacles are quite insurmountable. One can try to understand these allusions as one can try to learn a foreign language. I may have come intellectually a little closer than I was twenty-five years ago to understanding what cricket means to my English friends. Thanks to my son I may even be able to catch an allusion to W. G. Grace and his beard or to *Wisden's Almanack*. But I do not deceive myself. I could never learn to catch a cricket ball, and I could not respond to these allusions as one does to something one has known from childhood. To catch the ball or the real import of the allusion you must have assimilated the game into your flesh and blood. You must have grown into it so that it becomes part of your nature.

As you know, what might be called old-fashioned education emphasized the assimilation of knowledge rather than its acquisition. It is no accident, I believe, that this tradition stems from classical civilization with its tremendous emphasis on rhetoric, the mastery of language. Education was articulation; and the most articulate person was the one who had assimilated all the sources of metaphor with which to touch the chords of shared memories.

Our culture sets much less store by oratory. If it did I would certainly not have been honoured by the invitation to deliver an oration. And so, with this central purpose of assimilated knowledge gone, the question of what any person ought to learn and ought to know, what should or should not belong to general knowledge, became in one sense more worrying and in another less clear. Not that this dispute among disciplines is a new thing in education. It was in itself a favourite topic of the schools of oratory; you had to sharpen your wits by proving that medicine was more important than law or law more important than medicine, that the Quadrivium founded on mathematics imparted higher knowledge than the Trivium founded on language, or that language alone made human beings truly human. Not all of those who engage in these conflicts today know of their venerable ancestry. If they did, they would realize also, I believe, how inconclusive are the arguments from relevance and usefulness. Any piece of information, after all, can conceivably be important for something or somebody; but if that were the criterion for including it in the syllabus, the most important textbook would be the telephone directory. It certainly would not be a soft option. But though you could make your students learn it, I doubt if they could assimilate it. It could scarcely become part of their language, a source of metaphor shared by a culture.

It is easy to see and easier to say that language is not everything. A society where everybody could only talk and nobody do would not survive a day. But a society without the assimilation of general knowledge, starting from language and reaching out into the sources of metaphor, would cease to be a society. I shall not waste your time by labouring this point, for nobody thinks that this can ever happen.

Last year, I believe, my very illustrious predecessor Sir Geoffrey Crowther made your flesh creep by warning you of the dire consequences that would overtake us if more know-how in science was not spread sufficiently fast. I have no ambition to compete with him. If the tradition of general knowledge should break, you need not worry that it will hurt. Here ignorance really is bliss, for we certainly cannot miss what we never knew. Our distinctions would become a little cruder and our articulation more coarse-grained but our language would still serve us, as it has served those millions who were never in touch with these sources of metaphor.

But surely language and metaphor are not only of use, like the telephone-book, to communicate with others. They also help us to articulate and interpret our own world of experience to ourselves and it is here that the shrinking of these sources would ultimately affect us.

If we can believe the psychoanalysts—and here I am sure we can—our first sources of metaphor in this widest sense of the term spring from the earliest experience of our family situation. Mother and father provide for us the emotional models for all the clusters of feeling that go with motherly love or paternal authority. We learn to order and categorize our world of experience along those lines. Soon fresh experiences will provide fresh areas of comparison of a private nature: the toy-cupboard, the world of animals, fairy tales, and of course religion. For the growing child, the teachers at school quite frequently provide an additional range of models and types—and many of them would be surprised if they knew how the child's imagination transforms them into gods, daemons, and devils. Watch the conversation of schoolchildren and mark how much of it centres on the character, foibles and charms of their teachers. It is these common references, this shared knowledge, which welds the class together into a little sub-culture. Needless to say, there are other things which groups of adolescents share in our civilization. Television, radio and cinema provide a whole Olympus of stars and starlets, and those who are excluded by poverty or snobbery are soon made to feel outsiders. It is as embarrassing to those who share this culture to have to spell out an allusion to Cliff Richard (whose name I learned for the purpose of this oration), as it is to others to explain what is meant by the Mona Lisa smile. Everyday speech has become interlaced with phrases and catchwords from popular radio shows which for the habitué evoke a whole chain of associations and are forgotten tomorrow.

I do not think that this kaleidoscopic change of the area of reference is confined to radio and television addicts. Highbrows no less than lowbrows are constantly bombarded with insinuations that they must—or must not—know or read or take up this or that craze if they want to gain entry into some élite. I suspect indeed that some of our Sunday papers and our weeklies cater quite consciously for us busy people who want to have the feeling that though we have no time for reading or even for thinking, we remain in touch with the culture, all of whose members, in theory at least, might be sustained by the same papers in the same comforting illusion.

I am afraid, though, that there is still a difference between being in the swim and being in the culture: it is the same difference as between jargon and language. It is in this context that I can at least advertise my wares with some confidence. I must confess that I find many reasons given for a classical education unconvincing. I do not see, for instance, why the study of Greek and Latin should train the mind more effectively than would an equally intensive study of Chinese. The reason why people in our civilization should always have the possibility of studying the classics is, quite simply, that people in our past cultivated the classics. For in the classical heritage we have an area of metaphor, a common market of symbols and ideas that transcends the boundaries of both nations and periods in a way national literature never can. The Germans, for instance, are proud of having naturalized Shakespeare into their culture and *Hamlet* or *Lear* certainly do belong to general knowledge in German-speaking lands. But Jane Austen has not been admitted into that company. Proust, on the other hand, has been naturalized in England, but Goethe, who towers over the Olympus of German *Bildung*, is little known in the Anglo-Saxon world. It was different with the classics, at least up to a generation ago. They had become so profoundly assimilated into the tradition of general knowledge that they were not only less than general and less than knowledge, but also, in a curious way, more than knowledge and also more than general.

To pass from those psychological models of parents and teachers, and from the heroes of the hour, to less private and more universal symbols was to gain contact with the problems that helped to shape our civilization. Athenians and Spartans were to the growing mind not only names of peoples long dead, but also permanent possibilities interpreting the life and duties of man. To learn to hate the Spartans with their beastly ideals was an education in itself—all the more so since this education had to be gained in the teeth of our educators who never tired of extolling the noble virtues of these toughs.

In this way the Lycurgus of Plutarch, the Pericles of Thucydides, the Cato of Cicero have challenged the imagination of many generations to choose between different images of parental authority. Even today, our living language still carries the traces of these preoccupations: Draconian laws, Stoic endurance, Epicurean living, cynical indifference are not only allusions to be used or dropped at will, they are road signs erected at important crossroads. It is true, of course, that when we follow them we may find, for instance, the Epicurus was rather stoical and that many Stoics were rather epicurean. But do not these discoveries alert us to distrust hearsay? The fact that these names have become metaphors, that they stand for whole areas of experience, provides a stimulus to learn more about them. I believe that nearly all worthwhile research in the humanities owes its impulse to these still living forces in our culture. If I may take an example from an eminent member of this School, Karl Popper's criticism of Plato was such a revision, the realization that the political ideas Plato stood for in the pantheon of our culture were less beneficial than we had come to believe. By now it may have become general knowledge among the readers of weeklies that Popper is the anti-Plato. Those who follow this road sign and read his works will also have to revise that stereotype. Anybody deserving the name of a student must learn to mistrust what passes as general knowledge.

Yet our Olympus is not only populated by political father-figures. It merges into Parnassus, where artists survive in our tradition as lasting embodiments of human greatness, its triumphs and temptations. Michelangelo and

Raphael, Rubens and Rembrandt, Van Gogh and Cézanne are not only objects of art-historical study or investments or status symbols for collectors. They are centres of attraction and repulsion to be loved, admired, criticized or rejected, living forces with which we get involved. They are culture heroes, Gods of our secular Pantheon, beneficent or baleful, serene or capricious, but like Gods they must be approached with respect and humility for they can light up for us whole areas of the mind which would have been dark without them.

Take Raphael, now rather a remote deity in our Pantheon, but one whose name was once almost a synonym for divine beauty. To study him in the context of our culture is not only to study a historical figure but to examine our own relation to ideal beauty. I am very anxious not to be misunderstood here. I do not want to give my own field a bad name by suggesting that the study of art is necessarily more subjective than a study of scientific problems. There are rigid objective standards which the historian has to respect when he interprets texts and evaluates the authenticity of paintings. What is and must be subjective is the discovery of relevance. The Latin orators had a word for it; it was 'tua res agitur' which the modern advertising agent would probably translate as 'this is about you!' The study of Raphael, I suggest, is still about us. The stocks of beauty have fallen considerably during the last 150 years or so, for beauty has become suspected of dishonesty. The very name of the pre-Raphaelite movement was a declaration of war against an element in our culture and indeed an element in our religion, taking the word in its widest sense. By looking again at Raphael, we are led to examine the justification of this revolt in its turn.

How close must beauty lie to sentimentality? How far was the devotional trash of Victorian oleographs inherent, as a dangerous possibility, in some of Raphael's Madonnas? Personally, I have come to the conclusion that the revolt against Raphael missed its mark. The more I study him, particularly in his drawings, the more I come to admire his genius and the less does his art resemble the stereotype of hollow beauty. I have come to suspect that he is less easy to understand than Michelangelo, whose tremendous images take us by storm. The relationship is somewhat similar to that of Mozart and Beethoven, though Mozart's beauty does not need any defenders now, as it did during the Wagnerian era when many dismissed him as shallow because they had never fathomed his depth.

Thanks, perhaps, to the radio and the long-playing record, music has become the most precious of all shared possessions, of all sources of metaphor in our culture. Indeed, if there is anything that belies the modish talk of two cultures, it is the sight of any crowded concert hall. I have never noticed that scientists, engineers, or medical men cared less for this common possession than students of language and literature.

But not everybody is musical, and whether or not you are, you might get a lot out of other elements of our common heritage; a heritage that seems to be receding from our grasp as so many bridges to the past become impassable. It is for this reason that I deplore the fading of the tradition of general knowledge. Granted that it was no more than a cloud of rumours, often false or misleading; even hearsay has its value if it gives you news of something you might enjoy. Life is short and no one could ever follow up a fraction of those cues which the language of our tribe threw in our path. One day, I may really read *Don Quixote* or learn about the mystery of catalysts.

How can we make sure that these rumours and these possibilities continue to reach the next generation? Should we, at the university, give courses in General Knowledge?

Many colleagues advocate such courses under the name of General Studies, Surveys of Western Civilization or the History of Ideas. But though we all follow these experiments in the new universities and abroad with interest, many of us have still to be converted. Among most of my friends the word 'survey course' is still a dirty word. Having once written a survey of the history of art, I am barred from joining in these denunciations; but I may confess that I am also a bit sceptical, though not quite for the same reasons. What is usually alleged against these attempts is the sin of superficiality. We, it is said, want to teach the student a discipline, we want to build character by making him study a small area in depth. A smattering of this or that may have been good enough for finishing schools preparing for Claridge's; it has no place in the universities.

I hold no particular brief for finishing schools nor, as you know, for Claridge's, but I think this anti-snobbish attitude is tinged with snobbism. Go into any Senior Common Room and hear these same dons who champion specialization groan about some undergraduate who did not know whether the Greeks came before the Romans or when the Reformation happened.

The truth is that it was always a minority that had the unfair advantage of picking up this hearsay knowledge early in life, by actually hearing these things said during conversations at home, or by freely rummaging among their parents' books. By the time they arrived at the university they were aware of some of the landmarks on the traditional map of knowledge, they knew where they were and where they wanted most to go. It may well have made sense to submit these growing minds to a so-called discipline, to make them explore one area as thoroughly as their time permitted. It is a great comfort to acquire one small allotment in the vastness of the knowable where one feels a little more at home. Yet even this acquisition holds its dangers for the less intelligent. The more they hear about the contrast between a study in depth, which is a good thing, and superficial surveys, which are a bad thing, the more easily they may jump to the conclusion that they, at any rate, are now Masters of Arts. They forget to ask how deep this depth is anyway. Do we measure it in relation to what is knowable or to what is worth knowing? After all, our knowledge is always superficial. Whether we deal with a century in one page or in 5,000 pages, the relation to the infinitude of events is scarcely affected.

With all its imperfections, its social dangers and its temptations, the tradition of general knowledge at least kept alive the feeling that there was so much you did not know and ought to learn about; it constantly bombarded you with reminders that there were more classics to be read, more countries to be visited, more scientific theories to be grasped, more languages to be learned than you could hope to assimilate in a lifetime.

We must not snobbishly ignore the fact that increasing numbers of eager and impressionable young people now arrive at the universities who have had no opportunities of hearing these rumours and of forming ideas of these distant landmarks. Yet we propose to let these, too, learn just one square mile of knowledge to some degree of perfection during the three years' work for their B.A. Honours and possibly make them do ten square yards of micro-surveying within this plot for a Ph.D., to see them emerge from six years of successful grind with their character trained, and their minds closed. They may even be asked to teach in their turn without ever having seen a map of the whole country, let alone having crossed the frontiers. It is not all that easy, within our universities, to get permission to do so, as you know. Our students, at least here in London, are not even expected to stray into lectures outside their courses and those who want to change fields, as it is called, after their B.A., encounter further hurdles put up by our Boards of Studies in the form of so-called qualifying examinations to keep them, if possible, on the straight road. I should give such deviants a special bonus; but that is not a proposal likely to go through.

I know that I am neither the first, nor will I be the last, to bemoan the evils of specialization, but I may have explained the reason why I take an even more serious view of this state of affairs than do some of my colleagues. I do not claim to know how this situation affects economics or science; but the humanities certainly draw their strength, their nourishment and their *raison d'être* from the traditions and general concerns of the culture. To cut them off from these traditions is to kill them. One wonders, of course, how widely their death would be deplored.

But I am afraid their death may even be hastened if we concede to the tradition of general knowledge some place in the university curriculum. It could not survive the icy blast of the examination system. It is true that I read in last week's *Observer* that (I quote) 'General studies are *examinable* just as are the subjects of special studies.' What a word and what a commendation. The telephone directory may be examinable. Our involvement with our heritage is not. Imagine a question: 'Compare and contrast Raphael with Mozart and Beethoven with Michelangelo (as metaphors).' These are things you can talk about with like-minded friends late at night after a concert or a visit to a gallery. To make these private reactions the subject of examinations is to kill them for good.

No, I am afraid that, as long as the universities are identified in the public mind not with the passing on of traditions, but with the passing of examinations, those who have these traditions at heart must defend them against bureaucratization. I realize that this increasing bureaucratization of learning and scholarship has come about from the most admirable motives. The desire for examinable knowledge springs from the tradition of fairness to all, from the demand that justice should not only be done but be seen to be done. But unless we look out, this demand, backed as it is by a wonderful system of grants, may turn our academic institutions into a counterpart of the National Egg Marketing Board where eggheads are graded and stamped for the convenience of prospective purchasers. Far be it from me to question the reliability of our sister institution which, I believe, receives the same share of the national income as does higher education. They grade eggs according to size, and though it would be interesting to speculate whether this means height, girth or weight, I am sure they will know exactly by what criteria they have to sort their product. Who would not envy them their simple task? Having wielded the stamp myself, I confess to being increasingly perplexed as to how to plot such incommensurable qualities as originality and industry along one single co-ordinate or dimension, and declare first the paper and then the total result to be 53 or 57 out of 100. Most of us who are asked to play this game are agreed that it operates with fictions, particularly along that all-important zone of middling performance that divides the upper from the lower second. And yet it is here that our university places the all-decisive distinction between good eggs and bad eggs, the first to be used for hatching, the others, at best, for cooking.

However, I must not digress. Though I do not want the tradition of general knowledge to be caught in the sausage machine (radically to change the metaphor), I do think that our universities should not necessarily prevent the spread of general knowledge. I am afraid we are on the way to doing precisely this. I do not claim to be original in these strictures either; it has all been said often, and better than I could. It is bad enough that the importance attached to examination marks leaves the conscientious student no choice but to swot and memorize examinable knowledge. It is perhaps worse that our own dissatisfaction with the system of specialization so easily tempts us to overload the syllabus more and more till the undergraduates have to rush from course to course without a moment's time for reflection. I am sure that our first duty to the student is to resist this obvious temptation. We must protect him from all the clamouring bidders for his attention who want to save the idea of general knowledge by making the arts student attend courses on catalysts and the science student courses on the Judgement of Paris. What can be saved of this old tradition can only be saved by leaving the student more time to educate himself, more time to read rather than skim and skip, time to assimilate rather than acquire knowledge, to roam the country round his allotted field, to make his own discoveries and to enjoy looking down on it from a neighbouring peak without expecting a diploma in mountaineering to satisfy the bureaucrats that their grant has been well spent.

But though I am sure that we must always try to teach less rather than more, this does not absolve us from our responsibility to help the student to make good use of the time thus gained. On the contrary, we must try very hard to find worthwhile alternatives to yet more courses and examinations, so as to provide the student with the same kind of orientation, at least, which the tradition of general knowledge provided for earlier generations. We need not idealize this tradition, as we have seen. It was neither very coherent nor very accurate. But it cohered at least as much as our language and our culture cohered and it thus counteracted the fragmentation of knowledge into unrelated specialisms. The fact that this unity was subjective speaks in its favour, for what else could it be? Most systems of order are subjective, but that is just why they may help the growing mind to feel at home on the map of culture.

If modesty did not forbid it, I should say that for example the arrangement of the library which Aby Warburg thought out was intended as such a rough map of our cultural universe. Of course, being subjective, any such arrangement has its weaknesses and its idiosyncrasies, and I have sometimes cursed ours when I could not find a book. But this does not detract from the obvious merit of this model—it does not recognize any barriers between the so-called fields of study. The student of artistic traditions is made to realize that he should also read about the history of religion, science and the economics of patronage; the student of poetry that he should not forget mythology, music, pageants and social conventions. What is more, he can browse there at his leisure, almost as undisturbed as in an old-fashioned bookshop.

It is not only modesty, though, which prevents me from concluding with the fanfare that all our educational ills could be remedied if all students in these islands came to browse at the Warburg Institute. I surely must end with a more constructive suggestion of how to keep the map of culture before the minds of all these growing specialists.

Perhaps we might take a leaf out of the book of the oldest institution of learning that exists among us, far older and more experienced even than our old universities; I mean the Church. Not that I know anything about the theological syllabus, but I know at least that you cannot specialize in the First Person of the Trinity without having heard of the Second. The Church, it seems, has never had that morbid fear and snobbish contempt of superficiality that has invaded academic life with the rise of professionalism. There are all shades between the most humble and the most learned, but certain essentials of religious knowledge must be common to all. It has invented the Creed and the Catechism as a map of orientation for every-one who wants to be received into its community.

I know that the original purpose of the Creed was to fix the dogma, but the paedagogic wisdom of this simple device can be admired even by heretics who want to know the Creed in order to criticize its tenets. What we can learn from this example is to discard our fear of smattering, our all or nothing attitude to knowledge which is not only unrealistic and inhumane but also, I believe, the greatest obstacle to the survival of our traditions.

The classical tradition itself was only kept alive throughout the Dark Ages because a few learned churchmen such as Isidore of Seville were not ashamed of writing simple compendia to which they committed those few ideas about the universe and about the past which they considered indispensable. It was from writings of this kind that the idea of general knowledge could renew itself.

What I regret most, in the present eclipse of this tradition, is the loss of the historical frame of reference, the amputation of the time dimension from our culture. I think the Church would have known how to remedy this deficiency without imposing a burden. Indeed I have been toying with the idea of secular creeds, as brief and concise, if we can hammer them out, as the Athanasian Creed. It would not need a new course to teach them, for you would read them in three minutes and learn them in an afternoon. We could make such capsuled knowledge available to everybody in our schools irrespective of the type and level of their curricula. A secular creed of this kind should be packed so full with interesting rumours that the many and varied catechisms which should explain it somewhat more fully would always be in demand from the libraries. If we ever convoke such a Council of Nicaea to agree on

our creed, we might also, I suggest, invite delegates of the great cultures
from other continents to tell us their own, which should be available as
optional subjects.

It is with some trepidation that I submit for your criticism the first untidy
draft of such a creed, biased, subjective and selective, but containing the kind
of iron ration I should like to distribute before we are scattered to the four
winds:

I belong to Western Civilization, born in Greece in the first millennium
B.C. It was created by poets, philosophers, artists, historians and scientists
who freely examined the earlier myths and traditions of the ancient Orient.
It flourished in Athens in the fifth century, was carried East by Macedonian
conquests in the fourth century and in the first by Latin-speaking Romans
to large parts of Europe and North Africa.

It was transformed by Christianity, which arose among the Jews of Pales-
tine and spread throughout the Latin- and Greek-speaking world in the
second and third centuries A.D. It survived the collapse of the Roman Empire
under the pressure of Teutonic tribes in the fifth century, for the Greek and
Roman Churches preserved some of its organization, its literature and its
art during the so-called Middle Ages, when most of the barons and their
serfs were illiterate. It began to flourish once more in the twelfth and thir-
teenth centuries when the Gothic style of building spread from France over
Europe and when the growing universities of France, Italy and England
gained fresh knowledge of Greek science and learning through translations
made by Mohammedan Arabs, who had penetrated through North Africa
to Spain. These also brought Arabic numerals from India, and paper, gunpowder and the marine compass from China, thus assisting the emancipation
of the merchant cities of fourteenth- and fifteenth-century Italy, which
encouraged the recovery of Greek and Roman literature, art and building
styles that is called the Renaissance. Its New Learning was disseminated by
the printing press, which inaugurated the Modern Age and prepared the
ground for the Reformation that split Europe in the sixteenth century, while
voyages of discovery led to Portuguese, Spanish and English conquests and
settlements across the seas.

It was transformed once more at that time by the renewed faith in the
progress of human knowledge, exemplified in the mathematical theories of
experimental science created in Italy and developed in the seventeenth-
century Netherlands and Protestant England whence, in the eighteenth century, ideals of rationalism and tolerance spread to the Continent. It was thus
enabled to survive the rapid increase in population that favoured the Industrial Revolution, which led to nineteenth-century colonialism, the spread of

literacy and the mass movements of socialism and nationalism. It endangered and transformed, in our century, most other cultures of the globe, which has shrunk for us to sputnik size by the invention of flying. I hope there will be a twenty-first century. Amen.

In Search of Cultural History

PREFACE

THE publication of a lecture always presents the author with a dilemma which becomes the more intractable the larger the theme he has treated. To fit the discussion of such a theme into the narrow frame of an hour inevitably demands the sacrifice of many tempting topics and a certain sleight of hand in the concealment of all the lacunae of which only the speaker can be fully aware. When the occasion is over his sins of omission once more begin to haunt the author. There is no rational reason why the paragraphs he drafted and then discarded in the interest of brevity should not be restored for the published version. However, he is likely to find that any concession to these clamouring aspirants threatens to disrupt the superficial balance at which he had finally arrived. His text begins to ladder like a stocking and the distressing situation is hard to mend. The only real remedy would be to write a book, and that was not part of the bargain. A compromise has to be found which somehow preserves the text of the lecture and still saves the lecturer's conscience.

The pages in front of the reader are the result of such a compromise. The text of the lecture delivered at Lady Margaret Hall on 19 November 1967 survives almost intact, but additions have increased its length to more than double its original size. In particular I have allowed myself more quotations from the authors I discussed; the translations are my own. To make up for the inevitable loosening of the structure which goes with the increased length I have introduced subheadings. The notes are so plentiful because they are intended not only as references to my sources but also as pointers to further reading. The inclusion of a rather disproportionate selection of my own writings was to help me as far as possible to avoid repeating arguments I have presented elsewhere. I should like here to thank Dr. George H. Nadel, editor of *History and Theory*, for drawing my attention to recent discussions of cultural history. Professor R. L. Colie, Professor Philipp Fehl and my son Richard read the manuscript and suggested important improvements.

The Philip Maurice Deneke Lecture delivered at Lady Margaret Hall, Oxford, on 19 November 1967.

I. THE TERM AND THE THING

A FEW weeks ago I was travelling in a minicab across London when the conversation with the driver naturally turned to the overcrowding of the Metropolis. The driver was inclined to blame the lack of rival attractions in many provincial towns which had no theatres and no concert halls. 'I hate the word culture,' he said, in what I can only describe as a most cultured voice, 'I hate the word culture, but...' I was glad it was too dark for him to see me blushing. I am in charge of an Institute which was founded as *Die Kulturwissenschaftliche Bibliothek Warburg*. Its founder, Aby Warburg,[1] had been a student of Karl Lamprecht, the champion of cultural psychology who was engaged throughout his life in a running fight with those professional historians who confined their interest to political history.[2] Both Warburg and Lamprecht looked up in admiration to the towering figure of Jacob Burckhardt, whose central contribution to *Kulturgeschichte* will have to loom large in this lecture. Thus the rejection of the word 'culture' by English culture is a frequent cause of embarrassment to me when I am asked to explain what the Warburg Institute is about. It helps me little to point out that this rejection is of comparatively recent date[3] and that even the word *Kulturwissenschaft*, which sounds so quintessentially Teutonic to modern English ears, has a perfectly respectable English counterpart. The first chapter of Sir Edward Burnett Tylor's pioneering work on *Primitive Culture* of 1871 is headed 'The Science of Culture'.

Not that I have no sympathy for my driver's reluctance to pronounce the word. It had become tainted for him, as for many other sensitive people, by the highmindedness of Matthew Arnold with his eagerness to spread 'sweetness and light' among the benighted,[4] and by the lowmindedness of German propaganda during the First World War which invented a contrast between German *Kultur*, naturally a good thing, profound and strong, and Western civilization, a bad thing, a mere shallow addiction to gadgetry and materialism.[5] I do not propose to waste time on any of these phony distinctions,[6] but I must draw attention to a subtle change in the aura of the word which may soon render my driver's attitude somewhat obsolete. From the usage of anthropologists exemplified by Burnett Tylor the word has spread to social scientists, especially on the other side of the Atlantic.[7] In this sterilized meaning it has come into vogue again in such terms as 'working-class culture' or even C. P. Snow's 'two cultures' of unhappy memory. These are purely descriptive terms, stripped, it is often claimed, of any so-called 'value judgement'.

Human cultures, according to this tradition—which probably can be traced back to Hippolyte Taine—can be studied, as bacterial cultures must be studied, without ranking them in order of value.

It is not my purpose here to add yet further 'Notes towards the definition of culture',[8] for I believe that, whether we like the particular term or prefer another, we all know what it seeks to describe. At least everybody knows this who has ever travelled from one country to another, or even moved from one social circle to another, and has experienced what it means to be confronted by different ways of life, different systems of reference, different scales of value—in short different cultures.

Whenever peoples came into friendly or hostile contact they must have noticed the gulf that separated their own language and habits from those of the others. Naturally what struck observers in such situations was the unexpected feature or custom that contrasted with the norm to which the reporter was used. Whether you read Herodotus, Tacitus or Marco Polo, it is always these differences which are singled out for attention. But the experience cuts both ways. The variety of *mores* existing on the globe also provided a welcome topic for the moralist who wanted to hold up a mirror to his own people, and indeed the contrast in cultures becomes an effective device for satirists from Thomas More to Swift, from Montesquieu's *Lettres Persanes* to Sterne's *Sentimental Journey*. By then, of course, the travellers to foreign lands had long been joined by travellers in time, by historians. What motives had they to concern themselves with the conditions of past cultures rather than with events? The claims and contests of the mighty, which sent the historian back to old charters and chronicles, mainly fed the stream of political and constitutional history, but where traditional privileges and ancient laws came into play, power and custom could not be neatly separated. The search in the muniment room aroused interest in antiquities, particularly in England,[9] just as the interpretation of ancient laws focused attention on the changing conditions of society. It is hardly an accident that the pioneers of cultural as distinct from political history, e.g. Bodin, Vico and Montesquieu, were trained in the law. In addition there were the scholars interested in literary texts that needed an increasing amount of explanatory glosses, the knowledge of material culture (*realia*) cultivated by classical philologists and leading to the systematic study of 'antiquities'.[10] Last, but not least, there were the ancestors of my own subject, the early historians of art who, like Vasari, spurned the conception of the mere chronicler and concerned themselves with the conditions that favoured the progress of skill.[11] The question itself was not new. It had been debated in the ancient schools of rhetoric where both Longinus and Tacitus report discussions whether oratory could survive the conditions of democratic freedom that had brought it into being. Artists, in their turn, liked rather to draw attention to the effects of princely bounty and dreamed of Golden Ages of patronage.[12] But Vasari, for instance, was not blind to the importance of competition, and graphically described it in the *Life of Perugino*.[13]

And yet it could be claimed that such interest in the variety of cultural conditions alone would never have led to the emergence of cultural history had it not been for a novel element—the belief in progress, which alone could unify the history of mankind.

In the eighteenth century, when the words 'culture' and 'civilization' made their appearance and spread, they were indeed terms of value, to be used in contrast to barbarism, savagery or rudeness.[14] The history of civilization or of culture was the history of man's rise from a near animal state to polite society, the cultivation of the arts, the adoption of civilized values and the free exercise of reason. Thus culture could progress, it could also decline and be lost, and history was legitimately concerned with either of these processes. It was thus that Vico in the *Scienza Nuova* and Voltaire in his *Essai sur les Mœurs* had seen the problem, though neither of them used the term *cultura* or *culture*.[15]

In England it was that optimistic view of progress which Professor Butterfield has called the 'Whig Conception of History' that led to the first essays in this genre, notably William Roscoe's *Life of Lorenzo de' Medici* of 1795, which is really a cultural history of Medicean Florence in the early Renaissance. The same tradition was carried forward by the great Macaulay, whose famous chapter in *The History of England* on the condition of the country in 1685 is explicitly intended to bring home to the reader in 1849 the extent of the improvements which had been achieved in the intervening period.

But in a sense it was precisely this optimistic interpretation which led to a demand for a distinction between 'civilization' and 'culture'. For was it really true that all aspects of civilized life advanced together? Was it true that the arts, the sciences, goodness of manners and goodness of heart all kept pace in the process of civilization? There are implicit doubts in Vico and explicit ones in Rousseau. The very concern of the eighteenth century with the enlightenment, the creation of conditions favouring culture, also led to an increasing interest in the cultural conditions of the past. Winckelmann's praise for the arts of Greece went with a conviction that the whole of Greek civilization accounted for this efflorescence. His conclusion was that this made ancient civilization supreme, the model to which all others should aspire. It was easy, however, to turn the tables on these cultural expatriates and to point out to them that on their own reasoning these conditions could never come back. If art is embedded in culture we must accept that different cultures produce different arts. The Northern climate and the Christian religion both make it inopportune to build temples, but then the new conditions created a new flower in the Gothic cathedral. It was of course Herder, above all, who argued along these lines, and who therefore rejected the idea of a scale of excellence by which you could measure culture.[16] Not that he was a complete relativist. He still held fast to the idea of a divine plan which led mankind towards *Humanität*, but since history reflects such a grand design it would be arrogant to disregard the earlier stages; how could we, indeed, when God had manifested Himself among the Hebrew shepherds?

These sentiments, scattered about in the prolix and humane writings of Herder, were transposed into a metaphysical system claiming the necessary truth of logic by Georg Friedrich Hegel.[17]

II. THE HEGELIAN SYSTEM

Some people are allergic to Hegel and I confess that my own tolerance is low. But I do not want here to repeat what Schopenhauer, Bertrand Russell[18] and my friend Sir Karl Popper[19] have said with much greater authority; even less do I want to argue against those who may have been provoked by these denunciations into a defence of Hegel.[20] What I want to explain is merely why we are today in search of cultural history.[21] We are in search, I shall maintain, because *Kulturgeschichte* has been built, knowingly and unknowingly, on Hegelian foundations which have crumbled.

It is well known that Hegel wanted to build these foundations on a metaphysical system which he claimed to have developed out of Kant's critiques of metaphysics. But what is more relevant for the present context is rather Hegel's return to the traditions of theology. Admittedly his theology would have to be classed as heretical, for it disregards the Christian dogma of the creation as a one-time event and that of the incarnation as an equally unique occurrence in time. The history of the universe was for Hegel the history of God creating Himself and the history of mankind was in the same sense the continuous Incarnation of the Spirit.

In his book on *The Great Chain of Being* (1936) Arthur Lovejoy has described how, in the course of the eighteenth century, the new idea of Progress had gradually been fused with the old image of a hieratic universe. The ladder of existence from stones to plants, from plants to animals upwards to man and hence through the spiritual realm of the angelic orders to the divine apex was no longer conceived as static and immutable. There is a process of ascent along these rungs of the ladder leading the creation towards a divine culmination. Hegel translated this ascent into the terms of logical categories and thus turned the cosmic process into the progression of the divine spirit thinking itself, impelled by the need of resolving contradictions to move to a higher and higher plane of articulation. Human history, the rise of civilization, is part of this progress, indeed it repeats its essential and inevitable dialectical steps as an ascent through the logical categories till the divine at last comes to self-awareness in the mind of Herr Professor Hegel.

I know that this particular conclusion has been denied, but it certainly is part of Hegel's conception of History as an unfolding of divine reasoning that whatever is must also be right, right because meaningful as a step towards the self-realization of the spirit.

It is clear that within this system the contrast between the idea of culture as a term of value and its use as a merely descriptive word has no place; it is 'resolved', as Hegelians would say, on the higher plane on which every culture is right as a necessary stage. One does not argue with the Absolute. This applies not only to the past but also to the present. The critic can watch the signs of the times, he has no right to judge them. Every person can hope to be the mouthpiece, indeed almost the incarnation, of the spirit. Hegel called Napoleon 'the world spirit on horseback' and Gertrude Stein claimed to be the embodiment of the *Zeitgeist*. But in a sense everything is, at least everything and everybody can become, an instrument of the spirit. The invention of gunpowder in Hegel's view was such a manifestation of the divine. 'Mankind needed it, and lo, it was there.' The need arose because the feudal system had to be dissolved and, strange though we may find this, the invention led war on to a higher, because a more abstract, plane. Killing became more anonymous and so did courage.[22]

And yet, I want to maintain, this rather blasphemous and heretical interpretation is an extension, or possibly a perversion, of the Christian interpretation of providential history. Both in the Judaic and in the Christian tradition history was seen as part of a divine plan in which the actions of people and of nations were conceived as manifestations of the divine will. Not only the history of the Chosen People but even that of the Roman conquerors was so interpreted because the Plan of Salvation could only come into effect in 'the fullness of time' when the oecumene was sufficiently united by a common language to be ripe for the good news of the Incarnation.[23] From then on, of course, history is the stage for the battle between the militant Church and the adversary; but the outcome of that fight is assured with the Second Coming, announced by tremendous portents, when history as we know it will come to an end. The medieval abbot Joachim of Fiore had made these prophecies more specific and worked out a trinitarian system of history in which the Old Testament represented the realm of the Father, the Christian era the realm of the Son, which would in turn be replaced very soon by the third realm—*das dritte Reich*—the era of the Spirit.

The fateful expression to which I have just alluded reminds us of the spell which these chiliastic hopes exerted on successive interpreters of history. Lessing had referred to the visions of the abbot,[24] and similar mystical and especially Trinitarian speculations also played their part in Hegel's early development.[25] The degree to which these influences left their mark on his *Lectures on the Philosophy of History* still remains to be examined. Consider especially the pages in which he deals with the coming of Christ when, as he puts it,

> the identity of the subject and of God comes into the world in the fullness of time, the awareness of this identity is the recognition of God in His truth.[26]

Not surprisingly, perhaps, it is the Germanic peoples who are the instrument and the vessel of the new Spirit which unfolds in three phases, that of the conquest of the Roman world, that of the feudal monarchy of the Middle Ages and finally in the phase initiated by the Reformation. 'These three,' we read, 'may be described as the realm of the Father, the Son and the Holy Ghost'.[27] The same succession, he says in retrospect, can also be found in the pre-Christian stage of history where the Persians are thought by Hegel to represent the Father, the Greeks the Son and the Romans the Holy Ghost, each of course on a correspondingly lower plane.

Every one of these peoples, as we have seen, embodied a necessary phase of the ascending spirit; their individual spirit, their *Volksgeist*, was a temporary form of the absolute Spirit on its path through history. For this is the decisive aspect of Hegel's position for my purpose. Here are his own words as they were recorded by students who attended his course on the philosophy of history:

> World history represents ... the evolution of the awareness of the spirit of its own freedom.... Every step, being different from every other one, has its own determined and peculiar principle. In history such a principle becomes the determination of the spirit—a peculiar national spirit (*ein besonderer Volksgeist*). It is here that it expresses concretely all the aspects of its consciousness and will, its total reality; it is this that imparts a common stamp to its religion, its political constitution, its social ethics, its legal system, its customs but also to its science, its art and its technical skills. These particular individual qualities must be understood as deriving from that

general peculiarity, the particular principle of a nation. Conversely it is from the factual details present in history that the general character of this peculiarity has to be derived.[28]

I like to picture the content of this all-important paragraph diagrammatically as a wheel from the hub of which there radiate eight spokes. These spokes represent the various concrete manifestations of the national Spirit, in Hegel's words 'all the aspects of its consciousness and will'. They are the nation's religion, constitution, morality, law, customs, science, art, and technology. These manifestations, which are visible on the periphery of

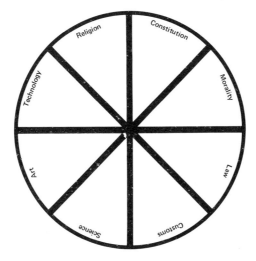

my wheel, must all be understood in their individual character as the realizations of the *Volksgeist*. They all point to a common centre. In other words, from whichever part on the outside of the wheel you start moving inwards in search of their essence, you must ultimately come to the same central point. If you do not, if the science of a people appears to you to manifest a different principle from that manifested in its legal system, you must have lost your way somewhere.

Hegel admits that you can only practise this art when you are familiar with the *a priori* knowledge deduced from his system, but he claims that the same is true of astronomers like Kepler, who must be familiar with the *a priori* laws of geometry to discover the cosmic laws of motion. The comparison is clearly misleading and I should like to replace it by another. Hegel's historian practises exegetics. His *a priori* knowledge is less like that of an astronomer than like that of a devout interpreter of the Scriptures who knows, for instance, that every event described in the Old Testament can be interpreted as foreshadowing an event described in the Gospels. The Jews crossing the Red Sea are a type for the anti-type of Christ's Baptism, Melchisedek offering Abraham bread and wine signifies the Eucharist. For God did not reveal His plan only through the mouth of the prophets, but also in ordering the events themselves.

I have given an example of this exegetic technique in Hegel's interpretation of the invention of gunpowder. I can only point briefly to one more, his interpretation of the Great Sphinx of Egypt. The sphinx, we read, can be seen as a symbol of the Egyptian spirit, the human head looking out of the animal body represents the spirit beginning to raise itself from the fetters of nature without, however, liberating itself fully. And just as the ingenuities of the allegorical interpretations of the Scriptures often compel admiration, so does Hegel's skill in representing every aspect of ancient Egyptian civilization in the light of this preconceived notion: Egyptian writing is still hieroglyphic, based on the sensuous image, not on abstract letters, Egyptian religion worships animals because the dim and inert spirit of the Egyptians cannot rise to a higher idea, and though the Egyptians were the first to believe in immortality they still clung to the body, the mummy.

Not all of Hegel's interpretations look as forced and Procrustean as his reading of Egyptian culture. On the contrary, his skill in imposing his scheme on a variety of cultural events must have been considerable if we are to explain the hold which his reading of history maintained on subsequent generations. His pages on the 'Dissolution of the Middle Ages through art and science' are a case in point. He sees the Renaissance on Herder's lines as 'a soaring of the spirit towards a higher humanity'.[29]

> The Grave, Death ... and the Beyond have been given up. The principle of here and now that drove the world to the crusades developed into a worldliness for its own sake.... But the Church remained and held on to externals. However, it so fell out, that this externalization did not remain crude, for it was transfigured by art. Art vivifies and animates ... the merely sensual and imbues it with form which expresses the soul, the sentiment, the spirit.... (p. 515)
>
> There is a great difference whether the mind is confronted by a mere thing such as the Eucharist or any stone, wood or crude image, or is contemplating a profound painting, a beautiful work of sculpture where soul relates to soul and spirit to spirit. In the first instance the spirit is ... tied to something totally other which is sensuous and not spiritual. Here, however, the sensual is also beautiful, the spiritual form that animates it, is also true.... (p. 515)

Yet in this way art transcended the principle of the Church. Being confined to sensuous representations, it was at first still considered to be safe. Hence the Church still accepted art, but became dissociated from the free spirit that had created art, when that spirit had risen to the realms of thought and of science.... (p. 516)

For art was assisted and uplifted by the study of antiquity (the name *humaniora* is very significant, for in these works of antiquity humanity and human education are honoured) ... scholastic formalism was replaced by a very different content: Plato became known in the West and with him there arose a new world of man.... (pp. 516/17)

The third main trend to be mentioned is the outward urge of the spirit, man's desire to get to know his earth ... the new technical means of the marine compass assisted shipping ... the means are found when the demand exists.

These three facts, the so-called revival of learning, the efflorescence of the fine arts and the discovery of America ... may be compared to the dawn, the harbinger of a new fine day after the long, fateful and terrible night of the Middle Ages.... (p. 518)

In Hegel's system this dawn announces the great 'all-transfiguring sunrise' of the Reformation, the modern age in the description of which his Theodicy culminates.

The interpretations of cultural history in these Lectures on the Philosophy of History are supplemented and partly expanded in Hegel's lectures on Aesthetics, in which he displayed much skill and even poetic gift in presenting the development of the arts as a logical process accompanying and reflecting the unfolding of the spirit. The whole system of the arts is here turned into a temporal hierarchy, beginning with architecture, the most 'material' of the arts, first appearing in the huge lumps of the pyramids, progressing to sculpture, which of course finds its apogee in Greece, and then to the even more spiritual, dematerialized medium of painting which, in Hegel's view, corresponds to the Christian Age of Faith. But painting, in its turn, tends increasingly towards the less tangible art of music, which must yield its place to poetry as even closer to pure thought. It is well known that Hegel believed that poetry, too, would be dissolved when the Spirit would no longer need images for its manifestation but would turn into abstract philosophy.

Whatever the validity of these individual interpretations, which are frequently presented with great persuasiveness, it was the technique itself which exerted a tremendous appeal. Those who accepted Hegel's logic now had the proof of what had before been a mere matter of intuition, the feeling that each art and each culture existed in its own right and could not be judged by other standards; and yet this proof did not invalidate the equally intuitive conviction that the history of civilization was and remained a history of growing values, a history of progress.

No type of historian has a greater stake in this approach than the historian of art. Indeed it might be claimed that a history, as distinct from a critical evaluation, of the art of the past only became possible in the light of this interpretation. For Vasari as for Winckelmann, art had indeed responded to favourable conditions but declined when conditions altered. Now there was no decline, only the logical progression of the *Zeitgeist* which had brought about changes in the monuments of the past. The changing styles of art thus became the index of the changing spirit. The Hegelian creed was formulated in the introduction of 1843 to a history of art by the now largely forgotten German art historian Carl Schnaase:[30]

> Art, too, belongs to the necessary expressions of mankind; indeed one may say that the genius of mankind expresses itself more completely and more characteristically in art than in religion. (p. 83)
>
> It is true that the keen eye of the beholder will also penetrate deep into the nature of a nation when examining its political life or its scientific achievement, but the most subtle and most characteristic features of a people's soul can only be recognized in its artistic creations. (p. 86)
>
> Thus the art of every period is both the most complete and the most reliable expression of the national spirit in question, it is something like a hieroglyph ... in which the secret essence of the nation declares itself, condensed, it is true, dark at first sight, but completely and unambiguously to those who can read these signs ... thus a continuous history of art provides the spectacle of the progressive evolution of the human spirit.... (p. 87)

III. BURCKHARDT'S HEGELIANISM

The historian who vindicated the approach to *Kulturgeschichte* through art in the eyes of the nineteenth century was of course not Schnaase but Jacob Burckhardt. It may appear outrageous to rank Burckhardt among the Hegelians, since he often expressed his dislike of Hegel's brand of philosophy. He always stressed that he distrusted systems and believed in facts. But I hope to show that Burckhardt here illustrates the important methodological truth that it is precisely those people who want to discard all 'preconceived' theories who are most likely to succumb unconsciously to their power. There is no more striking example of this truth than a letter which Burckhardt wrote at the age of twenty-four to his friend Karl Fresenius. It must therefore be quoted at some length:

> You have become a philosopher, and yet you will have to concede to me the following—a person such as myself who is quite unsuited to speculative theorizing and who never, even for a minute in a whole year, feels disposed towards abstract thought, such a person will do best if he attempts to approach the higher questions of life and of research in his own way and tries to clarify these issues as best he can. My own substitute, then, is my effort to achieve with every day a more intense immediacy in the perception of essentials. By nature I cling to the tangible, to visible reality and to history. But I have a bent for incessantly looking for parallels in co-ordinating facts and have thus succeeded on my own in arriving at a few generalized principles. I am aware of the fact that there exists a yet higher principle of generality soaring above these multifarious principles and, maybe, I shall be able to rise towards that level. You cannot imagine to what an extent this effort, however one-sided it may be, gradually lends significance to the facts of history, the works of art, the monuments of all ages, as witnesses of earlier phases in the evolution of the Spirit. Believe me, I often feel an awesome thrill when I see this age clearly present in ages past. The highest goal of human history, the development of the spirit towards freedom, has become my ruling conviction, and so my studies cannot betray me and cannot let me go under, but remain my tutelary guiding light as long as I live.[31]

Though Burckhardt believed that he was generalizing from the observed facts of history, what he ultimately found in the facts was the Hegelian world spirit he had rejected as a speculative abstraction. It is true that he was not entirely unaware of this situation. He admits a few lines later in the letter that, though the speculations of another man could never console or help him, he is still affected by them since they are part of the spirit which dominates the intellectual atmosphere of the nineteenth century.

> Indeed, it may well be that I am unconsciously guided by some of the threads of recent philosophy. But allow me to remain on this humble level, let me sense and feel history rather than understand it through its first principles. (Ibid.)

However, he promised he would read Hegel, and no doubt he did.

In his important introduction to Burckhardt's *Griechische Kulturgeschichte* Professor Momigliano has shown some of the links which connect even that series of lectures from Burckhardt's later years with the philosophical pre-occupation of Romanticism.[32] He has in particular pointed to the influence of one of Burckhardt's teachers, the classical scholar A. Boeckh, in whose writings the idea of a *Volksgeist* plays a central part.[33] Nor is the evidence lacking that the idea of the *Zeitgeist* was accepted by the young Burckhardt as a matter of course. In a letter to his friend Kinkel, who wanted to write on the arts of the Netherlands, he writes: 'Conceive your task as follows: How does the spirit of the fifteenth century express itself in painting! Then everything becomes simple.' (4 May 1847)[34]

It has often been deplored that Burckhardt never came to write such a history of art himself. In his first book on cultural history, *The Age of Constantine the Great* (1853), art plays indeed a rather subordinate role. Clearly Burck-hardt here tried to realize his ideal of a history based on *Anschauung*, imme-diacy. He aims at narration, quotation and depiction with little overt inter-pretation. Perhaps the subject of the book was especially favourable to this approach. The position of Constantine's reign as a turning point in history is so profoundly established in the reader's mind that the general framework is all but given—we look for signs of declining paganism and of the rise of the new age, and the historian hardly has to sketch in the context more firmly than Burckhardt did.

No doubt Burckhardt thought the same of that other age of transition to which he turned, the age of the Renaissance, to which he devoted his most famous masterpiece, *Die Kultur der Renaissance in Italien* of 1860.[35] But here it must be apparent to every reader that Burckhardt saw that civilization through the medium of its art.

He had begun his studies as a lover of Northern medieval art, but had experi-enced a kind of conversion on his Italian journeys. The outcome of this con-version had been his *Cicerone* of 1855, subtitled 'a guide to the enjoyment of works of art in Italy'.

There is also very little room for theory in this perceptive guide-book, but it is naturally pervaded by the interpretation of Renaissance art that had become commonplace by the middle of the nineteenth century and is still in evidence, I mean the contrast between the spirituality of the Age of Faith and the sensu-ality of the subsequent age. It was a polarity that had been created by the Romantics and used, of course, by Hegel. We have seen that for him the revival of the arts with their attention to the external world was one of the factors in the disintegration of the Middle Ages. The few but eloquent lines which Burckhardt devoted in the *Cicerone* to the 'New Spirit' that came over sculpture and painting in the fifteenth century conform to this conception of the Age.

> The generalized facial types are now replaced by individualities, the former system of expressions, gestures and draperies is replaced by an infinitely rich truth to life.... Beauty, formerly ... the highest attribute of Holiness ... now yields to ... clarity... However, where it still comes into existence, it is a newborn sensuous beauty which asks for its undiminished portion of what is earthly and real....[36]

Like Hegel, Burckhardt was convinced that this 'new spirit' transcended and therefore contradicted the demands of the Church. These demands, he suggests, are largely negative. The spirit of worship must not be deflected and diverted by anything that reminded the beholder of the realities of secular life. Wherever these are deliberately brought into art the picture will no longer look devout.

The lines of approach were therefore staked out before Burckhardt began to think of a book on the whole of the Civilization of the Renaissance. It may seem surprising that this work ultimately lacked a chapter on art, and Burckhardt himself referred to this *lacuna*. It is hard, however, to imagine how he could have made good this omission without repeating much of what he had written in the *Cicerone*.

We know something about Burckhardt's working methods during the four years in which he prepared *Die Kultur der Renaissance in Italien*. He obviously knew what he was looking for. He mentions[37] for instance that he collected seven hundred excerpts from Vasari's *Lives*, cutting up his notebooks in little slips for use in the appropriate places. There must have been similar numbers of slips from other texts of the period such as Vespasiano's *Memoirs* or Benvenuto Cellini's *Autobiography*, but what is impressive in the long run is not the number of pages he managed to read and excerpt, but rather his economy in their use, and the magic touch with which he turned these selected extracts into signs of the time.

In my youth the book was still a classic in German-speaking countries, and that meant that it was read by quite a large number of people as providing a passport to *Bildung*, to 'culture' in the Victorian sense of the term. Many may have found it a bit hard going, but they must also have enjoyed the wealth of memorable detail, the concise pen portraits of *condottieri* and of humanists, the tersely told anecdotes about vendettas and practical jokes, the quotations from poets and historians revealing their attitudes to subjects as diverse as scenery, honour or death. The villainies, the gaieties, the feats of prowess, the craving for fame, all this formed part of the panorama that was

Die Kultur der Renaissance. It was with these scenes and incidents that countless travellers to Italy peopled the streets of Florence, Siena and Venice in
their imagination.

Nobody can accuse Burckhardt of having failed to warn his readers that
his criteria of selection and arrangement were subjective. He said so in the
very first paragraph of the book, which he calls a mere essay in the original
sense of the term:

> The outlines of a cultural period and its mentality may present a different
> picture to every beholder and the same studies which resulted in this book
> might easily have led others to essentially different conclusions.

But though Burckhardt was fully aware of the part interpretation plays
in any such enterprise, neither he himself nor, as far as I know, any of his
subsequent commentators seems to have realized to what an extent his interpretation was guided by Hegel's theory of history.[38]

There must be a psychological reason for this reluctance, on the part of
German-speaking critics, to show up this connection. One feels in good company in attacking Hegel; but to criticize the intellectual foundation of Burckhardt's work is a different matter. He is the father-figure of cultural history,
whose very tone of voice carries authority. I feel that my own hand trembles
a little as I am setting out to sacrifice and dissect a work that has so largely
inspired the founder of the Warburg Institute.

The heart of the book, the main thesis, is expressed in the famous paragraph
in which Burckhardt contrasts the mentality of the Renaissance with that
of the Middle Ages:

> In the Middle Ages both sides of human consciousness—that which faces
> the outside world and that which is turned towards man's inner life—lay
> dreaming or only half-awake, as if they were covered by a common veil,
> a veil woven of faith, delusion and childish dependence. Seen through this
> veil reality and history appeared in the strangest colours, while man was
> only aware of himself in universal categories such as race, nation, party,
> guild or family. It was in Italy that this veil was first blown away and that
> there awoke an objective attitude towards the state and towards all the
> things of this world while, on the other side, subjectivity emerged with
> full force so that man became a true individual mind and recognized himself
> as such. (p. 95)

One does not need to know Hegel well to recognize in these polarities some
of his favourite categories. There is a constant play in Hegel with the inward
and outward turning of the spirit, and with its movement from the general

to the particular. Remembering Hegel's thesis that the Trinitarian or tri-
partite divisions of the Christian era repeat on a higher plane the evolution
of the spirit from Persia to Greece and from Greece to Rome, it becomes
even more significant that in Hegel the general principle of Roman history
(which corresponds to the Renaissance) is due to the inward movement of
the spirit producing *subjektive Innerlichkeit*, which leads to the juridical idea
of an abstract personality manifested in private property. It is this generalized
subjectivity which remains the ruling principle of the Germanic peoples, but
in the third phase, which ends the Middle Ages, the objective spirit can arise
when the subjective free spirit determines to adhere to form.

One must be grateful to Burckhardt for having kept this scaffolding largely
out of sight, but the basic Hegelian assumption is not concealed:

> Every cultural epoch which presents itself as a complete and articulate
> whole expresses itself not only in the life of the state, in religion, art and
> science, but also imparts its individual character to social life as such. (p.
> 257)

As to the state, this individual character is summed up by Burckhardt in
his famous opening chapter entitled 'The State as a Work of Art' (*Der Staat
als Kunstwerk*). This curious notion, which has been much debated, becomes
immediately intelligible when you remember that the third chapter in Hegel's
section on the Greeks is headed *Das politische Kunstwerk* ('The Political
Work of Art), a chapter, by the way, which is preceded by one on the shaping
of the 'beautiful individuality'.

Like Hegel, Burckhardt sees the progression of the spirit as an inevitable
process, and like him he sees it embodied in successive national spirits. Hence
his rejection of the conventional idea that the Renaissance is to be equated
with the revival of Antiquity.

> The Renaissance would not have been that exalted world-historical
> necessity it was, if that revival could be ignored. Yet it is one of the main
> tenets of this book, on which we must insist, that it was not this revival
> alone, but its close alliance with an independently existing Italian national
> spirit that achieved the conquest of the Western world. (p. 124)

Given this necessity, Burckhardt had little patience with the Romantics,
who regretted the passing of the Middle Ages; one does not argue with the
Absolute:

> It is certainly true that many a noble flower tends to perish in such a large
> process . . . but one should not therefore wish that the great universal event
> had never happened. (p. 124)

For ultimately the process of which the Renaissance formed part is progress. It is true that Burckhardt, later in his life, increasingly moved away
from an optimistic interpretation of history. But in his book of 1860 he not
only adopted the formula about the discovery of man and the world into which
Michelet had so skilfully distilled the gist of Hegel's interpretation; he also
opened his presentation on a note of Hegelian optimism:

> Freed from the countless barriers which elsewhere impeded progress, de-
> veloped into a higher degree of individuality, and schooled by Classical
> Antiquity, the Italian spirit turned towards the discovery of the external
> world and its representation in language and in art. (p. 202)

The breaking down of barriers and the new objectivity were really two
sides of the same coin. The new realism in art and the objective approach
to politics exemplified in Machiavelli, the egotism of rulers and the breakdown of conventional morality on which Burckhardt sometimes dwells with
suspicious relish, are represented as inseparable. Others, including Macaulay,
had emphasized before him that the freedom and moral licence of the period
went together. But Burckhardt was anxious to eliminate all vestiges of con-
demnation. The evolution towards egotism was not the fault of Renaissance
man; it was imposed by a verdict of world history, '*ein weltgeschichtlicher
Ratschluss*', which ultimately all Europe had to obey.

> In itself it is neither good nor evil ... it was the Italian of the Renaissance
> however who had to withstand the first tremendous surge of the new age.
> (p. 329)

I hope these quotations will suffice to show that Burckhardt's picture of
the Italian Renaissance was painted in a Hegelian frame. But I might be
accused of special pleading if I omitted to mention a remark in which he
dissociates himself from one of Hegel's tenets, the role assigned to the
Reformation in the evolution of the Spirit. Burckhardt raises the question
of why the Italian Renaissance, with its opposition to the medieval Church,
had not achieved the Reformation, why Italy had remained Catholic while
Germany went Protestant. His answer does not question the fundamental
truth of Hegelian determinism but introduces a note of warning against its
dogmatism.

> Such tremendous events as the Reformation of the sixteenth century may
> altogether elude all the deductions of the philosophers of history, as far
> as the details of their origin and their development are concerned, *however
> clearly it may be possible to prove their necessity in general outlines* (my italics).

The movements of the spirit, their sudden flashes, their extensions and their interruptions remain a mystery, at least to our eyes, since we can never see more than just a few of the sources at work. (p. 330)

It is certainly no accident that this mild caution occurs in connection with the problem of the Reformation. For in this respect Burckhardt did indeed interpret the plot of history differently from Hegel. To the Berlin professor the Reformation was almost the consummation of the entire historical process; it assured the hegemony of the Germanic nations and of Prussia, leaving behind the Catholic South, which had emancipated itself from the Church without being able to get rid of it. Burckhardt, who had begun his career as a student of theology only to abandon it for history, conceived of the development in terms of the growth of a new non-Christian *Weltanschauung*, the philosophy of the modern world.

It is in this light that we must read the concluding pages of the *Civilization of the Renaissance*, in which Burckhardt attempts to penetrate to the core of the period, which he finds in the Neo-Platonic revival of Lorenzo's circle.

> In the hymns of Lorenzo, which we are tempted to call the most sublime expression of the spirit of that school, theism is expressed without reservations, a theism grounded on the striving to see the world as a great moral and physical *cosmos*.
>
> While the men of the Middle Ages regarded the world as a vale of tears ... there arose here, in the circle of elect spirits, the conception of the visible world as a creation by God through Love ... of which He would remain the continuous Mover and Incessant Creator (*dauernder Beweger und Fortschöpfer*).
>
> Echoes of medieval mysticism here link up with Platonic doctrines and with a peculiarly modern spirit. Perhaps it was here that there ripened an ultimate fruit of that discovery of the world and of man for the sake of which alone the Renaissance in Italy must be called the leader and guide of our Epoch. (pp. 405–6)

Behind the reticence of this ending we can discern an avowal of Burckhardt's own faith in a God who continues to create in and through history, and this faith he never abandoned, however much he dissociated himself from the Hegelian progressivism of the nineteenth century.[39] Whether it was also the faith of Lorenzo de' Medici is of course an entirely different question. We are no longer under the Hegelian compulsion to find in all aspects of the Renaissance an adumbration of the Modern World.

Not that we should reproach Burckhardt for having built his picture of the period around a 'preconceived idea'. Without such an idea history could never be written at all. The infinite array of documents and monuments which the past has bequeathed to us cannot be grasped without some principle of relevance, some theory which brings order into the atomic facts as the magnet creates a configuration out of inert iron filings.

It is the secret of Burckhardt's strength that he built his masterpiece round a theory. Had he not done so the book would not have remained for a century the focus of discussion about the Renaissance.[40] There is hardly a single trait in his picture of the period which somebody or other has not wished to revise for good reasons, but few even of his critics have acknowledged the all-important fact that the picture is too consistent for such piecemeal alterations. If it does not stand up to a fresh reading of the evidence we cannot tamper with the image here or there. We must examine the methodological armature around which it was built. This armature is the Hegelian construct of cultural history with its corollary, the 'exegetic method'. Postulating the unity of all manifestations of a civilization, the method consists in taking various elements of culture, say Greek architecture and Greek philosophy, and asking how they can be shown to be the expression of the same spirit.[41] The end of such an interpretation must always be a triumphant Euclidian Q.E.D., since Hegel had bequeathed to the historian that very task: to find in every factual detail the general principle that underlies it.

IV. HEGELIANISM WITHOUT METAPHYSICS

Thus it is quite consistent that Burckhardt's successor in Basel, the great art historian Heinrich Wölfflin, writes in his first book, *Renaissance and Baroque* of 1888:

> To *explain* a style cannot mean anything but to fit its expressive character into the general history of the period, to prove that its forms do not say anything in their language that is not also said by the other organs of the age.[42]

Wölfflin was never quite at ease with this formula[43] but it still dominated his work and that of others. Not that Hegelian metaphysics were accepted in all their abstruse ramifications by any of these historians any more than they were by Burckhardt. The point is rather that all of them felt, consciously or unconsciously, that if they let go of the magnet that created the pattern, the atoms of past cultures would again fall back into random dustheaps.

In this respect the cultural historian was much worse off than any other historian. His colleagues working on political or economic history had at least a criterion of relevance in their restricted subject-matter. They could trace the history of the reform of Parliament, of Anglo-Irish relations, without explicit reference to an all-embracing philosophy of history.

But the history of culture as such, the history of all the aspects of life as it was lived in the past, could never be undertaken without some ordering principle, some centre from which the panorama can be surveyed, some hub on which the wheel of Hegel's diagram can be pivoted. Thus the subsequent history of historiography of culture can perhaps best be interpreted as a succession of attempts to salvage the Hegelian assumption without accepting Hegelian metaphysics. This was precisely what Marxism claimed it was doing. The Hegelian diagram was more or less maintained, but the centre was occupied not by the spirit but by the changing conditions of production. What we see in the periphery of the diagram represents the superstructure in which the material conditions manifest themselves. Thus the task of the cultural historian remains very much the same. He must be able to show in every detail of the period how it reflects its essential economic character.[44]

Lamprecht, whom I mentioned before as one of Warburg's masters, took the opposite line. He looked for the essence not in the material conditions but in the mentality of an age.[45] He tried, in other words, to translate Hegel's *Geist* into psychological terms. The psychology on which he relied, Herbarthian associationism, makes his attempt sound particularly old-fashioned today, but as an effort to rescue or rationalize the Hegelian intuition, his system is still of some interest. A similar turn to psychology was advocated by Wilhelm Dilthey, himself the biographer and a very sophisticated critic of Hegel, who yet, I believe, remained under his spell in the way he posed the problem of what he calls the 'structural unity of culture', especially in his later fragments. He there postulates as 'the most important methodological principle' that a culture should always be approached by the historian 'at its greatest height'.

> At this point a state of consciousness has developed in which the relationship of the elements of the culture has found a definite expression in its structure, values, meanings and the sense of life ... which is expressed in ... the configurations of poetry, religion and philosophy.... The very limitations inherent in any culture even at its height postulate a future.[46]

Dilthey is the father of the whole trend of German historiography significantly called *Geistesgeschichte*, the school which has made it its programme to see art, literature, social structure, and *Weltanschauung* under the same aspect.[47]

In my own field, the History of Art, it was Alois Riegl who, at the turn of the century, worked out his own translation of the Hegelian system into psychological terms.[48] Like Hegel he saw the evolution of the arts both as an autonomous dialectical process and as wheels revolving within the larger wheel of successive 'world views'. In art the process went spiralling twice: from a tactile mode of apprehension of solid matter to an 'optic' mode, first in the case of isolated objects and then in that of their spatial setting. As in Hegel, also, this process with its inevitable stages puts the idea of 'decline' out of court. By classical standards of tactile clarity the sculpture of the Arch of Constantine may represent a decline, but without this process of dissolution neither Raphael nor Rembrandt could have come into being.

Moreover this relentless development runs parallel with changes in the 'world views' of mankind. Like Hegel, Riegl thought that Egyptian art and Egyptian *Weltanschauung* were both on the opposite pole from 'spiritualism'. He postulates for Egypt a 'materialistic monism' which sees in the soul nothing but refined matter. Greek art and thought are both dualistic while late Antiquity returns to monism, but at the opposite end of the scale, where (predictably) the body is conceived of as a cruder soul.

> Anyone who would see in the turn of late antiquity towards irrationalism and magic superstitions a decline, arrogates for himself the right to prescribe to the spirit of mankind the way it should have taken to effect the transition from ancient to modern conceptions.[49]

For Riegl was convinced that this late antique belief in spirits and in magic was a necessary stage without which the mind of man could never have understood electricity (ibid.). And he proved to his own satisfaction (and to that of many others) that this momentous process was as clearly manifested in the ornamentation of late Roman *fibulae* as it was in the philosophy of Plotinus.

It was this claim to read the 'signs of the time' and to penetrate into the secrets of the historical process which certainly gave new impetus to art-historical studies. Max Dvořák, in his later years, represented this trend so perfectly that the editors of his collected papers rightly chose as title *Kunstgeschichte als Geistesgeschichte*[50] ('Art History as a History of the Spirit'), a formulation which provoked Max J. Friedländer to the quip, 'We apparently are merely studying the History of the Flesh' ('Wir betreiben offenbar nur Körpergeschichte'). The great Erwin Panofsky, like Dilthey, presents a more critical and sophisticated development of this programme, but those who have studied his works know that he too never renounced the desire to demonstrate the organic unity of all aspects of a period.[51] His *Gothic Architecture and Scholasticism*[52] shows him grappling with the attempt to 'rescue' the traditional connection between these two aspects of medieval culture by postulating a 'mental habit' acquired in the schools of the scholastics and carried over into architectural practice. In his *Renaissance and Renascences in Western Art*[53] he explicitly defended the notion of cultures having an essence against the criticism of George Boas.

But perhaps the most original rescue attempt of this kind was made by the greatest cultural historian after Burckhardt, his admirer, critic and successor, Johan Huizinga.[54]

It will be remembered that Burckhardt had advised his friend to ask himself: 'How does the spirit of the fifteenth century express itself in painting?' (See above p. 36)

The average art historian who practised *Geistesgeschichte* would have started from the impression van Eyck's paintings made on him and proceeded to select other testimonies of the time that appeared to tally with this impression. What is so fascinating in Huizinga is that he took the opposite line. He simply knew too many facts about the age of van Eyck to find it easy to square his impression of his pictures with the voice of the documents. He felt he had rather to re-interpret the style of the painter to make it fit with what he knew of the culture. He did this in his captivating book, *The Waning of the Middle Ages*,[55] literally the autumn of the Middle Ages, which is Hegelian even in the assumption of its title, that here medieval culture had come to its autumnal close, complex, sophisticated and ripe for the sickle. Thus van Eyck's realism could no longer be seen as a harbinger of a new age; his jewel-like richness and his accumulation of detail were rather an expression of the same late-Gothic spirit that was also manifested, much less appealingly, in the prolix writings of the period which nobody but specialists read any more.

The wheel had come full circle. The interpretation of artistic realism as an expression of a new spirit, which is to be found in Hegel and which had become the starting point for Burckhardt's reading of the Renaissance, was effectively questioned by Huizinga, who subsequently devoted one of his most searching essays to this traditional equation of Renaissance and Realism.[56] But as far as I can see, he challenged this particular interpretation rather than the methodological assumption according to which the art of an age must be shown to express the same spirit as its literature and life.

Critical as he was of all attempts to establish laws of history, he still ended his wonderful paper on *The Task of Cultural History*[57] with a demand for a 'morphology of culture' that implied, if I understand it correctly, a holistic approach in terms of changing cultural styles.

Now I would not deny for a moment that a great historian such as Huizinga can teach the student of artistic developments a lot about the conditions under which a particular style like that of van Eyck took shape. For obviously there is something in the Hegelian intuition that nothing in life is ever isolated, that any event and any creation of a period is connected by a thousand threads with the culture in which it is embedded. Who would not therefore be curious to learn about the life of the patrons who commissioned van Eyck's paintings, about the purpose these paintings served, about the symbolism of his religious paintings, or about the original context of his secular paintings which we only know through copies and reports?

Clearly neither the *Adoration of the Lamb* nor even the lost *Hunt of the Otter* can be understood in isolation without references to religious traditions in the first case and to courtly pastimes in the second.

But is the acknowledgement of this link tantamount to a concession that the Hegelian approach is right after all? I do not think so. It is one thing to see the interconnectedness of things, another to postulate that all aspects of a culture can be traced back to one key cause of which they are the manifestations.[58]

If van Eyck's patrons had all been Buddhists he would neither have painted the *Adoration of the Lamb* nor, for that matter, the *Hunting of the Otter*, but though the fact that he did is therefore trivially connected with the civilization in which he worked, there is no need to place these works on the periphery of the Hegelian wheel and look for the governing cause that explains both otter hunting and piety in the particular form they took in the early decades of the fifteenth century, and which is also expressed in van Eyck's new technique.

If there is one fact in the history of art I do not find very surprising it is the success and acclaim of this novel style. Surely this has less to do with the *Weltanschauung* of the period than with the beauty and sparkle of van Eyck's paintings.

I believe it is one of the undesirable consequences of the Hegelian habit of exegetics that such a remark sounds naïve and even paradoxical. For the habit demands that everything must be treated not only as connected with everything else, but as a symptom of something else. Just as Hegel treated the invention of gunpowder as a necessary expression of the advancing spirit, so the sophisticated historian should treat the invention of oil painting (or what was described as such) as a portent of the times. Why should we not find a simpler explanation in the fact that those who had gunpowder could defeat those who fought with bows and arrows or that those who adopted the van Eyck technique could render light and sparkle better than those who painted in tempera?[59] Of course no such answer is ever final. You are entitled to ask why people wanted to defeat their enemies, and though the question may once have sounded naïve we now know that strong influences can oppose the adoption of a better weapon. We also know that the achievement of life-like illusion cannot always be taken for granted as an aim of painting. It was an aim rejected by Judaism, by Islam, by the Byzantine Church and by our own civilization, in each case for different reasons. I believe indeed that methodologically it is always fruitful to ask for the reasons which made a culture or a society reject a tool or invention which seemed to offer tangible advantages in one particular direction. It is in trying to answer this question that we will discover the reality of that closely knit fabric which we call a culture.[60]

But I see no reason why the study of these connections should lead us back to the Hegelian postulates of the *Zeitgeist* and *Volksgeist*. On the contrary, I have always believed that it is the exegetic habit of mind leading to these mental short-circuits which prevents the posing of the very problem Hegelianism set out to solve.[61]

V. SYMPTOMS AND SYNDROMES

One may be interested in the manifold interactions between the various spheres of a culture and yet reject what I have called the 'exegetic method', the method, that is, that bases its interpretations on the detection of that kind of 'likeness' that leads the interpreter of the scriptures to link the passage of the Jews through the Red Sea with the Baptism of Christ. Hegel, it will be remembered, saw in the Egyptian sphinx an essential likeness with the position of Egyptian culture in which the Spirit began to emerge from animal nature, and carried the same metaphor through in his discussion of Egyptian religion and Egyptian hieroglyphics. The assumption is always that some essential structural similarity must be detected which permits the interpreter to subsume the various aspects of a culture under one formula.[62] The art of van Eyck in Huizinga's persuasive morphology is not only to be connected with the theology and the literature of the time but it must be shown to share some of their fundamental characteristics. To criticize this assumption is not to deny the great ingenuity and learning expended by some cultural historians on the search for suggestive and memorable metaphorical descriptions. Nor is it to deny that such structural likenesses between various aspects of a period may be found to be interesting, as A. O. Lovejoy tried to demonstrate for eighteenth-century Deism and Classicism.[63] But here as always *a priori* assumptions of such similarity can only spoil the interest of the search. Not only is there no iron law of such isomorphism, I even doubt whether we improve matters by replacing this kind of determinism with a probabilistic approach as has been proposed by W. T. Jones in his book on *The Romantic Movement*.[64] The subtitle of this interesting book demands attention by promising a 'new Method in Cultural Anthropology and History of Ideas'; it consists in drawing up such polarities as that between static and dynamic, or order and disorder, and examining certain periods for their bias towards one or the other end of these scales, a bias which would be expected to show up statistically at the periphery of the Hegelian wheel in art, science and political thought, though some of these spheres might be more recalcitrant to their expression than others. In the contrast between 'soft focus' and 'hard focus' the Romantic, he finds, will be likely to lean towards the first in metaphysics, in poetical imagery and in paintings, a bias that must be symptomatic of Romantic mentality.

Such expectations, no doubt, accord well with commonsense psychology; but in fact no statistics are needed to show in this case that what looks plausible in this new method of salvaging Hegel still comes into conflict with historical fact. It so happens that it was Romanticism which discovered the taste for the so-called 'primitives' in painting, which meant, at that time, the hard-edged, sharp-focused style of van Eyck or of the early Italians. If the first Romantic painters of Germany had one pet aversion it was the soft-focused bravura of their Baroque predecessors. Whatever their bias in metaphysics may have been, they saw in the smudged outline a symptom of artistic dis-honesty and moral corruption. Their bias in the syndrome—to retain this useful term—was based on very different alternatives, alternatives peculiar to the problems of painting. Paradoxically, perhaps, they identified the hard and naïve with the otherworldly and the chaste. It was soft-focused naturalism that was symptomatic of the fall from grace.

We have met this bias before in the discussions among cultural historians of the symptomatic value of painting styles. It might not have assumed such importance if it had not been such a live issue in the very time and ambience of Hegel and of the young Burckhardt. This was of course the time when the trauma of the French Revolution aroused a new longing among certain circles for the lost paradise of medieval culture. The German painters who became known as the Nazarenes regarded realism and sensuality as two in-separable sins and aimed at a linear style redolent of Fra Angelico and his Northern counterparts. They went to Rome, where most of them converted to Roman Catholicism, they wore their hair long and walked about in velvet caps considered somehow to be *alt-deutsch*. Now here the style of these artists and their *Weltanschauung* was clearly and closely related, their mode of painting, like their costume, was really a badge, a manifesto of their dissociation from the nineteenth century. If you met a member of this circle you could almost infer from his attire what he would say and how he would paint, except, of course, whether he would paint well or badly.

It is legitimate for the cultural historian to ask how such a syndrome arose which marks what we call a movement. It is possible to write the history of such a movement, to speculate about its beginnings and about the reasons for its success or failure. It is equally necessary then to ask how firmly the style and the allegiance it once expressed remained correlated; how long, for instance, the anti-realistic mode of painting remained a badge of Roman Catholicism. In England the link between Catholicism and a love of Gothic is strong in Pugin, but was severed by Ruskin, while the Pre-Raphaelite Brotherhood even aimed at a certain naïve and sharp-focused realism.

Even here, though, the style expressed some kind of allegiance to the Age of Faith. Judging by a passage from Bernard Shaw's first novel, this syndrome had dissolved by 1879 when it was written. In *Immaturity* Shaw wittily described the interior decoration of a villa belonging to a patron of the arts, a salon with its walls of pale blue damask and its dadoes 'painted with processions of pale maidens, picking flowers to pieces, reading books, looking ecstatically up, looking contemplatively down, playing aborted guitars with an expressive curve of the neck and fingers ... all on a ground of dead gold' (pp. 102–3). 'People who disapproved of felt hats, tweed and velveteen clothes, long hair, music on Sundays, pictures of the nude figure, literary women and avowals of agnosticism either dissembled or stayed away.' The syndrome, if Shaw was right, had changed from medievalism to aestheticism and a generalized nonconformism. Burne-Jones was now the badge of allegiance of a progressive creed.

I hope this little example may make it easier to formulate my criticism of Huizinga's Hegelian position *vis-à-vis* van Eyck's realism. For we can now ask with somewhat greater precision whether the style of van Eyck was felt in the Flanders of his time to belong to any such syndrome, whether, in other words, on entering a great man's hall and finding there a newly acquired painting by the master, you could expect certain other attitudes on the part of your host or his guests. I doubt it. Yet, if this sounds anachronistic, I would venture to suggest that if, only a little later, you had come into a room with a painting of Venus in a style *all'antica* this might have entitled you to expect the owner to want his son to learn good Latin and perhaps, generally, to meet a crowd hoping to discard and transcend the traditions of the past.[65]

VI. MOVEMENTS AND PERIODS

The distinction at which I am aiming here is that between movements and periods. Hegel saw all periods as movements since they were embodiments of the moving spirit. This spirit, as Hegel taught, manifested itself in a collective, the supra-individual entities of nations or periods. Since the individual, in his view, could only be thought of as part of such a collective it was quite consistent for Hegelians to assume that 'man' underwent profound changes in the course of history. Nobody went further in this belief than Oswald Spengler, who assigned different psyches to his different culture cycles. It was an illusion due to sentimentalizing humanitarians to believe that these different species of man could ever understand each other.

The same extremism was of course reflected in the claims of the totalitarian philosophies which stemmed from Hegel to create a new 'man', be it of a Soviet or of a National Socialist variety. Even art historians of a less uncompromising bent took to speaking of 'Gothic man' or 'Baroque psychology', assuming a radical change in the mental make-up to have happened when building firms discarded one pattern book in favour of another. In fact the study of styles so much fostered a belief in collective psychology that I remember a discussion shortly after the war with German students who appeared to believe that in the Gothic age Gothic cathedrals sprang up spontaneously all over Europe without any contact between the building sites.

It is this belief in the existence of an independent supra-individual collective spirit which seems to me to have blocked the emergence of a true cultural history. I am reminded of certain recent developments in natural history which may serve as illustrations. The behaviour of insect colonies appeared to be so much governed by the needs of the collective that the temptation was great to postulate a super-mind. How else, argued Marais in his book *The Soul of the White Ant*,[66] could the individuals of the hive immediately respond to the death of the queen? The message of this event must reach them through some kind of telepathic process. We now know that this is not so. The message is chemical; the queen's substance picked up from her body circulates in the hive through mutual licking rather than through a mysterious mental fluid.[67] Other discoveries about the communication of insects have increased our awareness of the relation between the individual and the hive. We have made progress.

I hope and believe cultural history will make progress if it also fixes its attention firmly on the individual human being. Movements, as distinct from periods, are started by people. Some of them are abortive, others catch on.

Each movement in its turn has a core of dedicated souls, a crowd of hangers-on, not to forget a lunatic fringe. There is a whole spectrum of attitudes and degrees of conversion. Even within the individual there may be various levels of conviction, various conscious and unconscious fluctuations in loyalty. What seemed acceptable during the mass rally or revivalist meeting may look pretty crazy on the way home. But movements would not be movements if they did not have their badges, their outward signs, their style of behaviour, style of speech and of dress. Who can probe the motives which prompt individuals to adopt some of these, and who would venture in every case to pronounce on the completeness of the conversion this adoption may express? Knowing these limitations, the cultural historian will be a little wary of the claims of cultural psychology. He will not deny that the success of certain styles may be symptomatic of changing attitudes, but he will resist the temptation to use changing styles and changing fashions as indicators of profound psychological changes. The fact that we cannot assume such automatic connections makes it more interesting to find out if and when they may have existed.

The Renaissance, for instance, certainly had all the characteristics of a movement.[68] It gradually captured the most articulate sections of society and influenced their attitude in various but uneven ways. Late Gothic or Mannerism were not, as far as I can see, the badge of any movement, though of course there were movements in these periods which may or may not have been correlated with styles or fashions in other cultural areas. The great issues of the day, notably the religious movements, are not necessarily reflected in distinctive styles. Thus both Mannerism and the Baroque have been claimed to express the spirit of the Counter-Reformation but neither claim is easy to substantiate. Even the existence of a peculiar Jesuit style with propagandist intentions has been disproved by the more detailed analysis of Francis Haskell.[69]

We need more analyses of this kind, based on patient documentary research, but I venture to suggest that the cultural historian will want to supplement the analysis of stylistic origins by an analysis of stylistic associations and responses. Whatever certain Baroque devices may have meant to their creators, they evoked Popish associations in the minds of Protestant travellers. When and where did these associations become conscious? How far could fashion and the desire for French elegance override these considerations in a Protestant community? I know that it is not always easy to answer these questions, but I feel strongly that it is this type of detailed questioning that should replace the generalizations of *Geistesgeschichte*.

VII. TOPICS AND TECHNIQUES

The historian does not have to be told that movements offer promising topics for investigation. The rise of Christianity, of Puritanism, of the Enlightenment or of Fascism has certainly not lacked chroniclers in the past and will not lack them in the future. The very fact that these movements detached themselves from the culture in which they originated offers a principle of selection. But it may be claimed that this advantage is bought at the expense of offering a panorama of the whole civilization such as Burckhardt or Huizinga tried to offer. The criticism of Hegelian determinism and collectivism therefore strikes indeed at one of the roots of cultural history. But there are other reasons for the malaise of the cultural historian.

The Victorian editor of Cicero's *Letters to Atticus* did not have to subscribe to Hegelian tenets to sketch in what was sometimes called the 'cultural background' in his introduction and notes. He had that unselfconscious sense of continuity with the past that allowed him to take for granted what was in need of explanation, and what was obvious to his readers. The modern student of Cicero's letters has lost this assurance. What is background and what foreground for him in such a cultural document?

But though there is a loss in this uncertainty of perspective, there is also a gain. He will be more aware than his predecessor was of the question he wants to ask. He may search the letters for linguistic, economic, political or psychological evidence, he may be interested in Cicero's attitude to his slaves or his references to his villas. Classical scholars were never debarred from asking this kind of question, but even classics are now threatened by that fragmentation that has long since overtaken the study of later ages.

That same fragmentation also threatens to eliminate another traditional form of cultural history—the old-fashioned biography of the 'Life and Letters' type, which used to present its hero in the living context of his time. I fear, if a survey were made, it would be found that books of this kind are more frequently written nowadays by amateurs than by professional historians. The average academic lacks the nerve to deal with a man of the past who was not also a specialist. Nor is his reluctance dishonourable; we know how little we know about human beings and how little of the evidence we have would satisfy a psychologist interested in the man's character and motives. The increasing awareness of our ignorance about human motives has led to a crisis of self-confidence.

Having criticized a Hegel, a Burckhardt, or a Lamprecht for their excess of self-confidence in trying to solve the riddles of past cultures, I am bound to admit in the end that without confidence our efforts must die of inanition. A scholar such as Warburg would not have founded his Library without a burning faith in the potentialities of *Kulturwissenschaft.* The evolutionist psychology that inspired his faith is no longer ours, but the questions it prompted him to ask still proved fruitful to cultural history. In proposing as the principal theme of his Institute *'das Nachleben der Antike'*—literally the afterlife of ancient civilization—he at least made sure that the historian of art, of literature or of science discovered the need for additional techniques to hack a fresh path into the forest in pursuit of that protean problem. Warburg's library was formed precisely to facilitate the acquisition of such tools. It was to encourage trespassing, not amateurishness.

Warburg's problem arose in a situation when the relevance of the classical tradition for the cultural life of the day was increasingly questioned by nationalists and by modernists. He was not out to defend it so much as to explain and assess the reasons for its long 'after-life'. The continued value of that question for the present generation lies in the need to learn more about a once vital tradition which is in danger of being forgotten. But I would not claim that it provides the one privileged entry into the tangled web of Western civilization.

Both the dilemmas and the advantages of cultural history stem from the fact that there can be no privileged entry. It seems to me quite natural that the present generation of students is particularly interested in the social foundations of culture; having myself been born in the reign of his Apostolic Majesty the Emperor Francis Joseph, who had come to the throne in 1848, I certainly can appreciate the rapidity of social change that prompts fresh questionings about the past. That all-pervasive idea of rank and hierarchy that coloured man's reaction to art, religion and even to nature, has become perplexing to the young. It will be the task of the cultural historian to trace and to explain it wherever it is needed for our understanding of the literature, the philosophy or the linguistic conventions of bygone cultures.

Perhaps this example also illustrates the difference between the social and the cultural historian. The first is interested in social change as such. He will use the tools of demography and statistics to map out the transformations in the organization of society. The latter will be grateful for all the information he can glean from such research, but the direction of his interest will still be in the way these changes interacted with other aspects of culture. He will be less interested, for example, in the economic and social causes of urban development than in the changing connotations of words such as 'urbane' or 'suburbia' or, conversely, in the significance of the 'rustic' order in architecture.

The study of such derivations, metaphors and symbols in language, literature and art provides no doubt convenient points of entry into the study of
cultural interactions.[70] But I do not think more should be claimed for this
approach than it is likely to yield. By itself it cannot offer an escape from
the basic dilemma caused by the breakdown of the Hegelian tradition, which
stems from the chastening insight that no culture can be mapped out in its
entirety, while no element of this culture can be understood in isolation. It
appears as if the cultural historian were thus still left without a viable programme, grubbing among the random curiosities of antiquarian lore.

I realize that this perplexity looks pretty formidable in the abstract, but
I believe it is much less discouraging in practice. What Popper has stressed
for the scientist also applies to the scholar.[71] No cultural historian ever starts
from scratch. The traditions of his own culture, the bias of his teacher,
the questions of the moment can all stimulate his curiosity and direct his
questionings. He may want to continue some existing lines of research or to
challenge their result; he may be captivated by Burckhardt's picture of the
Renaissance, for instance, and fill in some of the gaps left in that immensely
suggestive account, or he may have come to distrust its theoretical scaffolding
and therefore feel prompted to ask how far and by whom certain Neo-Platonic
tenets were accepted as an alternative to the Christian dogma.

Whether we know it or not, we always approach the past with some preconceived ideas, with a rudimentary theory we wish to test. In this as in many
other respects the cultural historian does not differ all that much from his
predecessor, the traveller to foreign lands. Not the professional traveller who
is only interested in one particular errand, be it the exploration of a country's
kinship system or its hydro-electric schemes, but the broadminded traveller
who wants to understand the culture of the country in which he finds himself.

In trying to widen his understanding the traveller will always be well
advised to treat inherited clichés about national characters or social types with
a healthy suspicion, just as the cultural historian will distrust the second-
hand stereotypes of the 'spirit of the age'. But neither need we ever forget
that our reactions and observations will always be dependent on the initial
assumptions with which we approach a foreign civilization. The questions
we may wish to ask are therefore in no way random; they are related to a
whole body of beliefs we wish to reinforce or to challenge. But for the cultural
historian no less than for the traveller the formulation of the question will
usually be precipitated by an individual encounter, a striking instance, be
it a work of art or a puzzling custom, a strange craft, or a conversation in
a minicab.

Take any letter that arouses our attention, says Burckhardt's letter to Fresenius on Hegel to which I have referred. Clearly we may use it as a document for a study of Burckhardt and his circle of friends, and try to build up, through careful reading and an expansion of the references, a picture of that 'sub-culture' in which the young Burckhardt moved. But we can also change the focus and use the letter as a starting point for very different lines of research—for instance into the history of epistolary styles. A hundred years earlier a student would have been most unlikely to pour this kind of confession into a letter to a friend, and if we go back to the Renaissance such a self-revelation, for which there is no Ciceronian model, would have been unthinkable. We might of course shift the focus even further and ask about the history of forms of address; we may wonder whether Burckhardt wrote with a quill and when this habit came to an end. We may speculate about the influence of postal services on the form of communications and blame the telephone for the relative decline of letter-writing today. By and large, therefore, we may either be interested in individuals and the situation they found themselves in, or in traditions passed on by hosts of anonymous people. If labels are needed we may speak of contiguity and continuity studies, though neither of these can be kept wholly apart from the other. The research into continuities may lead us still to individuals who stand out of the anonymous crowd for the impact they made on traditions, and the biographical approach will raise ever fresh questions about cultural conventions, their origins, and the time of their validity.

Either approach may thus lead us to consult works on economics or social science, on psychology or on the theory of communication; unless we do, we risk talking nonsense, but for the question in hand theories are critical tools rather than ends in themselves. It is true that the cultural historian may harbour ulterior ambitions; he sometimes dares to hope that there is a bonus in store for good work in this as in any other field. A worthwhile contribution to cultural history may transcend the particular, suggesting to other students of culture fresh ideas about the innumerable ways various aspects of a civilization can interact.

Of these interactions, the way forms, symbols and words become charged with what might be called cultural meanings seems to me to offer a particular challenge to the cultural historian. I have tried to hint at this problem at the outset of this lecture in drawing attention to certain overtones of the word 'culture' which can hardly be found in any dictionary. In our own cultural environment we catch these resonances without having to spell them out; the picture on the wall of the living-room, the accent, the handwriting, the manner of dress and the manner of greeting all reverberate for us with countless such cultural and social overtones, but if we are no Hegelians we also realize that these clusters of meaning cannot always be interpreted correctly in psychological terms. Much criticism of contemporary culture by the elderly misses the mark for this very reason. The widespread success of so-called psychedelic patterns is not really correlated to the strength of this silly and suicidal cult, but it still mildly partakes of the flavour of escapist conformism, which is not, I hope, a portent of things to come. It is only the Hegelian who believes that whatever is is right and who therefore has no intellectual defences against the self-appointed spokesman of the *Zeitgeist*.

I have alluded to styles in painting, in dress and in pattern-making, but the best example of what I mean by resonance is surely the realm of music. The jazzy rhythm, the folksy tune, the march, the hymn, the minuet, they all evoke clusters of cultural resonances which we do not have to have explained.

Or do we? I think my own roots are still sufficiently deep in the past for me to understand Beethoven's Pastoral Symphony. I do not claim that I have ever seen merry-making peasants quite in the style Beethoven saw, or that I have joined in a Thanksgiving hymn after a thunderstorm, but all these associations still come naturally to me as I can connect the 'awakening of cheerful emotions on arrival in the country' with my own memory of excursions from Vienna.

But today you leave the city by car along a motor-road which leads through ribbon developments to petrol stations. There are no merry-making peasants either in life or even in fiction, and attendance at Thanksgiving services is notoriously small. The mood of the 'pastoral' may soon have to be explained as elaborately as has the mood of 'flavour' of an Indian Raga.

Our own past is moving away from us at frightening speed, and if we want to keep open the lines of communication which permit us to understand the greatest creations of mankind we must study and teach the history of culture more deeply and more intensely than was necessary a generation ago, when many more of such resonances were still to be expected as a matter of course. If cultural history did not exist, it would have to be invented now.

VIII. ACADEMIC ATTITUDES

It seems to me that the academic world is very slow indeed in responding to this growing need. History in our universities still means largely political and perhaps economic history. It is true that a few other disciplines have also by now received a licence to make their own cuttings into the forest of the past in pursuit of the history of literature, of music, of art, or of science.

But unless I am much mistaken students are frequently advised to keep to these straight and narrow paths to the Finals and onwards to research, looking neither right nor left and leaving vast areas of the forest unvisited and unexplored.

I would hate the idea of my criticism of *Geistesgeschichte* giving aid and comfort to such enemies of cultural history. It cannot be repeated sufficiently often that the so-called 'disciplines' on which our academic organization is founded are no more than techniques; they are means to an end but no more than that. Clearly the historian of music must learn to read scores, and the economic historian must be able to handle statistics. But it will be a sad day when we allow the techniques we have learned, or which we teach, to dictate the questions which can be asked in our universities.

If the cultural historian lacks a voice in academic councils, it is because he does not represent a technique, a discipline. Yet I do not think he should emulate his colleagues from the departments of sociology in staking a claim to a method and terminology of his own.[72] For whatever he may be able to learn from this and other approaches to the study of civilizations and societies, his concern, I believe, should still be with the individual and particular rather than with that study of structures and patterns which is rarely free of Hegelian holism.[73] For that same reason I would not want him to compete for the cacophonic label of an interdisciplinary discipline, for this claim implies the belief in the Hegelian wheel and in the need to survey the apparently God-given separate aspects of a culture from one privileged centre. It was the purpose of this paper to suggest that this Hegelian wheel is really a secularized diagram of the Divine plan; the search for a centre that determines the total pattern of a civilization is consequently no more, but also no less, than the quest for an initiation into God's ways with man. But I hope I have also made it clear why the disappointing truth that we cannot be omniscient must on no account lead us to the adoption of an attitude of blinkered ignorance. We simply cannot afford this degree of professionalization if the humanities are to survive at all.

I know that sermons against specialization are two a penny and that they are unlikely to make an impression on those who know how hard it is even to master a small field of research. But I should like to urge here the essential difference, in this respect, between the role of research in the sciences and in the humanities. The scientist, if I understand the situation, must always work on the frontiers of knowledge. He must therefore select a small sector in which hypotheses can be tested and revised by means of experiments which may be costly and time-consuming. He, too, no doubt, should be able to survey a larger field, and be well-read in the neighbouring disciplines, but what he is ultimately valued for is his discoveries rather than his knowledge. It is different, I contend, with the humanist. Humanistic education aims first and foremost at knowledge, that knowledge that used to be called 'culture'.[74] In the past this culture was largely transmitted and absorbed in the home or on travels. The universities did not concern themselves with such subjects as history or literature, art or music. Their aim was mainly vocational, and even a training in the Classics, though valued by society, had its vocational reasons. Nobody thought that it was the purpose of a university education to tell students about Shakespeare or Dickens, Michelangelo or Bach. These were things the 'cultured' person knew. They were neither fit objects for examinations nor for research. I happen to have some sympathy for this old-fashioned approach, for I think that the humanist really differs from the scientist in his relative valuation of knowledge and research. It is more relevant to know Shakespeare or Michelangelo than to 'do research' about them. Research may yield nothing fresh, but knowledge yields pleasure and enrichment. It seems a thousand pities that our universities are so organized that this difference is not acknowledged. Much of the malaise of the humanities might disappear overnight if it became clear that they need not ape the sciences in order to remain respectable. There may be a science of culture, but this belongs to anthropology and sociology. The cultural historian wants to be a scholar, not a scientist. He wants to give his students and his readers access to the creations of other minds; research, here, is incidental. Not that it is never necessary. We may suspect current interpretations of Shakespeare or the way Bach is performed and want to get at the truth of the matter. But in all this research the cultural historian really aims at serving culture rather than at feeding the academic industry.

This industry, I fear, threatens to become an enemy of culture and of cultural history. Few people can read and write at the same time; and while we pursue our major and minor problems of research, the unread masterpieces of the past look at us reproachfully from the shelves.

But who, today, still feels this reproach? In our world it is the phrase 'a cloistered scholar' that reverberates with reproach. The cultural historian draws his salary from the taxpayer and should serve him as best he can.

I hope I have made it clear in what his service can consist. For good or ill the universities have taken over from the home much of the function of transmitting the values of our civilization. We cannot expect them to get more thanks for this from some of the students than the parental home sometimes got in the past. We surely want these values to be probed and scrutinized, but to do so effectively their critics must know them. Hence I do not see why we should feel apologetic towards those who urge us to concern ourselves with the present rather than with the past. The study of culture is largely the study of continuities, and it is this sense of continuity rather than of uncritical acceptance we hope to impart to our students. We want them to acquire a habit of mind that looks for these continuities not only within the confines of their special field, but in all the manifestations of culture that surround them.

Take the occasion of this paper. When I was honoured by the invitation to give the Philip Maurice Deneke Lecture, the question naturally struck me how the Institution arose in which I was to play a part. I knew that this particular series owes its existence to the beneficence of the Misses Deneke who instituted it in 1931 in memory of their father. But in making this benefaction they followed a tradition which is by now firmly established in the whole Anglo-Saxon world, the tradition of named lectures as monuments to private persons.

It took a 'traveller from foreign lands' to notice this tradition, for I found that my English colleagues took it so much for granted that I had to explain and confirm that there are no such lectures on the continent of Europe.

In England, it turned out, these lectureships developed organically out of the educational foundations exemplified by the colleges of the ancient universities which, in their turn, arose quite naturally from the medieval bequests for chantries. France still witnessed a parallel growth in the Sorbonne of Paris, called after a private founder, but soon the privilege of naming such institutions was apparently confined to princes and rulers. My own school in Vienna was called the Theresianum, after the Empress, but not before the nineteenth century were Austrian schools called after commoners. What was it that secured this continuity and ramification in England? What induced Lady Margaret Beaufort to found a Lady Margaret Readership and what part was played in the encouragement and preservation of this swelling number of benefactions by the Laws of Trust, which are also apparently peculiar to this country?[75] Admittedly I found it safer to ask these questions at the end of this paper rather than at the beginning, for I do not know the answers. But I believe that these answers could be found and that they need be neither vague nor, as the jargon has it, 'value-free'. Paying tribute to a great tradition, they would also help to vindicate the name and function of cultural history.

The Logic of Vanity Fair: Alternatives to Historicism in the Study of Fashions, Style and Taste

I. THE PROBLEM SITUATION

IN THE spring of 1936 I attended the meeting of Prof. von Hayek's London Seminar in which Karl Popper (not yet Sir Karl) presented the arguments which he later published under the title *The Poverty of Historicism*.[1] This deadly analysis of all forms of social determinism derived its urgency from the menace of totalitarian philosophies which nobody at that time could forget for a moment. But it also had a bearing on my own field, the history of art and of civilization. Indeed, one of Popper's main opponents had a foot in both camps, that of political utopianism and of historical holism; I am referring to Karl Mannheim, whose early studies on the sociology of art and of style[2] had made a considerable impression on those students of the subject who were eager to refine their methods and to substantiate the intuition that works of art do not emerge in isolation but are linked with others and with their time by many elusive threads. From my student days in Vienna I had shared this concern, but I had become increasingly sceptical of the solutions offered by Neo-Hegelian *Geistesgeschichte* and Neo-Marxist Sociologism.[3] This scepticism was not very popular with some continental colleagues, proud of being in the possession of a key that revealed the 'essence' of past ages. On the other hand, it may have seemed exaggerated to my new English friends, who found the whole issue remote.

Today, after thirty years, it is perhaps less the 'poverty of historicism' that needs pointing out, than the need for an alternative. The solutions offered by historicist theories are rarely taken very seriously in academic art history, but nothing very interesting has taken their place.[4] In contrast to the situation in my student days the prevailing mood is a desire for facts, a hope to get on with the business of cataloguing items without much interference from theorizers. No one acquainted with Popper's methodology need be told why this positivist attitude must be self-defeating. Not even a chronicle of art, let alone a history of styles, could ever be based on the collecting of uninterpreted data. This being so, the theories of previous generations are not so much discarded as taken as read. They often form the unexamined framework

Reprinted from *The Philosophy of Karl Popper*, ed. Paul A. Schilpp, 1974.

of teaching and research. Thus what we need is new and better theories that can be tested against the historical material as far as such tests are ever possible.

Such alternatives cannot be pulled out of a hat. But I have at least tried in my book on *Art and Illusion*[5] to explore the limited problem of the history of pictorial representation and to find more convincing reasons for the existence of period styles than the Hegelian 'spirit of the age'. I referred in its Introduction to a passage from the *Poverty of Historicism* which I should like to quote once more in slightly extended form:

> ... I have not the slightest sympathy with these 'spirits'; neither with their idealistic prototypes nor with their dialectical and materialistic incarnations, and I am in full sympathy with those who treat them with contempt. And yet I feel that they indicate, at least, the existence of a vacuum, of a place which it is the task of sociology to fill with something more sensible ... there is room for a more detailed analysis of the *logic of situations*.... Beyond this logic of situations, or perhaps as part of it, we need something like an analysis of social movements. We need studies, based on methodological individualism, of the social institutions through which ideas may spread and captivate individuals ... our individualistic and institutionalist models of such collective entities as nations, or governments, or markets, will have to be supplemented by models of political situations as well as of social movements such as scientific and industrial progress.[6]

The fourteenth chapter of the *Open Society and Its Enemies*, entitled *The Autonomy of Sociology*, explains a little more fully what Popper had in mind when he speaks of these models. It is here that he endorses Marx's opposition to 'psychologism' and analyses in some detail the reasons that lead him to reject the 'plausible doctrine that all laws of social life must be ultimately reducible to the psychological laws of human nature'.[7]

Art and Illusion was mainly concerned with such psychological laws. It did not (or only marginally) concern itself with the genuinely sociological problem of the unintended social repercussions of intentional human actions. A simple illustration of such a problem is taken by Popper from economics:

> If a man wishes to buy a house, we can safely assume that he does not wish to raise the market price of houses. But the very fact that he appears on the market as a buyer will tend to raise the market price.[8]

It is the purpose of this paper to apply the tool of situational logic to some recurrent problems of the history of fashion, style and taste.[9] If I have subsumed these in my title under the name of Vanity Fair it was not to 'debunk' art. It is true that today the element of fashion in the alternations of movements stares the historian in the face.[10] 'Pop' today and 'Op' tomorrow —they justify the joke in the *New Yorker* of the long-haired man's remark at the cocktail party 'I don't know anything about art, but I know what is "in".' Needless to say, this assimilation of art to fashion should not tempt us to think less highly of the great artists of the past or of today. It only makes it easier to recognize the poverty of those historicist philosophies which scrutinize all manifestations of style as the expression of the innermost essence of the 'age'—ours, or another.

II. COMPETITION AND INFLATION

The latest version of historicism current in the critical jargon of the press seeks for the sources of changing style and taste somewhere in the dark recesses of the Collective Unconscious. It may be all the more profitable, therefore, to start this investigation by testing the opposite approach, advocated by Popper where he recommends

> what may be called the method of logical or rational construction, or perhaps the 'zero method' ... the method of constructing a model on the assumption of complete rationality (and perhaps also on the assumption of the possession of complete information) on the part of the individuals concerned, and of estimating the deviation of the actual behaviour of people from the model behaviour, using the latter as a kind of zero-coordinate.[11]

Popper was thinking in the first instance of economic behaviour and the type of deviation from rationality represented by the 'Money Illusion', people's preference for a larger wage packet, even if it does not buy more than the smaller one. Now this model of inflation extends beyond the problems of money values to all tokens of value recognized in society, including fashion, language and art. The way, in fact, in which competition leads to unintended consequences is of prime concern to the student of fashion. All we need for an abstract model of such movements is the assumption that departure from a norm will arouse attention. Given the desire of a member of this group to focus attention on himself, the rational means for that purpose are therefore at hand.

There are closed societies where this game is institutionalized and almost ritualized, and where the auction for attention is confined to a particular area such as the number of heads hunted, or some other token of prowess. The ruinous expenditure on Potlatch feasts among the American Indians, the prestige attached to the possession of many heads of cattle regardless of the danger of overgrazing in certain African societies illustrates the departure from rational behaviour that Popper has in mind. These competitions have brought the societies concerned to the brink of destruction, and yet it is hard to see how the individual, caught up in the situation, can avoid these un-intended consequences of his bid without forgoing the necessary prestige. We are only too familiar with a similar threat summed up in the word 'escalation'.

What characterizes the situation on Vanity Fair is rather the fluidity of the game of 'watch me' that may be characteristic of Open Societies. For here there is no predicting what departure from norm will become a focus of attention. There are the notorious 'crazes' that sweep a school, of collecting cigarette cards or stamps, the performance of daring dos, or the flaunting of provocations, that are as remarkable for their intensity as for their volatility.[12] Satirists have inveighed against what they call the Follies of Fashion; but the folly of the game does not preclude rationality on the part of the players. For fashion can be described in terms of a rarity game. At one time it may be the display of rare lace that arouses attention and competition, at another a daring décolleté, the height of the coiffure or the width of the crinoline.[13] At various times competition has driven fashion to notoriously foolish 'excesses'—though what we call an excess here is harder to tell. Whatever rationalization we may be able to produce for our habit of shaving, to bearded nations or periods this fashion must surely look as unnatural and excessive as the wearing of powdered wigs looks to us. In all these matters some departure from the norm of apparel and appearance must at first have drawn attention for its rarity. If a game of display was in progress the choice in front of the other players was obviously whether to dismiss this particular move as an unprofitable eccentricity that should be allowed to remain one, or to emulate and top it. Once the battle is joined it lies in the logic of the situation that the particular departure from the norm must be trumped if attention is to be kept up.

As long as these games of 'one-upmanship' are played within a small section of people who have nothing better to do than outdo each other, fluctuations are bound to be rapid, so rapid perhaps that the rest of society will not be caught up in these superficial ripples. But occasionally the game catches on and reaches a critical size where all join in. Whether we have our hair cut or put on a tie, whether we drink tea or go skiing, we all join in the game of 'follow my leader'. Given time and sufficient documentation, each of these social fashions could of course be traced in its spread from the habits of a few to the custom of the majority. It would be tempting to attribute this spread of imitation to psychological causes, to man's desire to identify with leader- or father-figures. No doubt such a tendency exists and sometimes accounts for the wish of young people to model themselves on the idols of the screen in their 'set'. But within the context of this section it is more relevant to point out that even conformism is partly rooted in the logic of the situation. We have looked at fashion as a 'rarity game' played by some in order to attract attention. But there is usually also an opposite team, whose aim is to avoid attention. At first of course this team has an easy time. It just refuses to join in. Often, as we have seen, this refusal will do the trick and will leave only the players exposed to the gaze they covet. But the more members of that society imitate the move in order to attract attention, the more its original purpose will be defeated. Leaders of fashion will have to think up a new gimmick. But the opponents of the fashion will discover to their chagrin that now it is they who are conspicuous in the rarity game, they attract unwelcome attention by their refusal to fall in. In most cases there will be a point when even the diehards, the last-ditchers, will give in. They, too, will powder their hair or wear a wig, will shave off their beards or put on a black tie to avoid being stared at.

It is true that by this time fashion will generally have been shorn of its most impracticable extreme. The waves will have been somewhat levelled, but it is still a fact that a move made by a fop to impress his fellow-fops may start a trend that imposes itself on society.

That there is a competitive element in art which aims at drawing attention to the artist or his patron needs no lengthy demonstration. The following figures about the height of French Gothic cathedrals speak for themselves.

> In 1163 Notre Dame de Paris began its record construction to result in a vault 114 feet 8 inches from the floor. Chartres surpassed Paris in 1194, eventually reaching 119 feet 9 inches. In 1212 Rheims started to rise to 124 feet 3 inches, and in 1221 Amiens reached 138 feet 9 inches. This drive to break the record reached its climax in 1247 with the project to vault the choir of Beauvais 157 feet 3 inches above the floor—only to have the vaults collapse in 1284.[14]

The figures strongly suggest a game of 'watch me'—each city must have known what the previous record had been. They also remind us of the important fact that competition in art is not necessarily a 'bad thing'. There are beautiful structures on Vanity Fair which were stimulated by the desire to outdo the neighbour and there are great achievements in art which certainly were stimulated by the desire of artists to vie with their peers and to do even better than the best of them.[15] It is again part of the logic of the situation that where standards are high they may become even higher. After all not even all the excesses of fashion are unbecoming, whatever moralists may say; and, if tradition attributes a natural 'chic' to the Parisian woman, this is precisely because she has learned to care about her looks. Once more we are up against the limits of prediction. For it is clear that competition for attention can lead to the unintended consequence of simply lowering the value of what you have been doing before. This is particularly so where methods of emphasis are concerned, and emphasis is after all a special case of soliciting attention. Decoration is a frequent victim of such inflation. It is well known that within the tradition of Gothic ornament this need to outdo previous work in the admired feature of intricacy gradually led to the 'excesses' of the flamboyant Gothic style, much as the Renaissance tradition was driven—if that is the word—towards the 'excesses' of Baroque and Rococo exuberance in ornament.

In the nineteenth century attempts were made to explain these regularities in psychological terms, that is through the blunting of sensibilities in repetition, the fatigue aroused by forms that are seen so often that they are no longer noticed so that a stronger stimulus is required.[16] There is no need to deny that such psychological tendencies may exist. The instance of the drug addict who needs more and more of the stimulant for its effect to be noticeable provides an illustration. But even in this instance there may be a logical element that forms the background to this tragedy. The habit creates a level of expectation, a fresh norm, but the desire is for 'more'.

However that may be, there are many instances of inflation outside the field of art which illustrate the purely situational element. Take the case of titles and decorations. No one has felt fatigue at receiving a rare honour in a stable society; but once inflation sets in, the whole system is running downhill. The fuss made in England when the 'Beatles' received a decoration sprang from fear of such a precedent.

Hitler's war witnessed a particularly rapid inflation of this kind. At its start the German decoration for bravery was still the Iron Cross. Soon it was topped by the Iron Cross with Swords, which had to yield pride of place to the Iron Cross with Swords and Oakleaves, which was finally outshone by the Iron Cross with Swords and Diamonds. Every new move, of course, pushed the recipient of the previous top award down the ladder and probably made the next wonder what more additions were in store for his successor.

The example sums up the dilemma that is involved in all striving for extra emphasis. It thus serves to introduce the crucial problem of this kind—that of the corruption of language. In this corruption, I believe, both elements we saw at work and a few more can be discerned. If we use Bühler's terminology[17] distinguishing between the functions of symptom, signal and symbol, we may assign the ordinary influence of fashion primarily to the first function of drawing attention to the speaker. Affectations of every kind in the use of rare words fall under this category. We have all witnessed certain expressions becoming 'okay words', being adopted by increasing numbers till they are either replaced by others or become part of the ordinary vocabulary. The turnover of words is rapid in all urban speech. In the Rome of Horace the rights and wrongs of coining words must have been much debated:

> If it should be necessary to refer to recondite things by recent terms ... permission will be granted if it is done with modesty. ... It has ever been permitted and always will be to issue a word stamped with the mint mark of the day. As the woods change their leaves when the year declines and the earlier ones fall, so the old age of words comes to an end and those newborn bloom and thrive like youngsters ... all man-made things will perish, nor will the honour and splendour of language endure. Many will be reborn that have fallen, and those words will fall in their turn which are now honoured, if Usage so wants it, the arbiter judge and norm of speech ...[18]

In this drift of language, of course, the fashion element of 'showing off' plays only a minor part. The signal function, too, can be corroded, witness the fable of the boy who cried 'wolf' once too often. His fate, however cruel, concerns the student of situational logic less than that of the other shepherd boys whose signals he had rendered ineffective. How could they convince the villagers that their cry for help was not a hoax?

Inflationary debasement usually takes its departure from that need for increasing emphasis which we saw at work in the story of the iron crosses. Here the process of inflation really has more than a superficial resemblance to the debasement of currency. Words originally coined as the rarest tokens of exceptional emphasis rapidly sink down to the small change of the advertiser and of schoolboys' slang. It matters little here whether we class the advertisements of 'unprecedented offers', of 'gigantic successes' and 'tremendous sensations' as signals trying to outshout each other and blunting their own effect in the process, or as descriptions. In either case they are the victims of their own erosion neatly illustrated by the true instance of a toothpaste that is sold in three containers—'large', 'jumbo', and 'mammoth' size. 'Large' has come to mean the smallest. And yet one thing is sure. In such an environment it is pointless to try and shout even louder. The only chance for the judicious is negative emphasis, an attempt to return to the original gold standard.[19]

If we decide to call only a large thing 'large' we may re-establish a level where communication is again possible.

Popper has often stressed the responsibility of the individual to maintain the standards of clarity in language which, as a social institution, is as vulnerable as any to the seeds of corruption.[20] What makes it so vulnerable is the fact that, strictly speaking, the introduction of any new word or meaning subtly affects the whole instrument of language.[21]

Any such word will inevitably introduce an alternative, and thus increase the range of choice for the speaker of the language. To use one word (even the old one) thus implies rejecting another, and our appreciation of any statement will be affected by this novel element. When the word automobile received a competitor in the word car the earlier term did not change its meaning, but in England its use began to sound a little precious and affected. When barbers became hairdressers, and ratcatchers rodent operatives, the earlier word began by contrast to sound a trifle vulgar. One of the reasons why it is so hard to know a language well enough to appreciate style is precisely that we must always be able to assess the connotations of the writer's choice between existing alternatives. It is not enough to look up the German word 'Haupt' in the dictionary and find there that it means 'head'. We must also know that the more frequent word for head in German is 'Kopf' and that 'Haupt' is therefore poetic diction or elevated language. The degree to which we feel it to be a justified or a stilted word must depend on long familiarity with usages of every kind. But this familiarity will let us down when we do not know the region, the period or the set of the speaker. As new words come into use, they leave eddies of uncertainties behind and threaten that feeling for nuance on which civilized speech so largely depends. No wonder that some of the greatest lovers of language have also been the most intense haters of neologisms. Every new coinage somehow debases the value of the old mintings. However, it is easier to preach purism than to enforce it; and so we frequently find the purist or classicist in language on the side of authoritarianism.

Nobody has explored the links between fear of change and authoritarianism more convincingly than Popper. From the time when Plato inveighed against change in music, there has been indeed a tendency of conservativism in language and art to ally itself to restrictive governments. The cry, 'this lowers the tone', 'this should be forbidden', may not be commendable, but it is understandable when we find our language threatened. Academies under royal tutelage were the outcome of this desire to arrest the flux of language and of art. They had a case; but the price they wished to exact for the stabilization of currency was too high—as it so often is.

We find the same in all attempts to stem the tide of fashion and competition in a free society, the anti-luxury laws of medieval cities, which make such curious reading, the restriction on building heights or other items of 'conspicuous waste'. These, it seems, can be curbed only at the cost of a police state.

Granted the 'poverty' of historicism where it proclaims immutable laws of history, situational logic and the zero method may thus indeed fill something of the void which Popper's formidable axe has created in the study of movements and trends.

The study of language offers itself as the best testing ground. We need only return to those subtle students of speech, the ancient writers and orators, to find a storehouse of illuminating examples of inflation and its consequences. Discussing the pleasure of novelty and change in oratory Quintilian diagnoses its source correctly:

> Novelty and change are pleasing in oratory and the unexpected gives more delight. Hence we have exceeded all bounds and have exhausted the charm of the effect by too much straining after it (*est enim grata in eloquendo novitas et emutatio, et magis inopinata delectant. Ideoque iam in his amisimus modum et gratiam rei nimia captatione consumpsimus*).[22]

Quintilian wrote at a time when the introduction of verbal fireworks was a much-discussed problem in the art of rhetorics. Some teachers were so disgusted with this so-called Asiatic fashion that they advocated a return to Attic purity.[23] The extremists among these critics did, in Quintilian's words, 'shrink from and shun all pleasing effects in their language and approve of nothing except the plain, the simple and the unstrained'. He compares them to people who are so afraid of falling that they are always lying on the ground. Is a good epigram such a crime? he asks—True, the ancients did not use this device. But from what time on do you call an orator 'ancient'? Even Demosthenes introduced innovations. How could we approve of Cicero if we think there should be no change from Cato and the Gracchi? Before these, however, speech was even simpler.

> As for me, I regard these highlights of speech as something like the eyes of eloquence. I would not like the body to be full of eyes, however, for then the other parts of the body would cease to function. If I really had to choose I should prefer the roughness of ancient speech to the new licence. However, there is a kind of middle way here as well as in the style of life....[24]

There is an even more telling passage in which Quintilian comments on the similarity between language and fashion with urbanity and wit and draws his own conclusion.

Writing more than one hundred years after Cicero, he still considered Cicero the model orator. He was ready to concede, however, that Cicero's critics had a case in one respect. A few more 'epigrams' than the master used might even increase the pleasure a speech could give.

> This is not impossible even without interfering with the argument and the authority of our pronouncement, provided these highlights are used sparingly and not continuously, when they destroy their own effect. But having conceded so much, let nobody press me further. I give in to the times in not wearing a shaggy toga, but not in wearing one of silk; in having my hair cut, but not in arranging it in tiers and locks....[25]

Do tempori, I give in to the times, I yield to fashion. In this pregnant phrase Quintilian has posed the problem of any individual caught up in the situation created by the 'age'. Of course he did not have to yield. He could have refused to insert 'epigrams' in his speeches, worn a shaggy toga and left his hair uncut. But he was afraid that this course of action would have made him even more conspicuous; he feared the charge of affectation more than any other, and so he chose the 'middle road', not running after every innovation but not resisting those that had become generally current. It was a rational course to take.

III. POLARIZING ISSUES IN ART

Quintilian's problem, the problem of change and of the self-consciousness to which it can give rise may be a problem of 'Open Societies'. Not that the closed societies of tribal cultures never witness alterations of style. But, generally speaking, these alterations are gradual and imperceptible, they do not give rise to discussion and do not force the individual to take sides. Where Custom is King and standards are uniform, innovation will generally be frowned upon, and if togas are worn shaggy by one generation, they will continue to be so worn, at least new styles will not be introduced with a flourish.

It is precisely any departure from the accepted norms of tradition that can turn into an 'issue'. We are all familiar with the dilemmas posed by the logic of certain situations. We would not mind, maybe, on a cold day asking the dustman in to join us for lunch; we are certainly not held back from this charitable act by the same kind of social tradition that would make such an

idea unthinkable to a Brahmin. What may hold us back is rather the knowledge that, having done it once, we would have to do it again even when we
have no time or inclination. A failure to call him in a second time would make
him wonder whether he had made some blunder. If, to avoid this unintended
impression, we call him once more, we are on the way towards a tradition
which becomes increasingly hard to break, for not to ask him now becomes
a withdrawal.

To some extent we all constantly act like the timid civil servant who would
like to do a certain thing but refrains for fear of creating a precedent. The
trouble is that this fear is often quite justified within the logic of his situation.
If you depart from the norm in one case, however deserving—for instance in
admitting a student to the University without the required paper qualification
—you make it correspondingly harder for yourself and your successor to
apply the existing rules. No wonder that such concessions are so often
accompanied by the request not to talk about it to anyone. The knowledge
of a rule broken is the knowledge of it being breakable. What is worse, the
knowledge that you did relent once makes any future refusal to relent look
doubly harsh. Where there was no alternative, there could be no complaint.
Where one has been shown to exist, the complaint is only too justified.

At this point a psychological consideration comes in—an expectation unfulfilled seems to register more violently than one fulfilled. This special
weight attached to the negative instance may well be connected with the
survival value of negative tests which Popper has taught us to see.

There are many idiomatic expressions referring to the danger of creating a
situation from which there is therefore no easy way out. 'Where would we
get to?' asks the reluctant bureaucrat, 'we cannot have that'. 'Once you start
it, you are in for it.' German (or Austrian) parlance is even more explicit:
'Fang' dir nichts an, du kannst dir das nicht einführen'' ('Do not start things,
it must not become an institution').

The 'it' which is to be avoided is always in such cases the emergence of
a new tradition which will exact the repetition of an act or a favour which
was intended to be taken in its own right.

The link between this problem and that of inflation is obvious. What was
to make an effect as an exception becomes a norm and has to be outbid if the
effect is to remain. Start writing to someone once at Christmas and he will
be expecting that card and get worried or annoyed if it fails to come. The
same might be true if you wrote every month, every week or every day. It is
the relation to the norm that matters, not the actual frequency of writing.

Our reactions to art are particularly closely bound up with the fulfilment
and denial of expectations.[26] Hence the relevance of norms and the dangers

of inflation discussed in the last section. But however much this consideration may support the case for classicism and conservativism in art, new moves will be made and precedents will be set which alter the situation irretrievably.

It is not surprising, therefore, that such moves can arouse real passions both on the part of those who wish to preserve the norm as on that of the innovators who want to establish a new tradition. The historian of art concerned with the changing styles of Open Societies is familiar with typical situations of this kind. A banner is raised and the world of art is ranged for or against the 'revolution'.

The hostility and mutual contempt with which these warring camps look at each other sometimes recall the fervours of religious wars. For a French classicist it was an outrage which stamped the perpetrator a barbarian to break the Aristotelian Unities of place, time and plot in a play. To the admirers of Shakespeare, determined to break this bastion of conservatism, the Aristotelian Unities were as the red rag to the bull. For a champion of Ideal Beauty in painting the *'naturalisti'* who followed Caravaggio[27] were dangerous subversives; the Spanish writer of the seventeenth century who called Caravaggio the anti-Christ of art[28] did not try to be funny. In Vienna, towards the end of the last century, the followers of Wagner and of Brahms were irreconcilable. When Hugo Wolf heard somebody at a party praise Brahms he sat down on the keyboard with the words 'That is how I play Brahms.'[29]

All these and similar battles in the arts were fought for or against certain principles which I propose to call 'polarizing issues'. Not every challenge to tradition becomes such an issue. Some remain unnoticed or are shrugged off, others may be so successful that they rout the opposing party before it can make a stand. If we can believe historians of literature this is what happened when Cervantes published *Don Quixote*, that deadly satire of Amadis of Gaul and similar Romances of Chivalry. It certainly might have happened that the literary world had been split for and against Amadis. But it appears that this literary survival of a medieval tradition was killed outright, and that no further imitation of the Amadis novels came out after *Don Quixote*, but plenty of continuations and imitations of Cervantes. A new bandwagon was rolling on Vanity Fair.

There certainly is an aspect of all stylistic history that can be described in terms of such triumphs, whether with or without a preceding fight. The spread of the Renaissance was the submission of Europe to the banner of *'all'antica'*. The victory of Neoclassicism was the triumph of the standard of 'noble simplicity' championed by Winckelmann over the playful complexity of the Rococo fashion. Classicism in its turn, of course, succumbed to the bandwagon of Romanticism flying the flag of variety and originality, only to be trumped by Realism and Impressionism enlisting the support of 'scientific truth'.

What should interest the historian who tries to track down these changes is to observe the polarizing issues in *statu nascendi*. The type of documentation I have in mind is exemplified by a passage in the memoirs of an English painter who mixed with the avant-garde in Paris before the First World War. It need not be taken as gospel truth to remain a neat illustration of the Vanity Fair aspect of stylistic change:

> When I used to visit Paris at the beginning of the present century my artist friends in the Latin Quarter would explain that what seemed strange to me in their pictures was due to my own slovenly habits of vision. If I suggested that shadows were grey and not purple they would say, 'That is because you do not use your eyes'; and when we were walking along the boulevards ... I discovered that they were right and I wrong...
>
> But ten or a dozen years later I found that the young artists of Paris had totally altered their attitude towards art. All references to vision were impatiently brushed aside with the remark, 'Yes, yes; but the important thing is not to paint what you see, but to paint what you feel'....
>
> My friends spoke little of things seen; but they were full of ideas, full of theories. A new phrase was an inspiration, a new word a joy. One day a painter I knew accompanied a friend of his, a student of science, to the Sorbonne and there heard a lecture on mineralogy. He returned from an improving afternoon with a new word—*crystallization*. It was a magic word, destined to become a talisman of modern painting. Some nights later while sitting with some friends in the Closerie des Lilas, on the Boulevard Saint-Michel, I incautiously let drop a confession that I admired the work of Velazquez. 'Velazquez!' said the most advanced of our party promptly, 'but he has no crystallization!' ... a new theory of art was being constructed, based on the idea of the crystal being the *primitive form* of all things. Velazquez, I was given to understand, was a Secondary Painter because he employed rounded—that is to say secondary—forms. A Primary Painter, I was told, would preserve sharpness in the edges of his planes and accentuate the angles of his volumes.[30]

The author is not unprejudiced and his suggestion that it was this chance encounter with a word that led the young painters to Cézanne need not be taken seriously. On the contrary, it was their desire to find an alternative to Impressionism that led them to discover Cézanne and sent them in search of a fresh theory and a fresh slogan.[31] And yet this little snapshot from Vanity Fair seems to me more illuminating than many a more pretentious history of modern art which describes the rise of Cubism as a symptom of a New Age.

I believe that here, too, the historian's first concern should be with what Popper calls the logic of the situation. Popper called for 'individualistic and institutionalist models'[32] which allow us to look at such a situation in purely sociological rather than psychological terms. I believe that an almost ideal model of such a 'polarizing issue' lies at hand. It is to be found in Jonathan Swift's famous account of the war between Lilliput and Blefuscu.

It began upon the following occasion. It is allowed on all hands, that the primitive way of breaking eggs before we eat them, was upon the larger end: but his present Majesty's grandfather, while he was a boy, going to eat an egg, and breaking it according to the ancient practice, happened to cut one of his fingers. Whereupon the Emperor his father published an edict, commanding all his subjects, upon great penalties, to break the smaller end of their eggs. The people so highly resented this law, that our histories tell us there have been six rebellions raised on that account; wherein one Emperor lost his life, and another his crown. These civil commotions were constantly fomented by the monarchs of Blefuscu; and when they were quelled, the exiles always fled for refuge to that empire. It is computed, that eleven thousand persons have, at several times, suffered death, rather than submit to break their eggs at the smaller end. Many hundred large volumes have been published upon this controversy: but the books of the Big-Endians have been long forbidden, and the whole party rendered incapable by law of holding employments. During the course of these troubles, the Emperors of Blefuscu did frequently expostulate by their ambassadors, accusing us of making a schism in religion, by offending against a fundamental doctrine of our great prophet Lustrog, in the fifty-fourth chapter of the Blundecral (which is their Alcoran). This, however, is thought to be a mere strain upon the text: for the words are these; *that all true believers shall break their eggs at the convenient end:* and which is the convenient end, seems, in my humble opinion, to be left to every man's conscience, or at least in the power of the Chief Magistrate to determine.

Now the Big-Endian exiles have found so much credit in the Emperor of Blefuscu's court, and so much private assistance and encouragement from their party here at home, that a bloody war has been carried on between the two empires for six-and-thirty moons with various success; during which time we have lost forty capital ships, and a much greater number of smaller vessels, together with thirty thousand of our best seamen and

soldiers; and the damage received by the enemy is reckoned to be somewhat greater than ours.[33]

Swift no doubt intended his story as a parable of human folly, a castigation
of stupidity explicable in psychological terms. But he has done more. He has
devised a convincing caricature of a social situation with a logic of its own.
For the purpose of our analysis we can disregard the story of terror and
persecution Swift unfolds. For even without these outward means of compulsion the situation allows of no easy escape. It is not only the foolish Lilliputian
who is caught up in this quarrel over eggs. Even the most intelligent of his
countrymen who wants to eat a boiled egg has to open it somehow—and try
as he may, he cannot empty his action of significance. If he opens it at one
end he will either show himself to be pro-Lilliput or pro-Blefuscu and if he
laboriously opens it at the side to display his neutrality he will have been
compelled by a foolish situation to perform a foolish act. The same applies
if he decides to give up boiled eggs altogether, which is a poor solution,
particularly if he likes them. Moreover, there may be social situations such as
communal breakfasts in which the withdrawal would be interpreted as an
act of disloyalty by both sides. His best hope, maybe, would be to act the
madman and thus to deprive his actions of any social significance, but the
need for such a desperate course only underlines the power of a situation
from which there is no opting out.

Of course, we must be careful, lest this analysis prove too much. If it were
quite correct, polarizing issues could never loosen their grip, and the war
over the eggs would be doomed to last for ever. Perhaps it is here that psychology comes in; for people do get tired of issues, particularly if a new excite-
ment diverts attention from the old one. It would not be true, moreover,
that the wise Lilliputian could not contribute to this breaking of the deadlock,
particularly if he had the talent of a Jonathan Swift in showing up the
ludicrous side of such quarrels. But attend to it in one way or another he
must, if he is caught up in his society.

There are historians who will deny the relevance of the issue. The story
of the eggs, they will argue, was a mere pretext, an irrelevant frill in the long
chronicle of strife between Blefuscu and Lilliput. Their *real* dispute was over
issues of power, not over the ludicrous myth told to the populace. Though
the secret archives of both islands appear to be irretrievably lost, we must
grant a certain plausibility to this hypothesis. Had the Blefuscudians not
hated the Lilliputians they would not have made an issue of the enemy King's
decree, by aiding and abetting its opponents. But this is precisely what our
analysis would have led us to expect anyhow. The existence of this hostility

does not prove that there was not also an autonomous social situation deriving from the polarizing issue of where to open the egg. Moreover no amount of investigation of the conflict of interests between the two islands would allow us to predict that this particular issue would arise, let alone which side would favour which solution. What could be predicted is only that, if there was any issue, the camps would be likely to divide along party lines.

Actually Swift tells another story earlier in the same chapter, about the internal politics of Lilliput, which confirms this interpretation. The two opposing parties—modelled of course on the Whigs and Tories, or cavaliers and roundheads—are marked by a badge of allegiance that cannot but be fortuitous in its absurdity:

> For above seventy moons past there have been two struggling parties in this empire, under the names of Tramechsan and Slamecksan, from the high and low heels on their shoes, by which they distinguish themselves. It is alleged indeed, that the high-heels are most agreeable to our ancient constitution: but however this be, his Majesty has determined to make use of only low heels in the administration of the government, and all offices in the gift of the Crown, as you cannot but observe; and particularly, that his Majesty's Imperial heels are lower at least by a *drurr* than any of his court; (*drurr* is a measure about the fourteenth part of an inch). The animosities between these two parties run so high, that they will neither eat nor drink, nor talk with each other. We compute the *Tramecksan,* or High-Heels, to exceed us in number; but the power is wholly on our side. We apprehend his Imperial Highness, the Heir to the Crown, to have some tendency towards the High-Heels; at least we can plainly discover one of his heels higher than the other, which gives him a hobble in his gait.

It will be noticed that the two stories do not duplicate each other entirely. In foreign politics, as with the opening of eggs, there is only the stark choice between two alternatives, in internal politics there is a spectrum extending between the two extremes. But this gradualness of transition does not materially change the logic of the situation. A Lilliputian ordering a pair of shoes will still be presented by the cobbler with the awkward and inescapable question how many *drurrs* he wants his heels to be. Even if, like Quintilian, he opts for the middle way, he has to place himself somewhere along the scale.

We need not go far to find an application of these models in the field of art. The most conspicuous polarizing issue in contemporary painting is a case in point. I refer to the issue of 'abstraction'. Whether he wants to or not, the artist today is compelled to attend to this issue. He is of course quite free to shun exercises in what is called 'nonobjective' painting; but he cannot avoid the result that the representational paintings he produces in this situation will be 'non-nonobjective'. He might long for the lost age of innocence, where to paint an apple and a jug meant precisely painting an apple and a jug. But while the polarizing issue looms over him, this innocence is not to be had. Painting a still life becomes, among other things, an affirmation in a situation not of his making. And, though he can preach against the artificiality of the issue, even this will only increase the attention he has to pay to it. Again, it is easy to ascribe the resulting tension to underlying conflicts of power. For, by and large, we find that the geographical distribution of the most vocal partisans pro and con abstract art coincides with the cold war frontiers. There are exceptions, but they confirm the rule. It is of political rather than artistic interest that abstract art is cultivated in Poland and Yugoslavia as an affirmation of independence from the party line that still enforces 'social realism' in Russia and in China. But, though the polarizing issue has been thus drawn into the political arena, it would still be misleading to identify the two. There is no intrinsic reason why Communists should side against abstract art rather than for it. However much they may at present rationalize their hostility in terms of Marxist aesthetics, the fact remains that, at an earlier phase, it was in Soviet Russia that extreme abstract experiments were launched (by Malevich), to be promptly denounced by the Right as '*Kulturbolschewismus*'.

Of course, the fact that the constellation of parties in such an issue can be fortuitous does not mean that it must always be fortuitous, even less that it must be felt to be fortuitous. Reasons can be given for the switch of Soviet art policy from modernism to socialist realism no less than for the official backing 'experimental' art is receiving on the other side of the iron curtain.

It may have been hard to predict which party in Lilliput would wear the high heels, but it is quite intelligible that it was the middle-class party in the English Civil War which had no use for the long hair of the cavaliers and became the 'roundheads' just as their extremist successors in France became the '*sans culottes*'.

It is for this kind of intelligibility that the Hegelian looks in the formation of styles. He wants to identify Gothic elegance with courtly aristocracy and the realistic reaction with the hardheaded middle class. He is sure that the frivolity of the Rococo expressed the decadence of the doomed aristocracy and the severity of Neoclassicism the ideals of the classes which triumphed in the French Revolution. The historian can be forgiven if the crudity and triviality of such interpretations provoke his scepticism;[34] but, though the

Hegelian and Marxist theories of determinism are as fallacious here as in other fields, there is no harm in conceding that even in artistic preferences the dice will sometimes be loaded. There are occasionally elements in an artistic issue that will become fused with a social or political tension.

One style of church buildings was felt to be appropriate for Protestants, another for Catholics, and, though the idea of a Jesuit style used for propagandist purposes has been exploded,[35] the fact remains that the very austerity of the Protestant camp in matters of art created an issue that made the Catholic camp all the more eager to exploit the effects of images and lavish ornament.

It is even possible that the young men of 1912 who rallied round the slogan of crystallization were dimly attracted by the glamour of a scientific term and by some unformulated identification of such hard and cold forms with an antiromantic bias in other spheres of life. In other words, it is possible that the polarized issue becomes a symbol or a metaphor for issues which are less articulate. Possible, but not necessary. Hence it is better at this point to break off this particular trend of thought, lest we are led from a logic of situations into the swamps of psychological speculations.

IV. ART AND TECHNICAL PROGRESS

In language and in art we feel entitled to deplore innovations that turn into issues (though this will not help us much); in other fields we do not, for some innovations may be real improvements that save lives and diminish suffering, in others (and I refer to science) they may bring us nearer to the truth we wish to find. Given these aims (about which there can be little quarrel) it is often easy to say which departure from tradition will be adopted in a rational society. The history of technological progress and of scientific advance is thus to some extent the history of rational choices within an open society. Once bronze was shown to cut better than stones, iron better than bronze and steel better than iron, these alternatives had only to be invented and presented for rational men to use them for their cutting tools.[36] Similarly, Popper has discussed the progress of science, and has asked what social conditions would stop or impede such progress—for instance a ban on free inquiry.[37] The refusal of certain societies to adopt technical improvements is an equally topical problem, for it has turned out to be far from easy to introduce, for instance, better methods of farming in the so-called underdeveloped countries. The reasons have been frequently discussed. To quote the words of a recent broadcast:

They have not passed the first intellectual hurdle, the great innovation which is acceptance of the idea of innovation itself. The annual agricultural round is part of a whole pattern of existence, and it is often religiously sanctioned. The seeds have to be blessed this way; the ploughing should not begin until after a certain saint's festival; only men may prune the olive trees; only women may gather the olives—and so on. Deviation means anxiety about the possibly fearful consequences. And it is not impossible to appreciate this point of view even for a product of a scientific Western culture. A fertility rite usually does look much more impressive than a dressing of ammonium sulphate, besides usually being more fun.[38]

The detailed analysis of any such situation in which improvements are resisted might be an excellent way to test the capacity of Popper's 'zero method' to lead cultural studies out of its reliance on organicistic holism. To put it briefly, any tool or action that serves a great multiplicity of purposes will be much harder to change and therefore to improve than anything that serves only one particular aim. A cutting tool, as we have seen, can certainly be improved by sharpening and hardening the cutting edge. A knife that one also wishes to use as a paper-knife should not be too sharp, for, if it is, it tends to slash the pages. Improvement in one respect makes it useless in another. If this is true of such simple and perfectly rational aims, the situation becomes more acute where some of the purposes are strongly charged with emotions. We are told that for a time Picasso never shaved without drawing lines in the lather and turning his face into the mask of a clown. As long as this habit lasted he would not have been a likely customer for an electric razor, however much the new device may be superior to the older ones. There can, of course, be few technological improvements that do not disrupt some habit and threaten some aspects of a way of life.

In many cases, therefore, technological change is at first confined to strictly utilitarian functions, while other spheres even in our society tend to respond more slowly or resist them altogether. The ceremony of Knighting is still performed by the Queen with the technologically obsolete sword, not with the butt of an automatic rifle. Candles are still lit in church, and cumbersome seals are still appended to important documents, though one could think of many means of achieving their purpose more easily and more lastingly.

But this special aura that for us surrounds the technically obsolete and the archaic, the judge's wig, the don's gown and the guardsman's gala uniform, only serve to confirm the influence which an increase in alternatives has on the gamut of expressive symbols. It was the invention of paper that made vellum look solemn.

Some idea of progress (as a possibility rather than as an impersonal force) is inseparable from the Open Society. Its members must believe that things and institutions can be discussed and improved. Its champions, therefore, can be forgiven when they look with exasperation at their opponents, who fight for the status quo at any price. For good or ill this issue of 'progress' has become the dominant problem of Western Society ever since the Enlightenment proclaimed its faith in the perfectibility of man and society. The French Revolution notoriously consolidated this issue in the 'polarization' of politics with the 'radicals' on the left, the 'reactionaries' on the right. And just as eggs and heels in Lilliput were turned into issues, with the camps aligned according to these dominant tensions, so art has been caught up in the political problem of the nineteenth century and become 'polarized' in progressivist and conservative schools. It is not surprising that even the advocacy of technical innovations in art was seen as a symptom of radicalism and that a resistance to such innovations tended to brand the critic as a stick-in-the-mud. What is more surprising is rather that the fit is far from perfect.[39] Artists of the 'avant-garde' (such as Degas and Cézanne) were sometimes found on the political right while their medievalizing opponents (such as William Morris) were on the political left.

The poverty of the kind of historicism that applies the idea of progress to art has often been castigated but never been exorcized. Maybe the logic of situations and the zero method can help here, too, to clarify this all-important matter.

What we call 'art' in primitive societies is obviously so deeply embedded in the ritual and life of the community that its multiple purpose makes change very precarious. Painting and carving for instance may have a magic or religious as well as a decorative and prestige function. The age of these traditions is often felt to be the guarantee of their value and efficacy; and since no rational criteria can exist to decide which image is more efficacious such changes as occur must be due to accidental 'mutations'.

But this ritualistic conception of painting and sculpture may be losing its grip in a society that is exposed to many influences from outside. The travelling merchant may come home with tales of images seen elsewhere that surpassed, in his judgement, anything his native craftsmen had ever done. In stressing this role of culture clash in the emergence of Open Societies I am of course following Popper's lead.[40] Where art is thus prized loose from its multiple allegiances, the question of standards can come up with new force.

I have tried to argue elsewhere that in the first Open Society, that of

Greece, a technological and even scientific element did indeed enter art, as can always happen where one rational purpose is regarded as overriding. I have suggested the hypothesis that for the Greeks this aim was the representation of a sacred story as it might actually have looked to an eyewitness.[41]

Granted a specific demand of this kind, technical progress towards its achievement is certainly possible.[42] The stylistic changes in Greek art from the archaic representations of the sixth century to the illusionistic illustrations of the third constitute the most famous advance of this kind, which was recapitulated in the Renaissance development from Giotto to Leonardo da Vinci. It is true that, in postulating such an underlying purpose that would explain the successive innovations of these styles, we are using our hindsight. We cannot prove that the sculptors of the Temple of Aegina wanted to render the human figure as naturalistically as did their successors on the Parthenon pediments, nor can we give evidence to show that Giotto would have admired Leonardo. All we can demonstrate is that naturalistic inventions spread with the same rapidity as did other technical innovations. The mastery of the nude in Greek art impressed sculptors as far as Afghanistan and Gandhara; the invention of perspective in Florence conquered France and Germany within a century.

Even in a case like this the disruptive effect of this improvement on other functions of art was very serious indeed. The illusion of depth threatened the decorative unity of painting that displayed its lucid pictograph on a ground of gold. The mastery of the nude in Greek art led away from that simplicity and grandeur of form we admire in Egyptian statuary.

Speaking more generally, the technical innovations threatened the artist's tasks of creating a rich and satisfying order with his well-tried elements.[43] It is in this way that progress creates a polarizing issue in art, for it presents the painter or sculptor with a choice of priorities. Are you ready—for instance—to risk disruption for the sake of this increase in naturalism or would you rather confine your art to the traditional game? Art is not a game; but there are important elements these two pleasures share—in both activities there are rules and there is mastery. The mastery is achieved within the rules through years of practice that explores the possible initial moves and their potentialities for further achievements. This mastery depends to no small extent on the exact knowledge of means. The weight and size of tennis balls is fixed and so are the dimensions of the court and of the net. It is within these fixed conventions that the champion develops his capacity to calculate and predict. Of course, a good player may take some change in these conventions in his stride; but the idea of 'improving' tennis by giving his balls more bounce or his racket a boosting device would strike him as silly.

The champion's fans, in their turn, who flock to Wimbledon would certainly stare in incomprehension if it were suggested to them that times had changed and that they should learn to appreciate a new game. If one struck their fancy and they wanted to understand its finer points, well and good; but where was their obligation to do so?

If art were nothing but a game this comparison would completely dispose of all historicist arguments in criticism. Neither players nor connoisseurs are interested in changing rules, let alone games. It is possible that only in such situations art can blossom to real refinement. The Chinese scholar looking at a painting on silk of some bamboo stems shares with the connoisseur of games something of this developed pleasure in *finesse*. The suggestion that this art could be improved by changing tools or media he would probably dismiss as barbaric.

But, for good or ill, as we have seen, art as it is functioning in our society is not only a game of this kind. It derives from its functions a technical component that is intrinsically unstable and shares with language the drift towards inflation. These two sources of instability may well belong together. At any rate, each of them can result in that disturbance I have called a 'polarizing issue'. What appears as an improvement to one side, may be felt as a disruption by the other. But once the initiative is with the innovator, the defence of the status quo becomes increasingly difficult. When more and more artists have gone over to more naturalistic methods, the old game will acquire a precious or a musty look. More and more gifted artists will be attracted by the challenge of the new one, and the old playgrounds will be increasingly deserted of players and spectators. The game may survive for a time as an archaizing ritual played by defiant outsiders who may have all the right arguments but meet with no response. Their decision to keep up their little cult will impress their contemporaries as preciousness and affectation. When this moment comes, one of two equally undesirable things may happen according to the logic of Vanity Fair—either the game dies out, or the preciousness will attract the snobs and will bring the game back into fashion, but with very different social overtones. And, whether we want to or not, we cannot easily disregard these overtones.

V. SOCIAL TESTING AND THE PLASTICITY OF TASTE

During the last few years of the nineteenth century the polarizing issue in architecture was the question of the use of iron. Was the Eiffel Tower to be accepted as a work of architecture or was it just a feat of engineering? More was involved in this dispute than a mere verbal quarrel. The architects felt that the integrity of their art was threatened by the new material. Perhaps their attitude becomes more understandable if we look at it in the light of the first section. For architecture as an art also works with accents of emphasis. A high tower, a vault of wide span are the high-points of the architect's vocabulary. We still marvel at the lofty vaults built by the Romans and by the cathedral builders. These famous buildings established the scale within which the tradition of architecture worked. Now the use of iron threatened this scale and upset the whole hierarchy of values. Any railway station could boast of a wider span than the most monumental of classical interiors. No wonder that architects tried to resist this dislocation, which upset their whole game. Let the engineers construct what they liked, but let architecture retain its established vocabulary.

In this situation before the turn of the century, a German critic and historian wrote a passage that seems to me to sum up the most important problem which concerns us:

> It is not much use to dismiss the impression (made by iron constructions) as inferior. After all, it looks as if the majority of people and a large section of the architects were increasingly accepting these impressions as satisfying. If the others, who are trained in the theory of art, continue to disapprove, this may easily bring them into an opposition to the progress of the world, in which they will certainly be the losers. The question therefore is not how to mould iron to make it conform to our taste, but the much more important one, how to mould our taste to make it conform with iron?[44]

At first blush this looks a cynical pronouncement. 'Jump on the band-wagon and learn to like it.' Indeed, when I once quoted it to a group of architects, they became downright abusive. Not that they disliked iron, but they were rightly suspicious of the relativism this advice seemed to imply. It appears to challenge the belief in objective solutions which are 'liked', because they are good. It undermines the idea of art as an autonomous realm realizing values which are and remain independent of technical change. As an admirer of Popper's social philosophy my immediate reaction to this pronouncement was equally hostile. It seemed to me the embodiment of historicist opportunism. Moreover, I remembered an important passage in the *Poverty of Historicism* in which Popper takes issue with Mannheim in a related context. Mannheim had suggested that the political problem was to organize human impulses in such a way that they will direct their energy to the right strategic points and thus lead to the transformation of society in the desired direction. Popper points out to the

> well-meaning Utopian that this programme implies an admission of failure ... for ... the demand that we 'mould' these men and women to fit into his new society ... clearly removes any possibility of testing the success or failure of the new society. For those who do not like living in it only admit thereby that they are not yet fit to live in it; that their 'human impulses' need further 'organizing'. But without the possibility of tests, any claim that a 'scientific' method is being employed evaporates. The holistic approach is incompatible with a truly scientific method.[45]

As an admirer of Popper's methodology, however, I have also learned from him that one must be critical of one's own reactions. Maybe there is something in the German critic's formulation that we can and sometimes must mould our taste. If it is, this would prove to be a source of weakness in art, but it may not be uninstructive to probe this possibility.

Clearly, architecture is one of those multiple-purpose activities in which the artistic aim is only one of many. If the use of iron allows us to house many people better, it would be criminal to reject it for aesthetic reasons. We still have a right to regret the passing of the timber age and of the beautiful stone buildings of the pre-industrial era; but our regrets are irrelevant to the architect working today. But should we not rather accept this change as a necessary evil, should we not face the fact that art had to be sacrificed to efficiency and hygiene? Not, surely, if we are architects. To an architect the new material does present a challenge, and an exciting one; he must try to subdue it into order and beauty, to create a new game that can be played with iron, and the greater the problem, the more he will perhaps come to 'like it'. He must discover the potential of the new material, and when he has found it, we too may see the point and 'like it', provided we share in his adventure. Thus the plasticity of our aesthetic reaction, which the critic's pronouncement implied, may be a fact, although a disturbing one. Is all taste acquired taste?

These questions may lose some of their sting if we return to the difference between the problems of technology and science on the one hand, and those of art on the other. In technology progress can be specified once aims are stated; in science the aim is implicit in the search for truth. If there were something corresponding in art, it should be the creation of something we can 'like'. There have, indeed, been attempts to describe art in some such terms as a technology for the achieving of certain pleasures, the creation of that 'aesthetic experience' about which we read so much.[46] One would like this to be true; for, if it were, our spontaneous reactions to works of art would be the sole and safe criterion of their excellence. I would still defend the position that Mozart has found means of giving real pleasure to human beings which are as objectively suited to this purpose as are aeroplanes for flying, that Fra Angelico has discovered ways of expressing devotion or Rembrandt of hinting at mysteries anybody can learn to see because they are 'there'.

And yet we know from history and from our own experience that there were and are large groups of people who never 'liked' Mozart, Fra Angelico or Rembrandt, and who totally failed to appreciate their miraculous achievements.

It is perhaps important at this point to stress that a belief in the objectivity of artistic standards is not necessarily refuted by the undoubted subjectivity of likes and dislikes. Clearly those who do not like a game will not become good judges of players, and those who do not want to touch wine for whatever reason will not become connoisseurs of vintages. With most people, at least, liking is a preliminary condition of appreciation. Only if certain types of art hold a promise of pleasure for them will they make the effort of attending to the individual work. They may find they like ballet and dislike opera, enjoy eighteenth-century music but avoid the Romantics, or prefer Chinese to Indian art. Naturally, they would not claim to be able to distinguish excellence from mediocrity in the products of art forms or schools that 'leave them cold'. The professional critic, it is true, can attempt to surmount this subjective reaction. He may, on occasion, be able to appreciate artistic achievement in an artist or period that does not much appeal to him. He may for instance find Rubens not very sympathetic but come to admire his verve, skill and imagination. Or he may fail to respond to Poussin and still learn to understand what his champions see in him.

And yet it may be argued that this 'cold' appreciation of what we really do not like is a poor substitute for the experience a work of art can give us. This experience is bound up with love. There is an element of initial yielding in this response that can perhaps be compared with what psychoanalysts call transference. It includes a willingness to suspend criticism and to surrender to the work of art in exploring its complexities and its *finesse*. If we try to be merely unprejudiced in our approach we shall never find out what the work can offer us.

We know from Popper, moreover, that this demand for unprejudiced objectivity represents altogether an impossible and erroneous methodological position. The objectivity of science does not rest on scientists being free of preconceived views and theories, but on their readiness to test them and to listen to arguments leading to their refutation. But, if I am right that, as far as the testing of artistic excellence is concerned, such a critical attitude may impede the test, it becomes clearer why dogmatism and subjectivism are so prevalent in artistic matters. In this respect artistic creeds are indeed closer to religion than to science. The awe and consolation connected with religious experience also depends on such an initial readiness on the part of the worshipper and this readiness he mostly derives from tradition. In growing into the group he learns what to revere and what to abhor, and, whenever he is doubtful, he will anxiously look to other members to see whether he adores the right thing and performs the right ritual. The places of worship of rival sects may not only leave him cold, but appear to him as abominations. But the only test he has to distinguish between the holy and the unholy is the reaction of his group.

It is the probing of this reaction that I propose here to call 'social testing'. It need not take the form of a formulated question—we soon learn to feel how our actions or utterances are 'taken' by those around us. It is well to remember, moreover, that this kind of 'social testing' is the rule rather than the exception not only where religious beliefs are concerned, but also in matters of behaviour and even of ordinary beliefs. The child will try out an opinion and search the face of his mother or, later, of his companions to find out whether he has said something silly. In most cases, in fact, there is little else he could do to form his opinions. It is through social testing that most of us have arrived at the opinion that there are no witches; just as our ancestors arrived at theirs, that there are. Even the rationalist, as Popper has pointed out, must take a lot on trust in what passes for knowledge.[47] He only differs from the dogmatist in his awareness of limits, his own and those of others. He is ready at least in principle to test any opinion and to ask for credentials other than social ones.

It is here, of course, that the difference between scientific beliefs and artistic taste is crucial. For, in art there are no credentials that could be probed in the same systematic way. Debates about artistic merit, though I do not consider them empty, tend to be laborious and inconclusive. What wonder, therefore, that there are few areas where 'social testing' plays a greater part than in aesthetic judgements? The adolescent soon learns that the group can be a dreadful spoilsport if he confesses to liking something that has fallen under a taboo. Imagine a young Spaniard in the first decade of the seventeenth century meeting his friends after a longish absence abroad and mentioning casually that Romances of Chivalry are his favourite reading. Suddenly he finds himself the centre of mocking attention; he is called Don Quixote, or the Knight of the Sorrowful Countenance, and may never live this down. It would need a strong character in a similar situation to stick up for Amadis of Gaul and to discourse on its artistic merits which, after all, had recently been apparent to everyone. Even if our imaginary victim tried, the defence would die on his lips. He would find in his heart that maybe Amadis was all a lot of nonsense and that he was silly to have been taken in by that bombast.

The more seriously art is taken by any group, the more adept will it be in such brainwashing; for to enjoy the wrong thing in such a circle is like worshipping false gods; you fail in the test of admission to the group if your taste is found wanting. In the light of these solid facts it is curious to reflect on Kant's opinion that the aesthetic judgement is entirely 'disinterested', entirely free, grounded only in the conviction of what every developed human being would enjoy. One wonders whether that was true even of the Sage of Koenigsberg. Whether not even he was influenced in his preferences by his group and by its ideas of 'good taste'. He probably never observed the nexus between aesthetic and social appeal, because he lived in a relatively closed milieu and because he was not very much involved in artistic matters. Had he been, he might have had occasion to see the pathetic desire of the socially insecure to 'like' the 'right thing', and the feeling of anxiety that can arise in a situation where an unlabelled and unconnected work of art is displayed that does not seem to fit any pre-existent aesthetic pigeonhole. Contrary to Kant's opinion, it sometimes looks in such situations as if the expression 'I like it' really implied, 'I believe that is the kind of thing my group accepts as good. Since I like my group, I like it, too.'

Here are the roots of the unholy alliance between snobbery and art that no observer of our social scene can have missed. There is every reason to combat the attitudinizing to which it leads; but not everything is snobbery that is sometimes branded with this stigma.

Much has been written and talked, for instance, about the way art lovers have been known to enthuse about forgeries, which they then discarded contemptuously, once the fraud had been exposed. The suspicion is always voiced that this transformation of liking into disliking reveals the first as mere sham and the outcome of snobbery. It is an understandable suspicion and one which may not be totally off the mark in many cases, but, in so far as it implies that hidden postulate of an entirely unprejudiced appreciation, it is mistaken. We are never uninfluenced by our previous experience and expectations. We cannot approach all works of art without a theory, nor can we set out independently to test every reputation. There is just no time, nor, perhaps the fund of emotional response, to enter into every encounter with a work of art with such a mixture of readiness and critical detachment. Tradition, even where it is not accepted dogmatically, presents a tremendous economy. It is something to be told that among the countless items in our heritage the works of Homer, Shakespeare or Rembrandt have given much enjoyment to those who surrendered to their magic. If I am told, therefore, that a drawing is by Rembrandt, I shall approach it with the expectation of finding a masterpiece. I shall look for the signs of mastery to which I have responded before in Rembrandt and will surrender myself to the promised pleasure. This means no more than that I have learned to have confidence in Rembrandt and that I take his lines on trust even where I may find them at first a little puzzling. Can I be blamed if my enjoyment turns into embarrassment and disgust on finding that my trust has been betrayed?

Take the case of 'Ossian's' poems, which were hailed with such enthusiasm in the eighteenth century not only by snobs but by people who cannot be accused of ignorance of poetry—Goethe, for instance. Surely it does make a difference to our attitude whether we read them as the genuine creations of a primitive and heroic tribe or whether we know them to be little more than a literary fraud concocted by a sophisticated antiquarian. The uncritical acceptance of this fraud, incidentally, is instructive within the present context. It was perpetrated within a situation created by a polarizing issue. Reaction against the dominance of the classical dogma in poetry was the overriding problem of poetry, particularly in the non-Latin countries which resented the pretensions of the French to be the guardians of the one and only classical standard. The rejection, by this standard, of Shakespeare as 'barbarian' naturally invited the retort that, maybe, the French were not barbaric enough? Rousseau had provided enough ammunition for such an attack. And was not Homer, the expression of an heroic age, still ignorant of rules and polite conventions? Were not folk songs pure poetry? It was this debate that explains not only the forgery of a large body of barbaric poetry from the wilds of Scotland but also its reception. Ossian was a godsend, a confirmation of the theory that the anticlassicist camp was in the process of formulating. Moreover, it bolstered the self-respect and self-confidence of those nations that could not boast of a Roman lineage. What wonder that the champions of this movement 'liked' Ossian and failed to notice the false notes of inflated pathos and overemphasis that strike us today as obviously jarring?

Such are the perils and pleasures of Vanity Fair. The classicists who had been conditioned to respond to Virgil, Racine and Poussin never explored the alternative traditions, for they were 'put off'—as the excellent idiom has it—by certain external irregularities. And, though some of them might have had the satisfaction of not having 'fallen for' the Ossian fraud, they might have paid for it in not appreciating Shakespeare either.

We have here come back to the problem of polarizing issues from another angle.[48] The situation tends to create self-confirming aesthetic theories. Each side in such a dispute will tend to look first at the badge on any work of art that comes its way. How does it stand with regard to the dominant dispute? If they find signs that it comes from the 'right camp', they will receive it with a warm glow which in itself will be pleasurable to experience and will be productive of more pleasure as the work unfolds its qualities. A work of art would have to be very poor indeed not to be 'likeable' in such favourable conditions. If, on the other hand, the work comes in the hated wrappings of the hostile camp, the partisan art lover will scarcely bother to cut the strings and have a look. In this climate of opinion even a good work will be likely to wither and die. It is true that history records enjoyable exceptions to this rule. Hugo Wolf, who treated Brahms with such contempt, was heard to mutter at a first performance of a Brahms symphony: 'Hell, I like it.' (*Teufel, mir gfallts.*)[49] What was said of the influence of the planets also applies to social pressures—'they incline, but do not compel'.

If this analysis has been correct, the situation in aesthetics is not dissimilar to the one in ethics. In both areas of value the standards of the group influence our decisions, in both they become internalized in the voice of the conscience or what psychoanalysts call the superego. There is an anxious creature hidden in us that asks 'may I do this', or 'may I like this?' Yet in one respect there is surely a great difference between ethics and aesthetics. Where moral issues are concerned we must obviously battle against conformism and preserve our critical independence in the face of social pressures as far as is humanly possible. For ethics is not part of Vanity Fair.

Art, too, is important; and those of us who believe that it is must certainly do their best to remain as honest in their own reactions as Hugo Wolf could be. They must try what they can to ignore their fond prejudices and to see the possibilities of achievement on the other side of the fence. A distaste for the devotional art of nineteenth-century pseudo-Gothic should not prevent us from looking at such church furnishings and glass with a certain awareness that our rejection of this kind of product is socially conditioned; nor should our readiness to admire children's art make us incapable of remembering adult standards. But there clearly is a limit to this process of self-criticism in matters of taste, and it may well be that we may have to accept this social element in our reactions as the price we pay for untroubled enjoyment. Hugo Wolf's—as we have seen—was not untroubled. We may have to admit, in other words, that something of this enjoyment belongs to the pleasures of the Fair. I do not think (to repeat) that such an admission would have to destroy our belief in standards. Nor is it necessarily good for art to be set up on a pedestal high above the market place. *Ernst ist das Leben, heiter ist die Kunst.*[50] Too much moral solemnity may kill it.

VI. HISTORICISM AND THE SITUATION IN MUSIC

I have left the problem of music to the last, not only because it lies largely outside my competence, but also because music presents a special case. It is a game and an art that relies on the listener's memory for what has gone before, for only this recollection will allow him to build up expectations, and experience delight at the transformation and elaboration the composer introduces. Small wonder that for the less musical a work gains in beauty on several hearings and that for many familiarity is a condition of complete enjoyment. If not familiarity with the individual work (which is the ideal case) then at least familiarity with the composer's idiom which allows the listener to 'follow' more easily, even though he may not know the name and function of the various conventions which he has learned to recognize. But if music is in this respect a special case, it is also one that for this very reason shows the mechanism of self-reinforcement particularly clearly at work. Few music lovers want to attend to a work of which they do not know and like the idiom; fewer would want to give it a second hearing. Hence it is the constant complaint of professional critics that the public boycott new music, that they only flock to hear what these critics contemptuously dismiss as the 'old war horses', such as Beethoven's symphonies or Handel's 'Messiah', and that the presence of an unknown work by a modern composer on the programme means the risk of financial failure.

As one who still likes Beethoven symphonies and is likely to stay away when a modern work is announced, I must confirm the existence of this situation, though I resent the critic's tone. If he hears these symphonies too often, this is an occupational hazard which is pretty irrelevant to the general argument. Moreover, the argument he generally uses or at least implies is pure historicism of the brand Popper should have disposed of for good and all. We are told that we must 'go with the times', that each age has its own idiom or style, and that Beethoven, who may have been all very well for the early nineteenth century, has nothing to offer to the second half of the twentieth.

In conversation Popper has often drawn my attention to the devastating effect that Wagner's Hegelian futurism has had in this respect on the theory of music. It is Wagner who is largely responsible for this 'polarizing issue' of musical thought in the last century. It was he who wedded the historicist belief in progress and evolution, which so preoccupied the nineteenth century,

to the genius worship of the Romantics and turned himself into the exemplar
of the genius who is spurned by the multitudes but worshipped by the elect.
I remember an old lady in Vienna who was born in the 'fifties of the last
century telling me how Wagner's writings and prophecies had impressed
her and her friends in their youth and how she had become a 'Wagnerian'
before having had an opportunity of hearing any of his music. She still remembered how shocked and bemused she felt when *The Valkyrie* was at last
performed in Vienna and the prelude contained no recognizable tune. Were
the critics who attacked Wagner perhaps right after all, or was she possibly a
philistine herself? It is an unpleasant situation to be in, and as far as I know
she quickly climbed out of it. Being disposed to like Wagner, she looked for
the features she could like and so she could again feel happy in the company
of those brilliant people she respected and loved. Brainwashing in art is quite
possible; and if one makes the effort one can no doubt make oneself like
something that one did not care for before. We conservatives in music (and I
know I can include Popper here) find it hard to get rid of the suspicion that
many critics and other partisans of serialism have undergone a similar forced
conversion. They were first converted to historicism and futurism, to the
Hegelian creed of the march of the mind to its predetermined goal, and then
considered it their duty to side with contemporary experiments. The more
their self-respect depended on their liking what they approved of, the more
they invested in efforts at appreciation. If they now had to confess that really,
after all this effort made for extraneous reasons, they found the game not
worth the candle, they would feel traitors to their cause. I have spelt out this
suspicion of the antihistoricist in music, but I admit that it is both libellous
and self-reinforcing. I cannot disprove the claim that people really like
Schoenberg; in fact the evidence is that some really do. What would be open
to me is to taste and test a serialist piece by Schoenberg myself more seriously and more earnestly. But here my suspicion stands in the way. Not that
I have never tried to listen; but by and large such efforts as I have made
flagged after a time when I was 'put off' by a specially ugly sound or a
particularly historicist defence. Popper, I know, has made great efforts in his
youth, when he was well acquainted with Schoenberg's circle, and has still
found his suspicion confirmed that the moving ideology behind these innovations was historicism. Maybe his and other people's personal accounts have
'brainwashed' me in my turn and made it harder for me to see (or rather
hear) the other side of the issue. Theoretically I must grant the possibility
that, despite the historicist nonsense talked by Schoenberg's champions,
there are fascinations in the serialist game which long effort and familiarity
would reveal. And I must concede it to my opponents that I do not make the

effort because I am dogmatically convinced that Mozart will be more worth-while every time. At the same time I must admit that one of the unintended consequences of my dogmatism is in fact a worsening of the situation for composers writing now. For, if my arguments in this paper hold, it is not only the historicist creed that prevents them from writing now in Mozart's or Beethoven's idiom. They may curse or at least deplore the changes Wagner or Schoenberg introduced into the language of music, but they can-not wholly undo them. To be sure, it is open to anyone today to write in a classical or preclassical idiom, and I hope I am not betraying any secret if I mention that Popper has taken this course, writing fugues in the strict style of Bach. I do not know whether he would do so if he were a professional composer rather than a philosopher. At any rate, whether he would or not, he could not prevent his choice from meaning something different to what it meant in Bach's time. Not that Johann Sebastian himself was a vanguard or fashionable composer. On the contrary. He was certainly somewhat out of touch with latest developments. But he did not try to write like Lassus or Palestrina.

I cannot write fugues in any case; but I am not sure that, if I could, I would not be swayed by the consideration summed up in the Latin proverb 'si duo faciunt idem, non est idem'. In other words I would find it a problem how far to 'give in to the times'.

It is this logic of the situation that makes artists and critics so susceptible to the historicist's message. If the past cannot be retrieved, why not enjoy the drift to the future? The Hegelian theories they like to appeal to are, from this point of view, little more than what psychoanalysts call rationalizations. They provide a grand excuse for what Quintilian did with a shrug of his shoulders. They neither have his wisdom nor his humility to use his argument; for to 'make concessions' is the worst sin in their code, 'to be committed or engaged' the greatest virtue.

It is here, I think, that the nonhistoricist could help to break the dead-lock by pointing out that life consists in making concessions and that situa-tions in art may occasionally exact them, not, indeed, as virtues but neither as terrible vices.

All artists must be opportunists if we mean by 'opportunism' the desire to be liked, to be heard and considered, especially by their friends and their friends' friends. It is in this way that the polarization of opinion will generally react on the artist who is reluctant for his work to appear in a garb that will 'put off' his friends. The difference here between the genuine artist and the mere time-server is not, therefore, that the one forges ahead regardless of anyone, while the other wants to please the right people. It is that for the real artist concessions will be mainly matters of avoidance. He will instinctively turn away from methods or styles that have come to sound hackneyed or un-promising; but he will leave all these considerations aside once he has found his problem and has started to wrestle with his material. In other words, the real artist will obviously do his best in a situation in which the plasticity of taste and the corruptibility of his medium will have deprived him of any firm standards except those provided by his artistic conscience. He will neither eat out his heart in nostalgia, nor set his sights on a future which may never come, but will use the material at hand. As a painter who was himself critical of abstract painting and had succumbed once said to me—one must go where the fighting is! Rationalization or not, it is hard to see how this reaction can be wholly avoided in the situation in which artists find themselves. Even after the hoped-for demise of historicist creeds the whirligig of fashion will turn on Vanity Fair. It lies in the logic of the situation, as I have tried to show, that those arts which are no longer anchored in practical functions will be most easily drawn into this giddy movement. This is one of the unintended con-sequences of that emancipation from utilitarian ties for which so many great artists strove. No wonder artists today tend not only to be historicists but also romantics longing for a return to the shelter of a closed society, past or future. But if that is the choice, the fair is preferable to the barrack square.

The results to which I have come in this paper are a little distasteful to my own inclinations and prejudices. I certainly would not want them to provide ammunition for those who talk of the 'inevitability' of any particular development in modern art, nor would I want to cheer the trimmers and opportunists on their way to success. I would therefore not have ventured to draw such dangerous conclusions from the flimsy premises of Vanity Fair if I did not hope that they may provoke Sir Karl Popper to a critical reaction that will restore the independence of art from social pressures and vindicate the objectivity of its values.[51]

London, November 1965.

Myth and Reality in German Wartime Broadcasts

THE CHOICE of a subject which is bound to evoke so many grim and painful memories requires a brief word of explanation. It is true that the study of myth is germane to the work of the Warburg Institute, and that the relation between reality and illusion has concerned me in my own research. But the pursuit of these problems has taken me across the boundaries of many fields, and when I was honoured by the invitation to give this lecture, which commemorates a great historian, I naturally looked for a historical subject in which I had really specialized. I am afraid I found only one. From the age of thirty to thirty-six I was concerned with the body of documents I propose to bring to your attention today. Working at the Listening Post of the B.B.C. first as a so-called monitor and then as a monitoring supervisor I must have heard, recorded, translated, or read a considerable proportion of all German broadcasts for the German people from December 1939, when I joined the service, to December 1945, when I left it.[1] As a historian I witnessed the war not only through the British news media and the realities of life 'somewhere in the country', as the formula was, but also through the distorting mirror in which Goebbels wanted the German people to perceive it.

As you may know, a fresh body of documents has come to light fairly recently which adds yet another dimension to my wartime experience. I mean the confidential minutes of the meetings Goebbels held almost daily with his propaganda team and which have been published *in extenso* covering the period from October 1939 till 19 June 41,[2] and at least in ample extracts till 13 March 1943, that is till after Stalingrad.[3] I do not think it is an exaggeration to say that these publications render all earlier books about Goebbels and German propaganda obsolete.

Let me give you an example: We monitors were only too familiar with the habit of the German Home Service of interrupting its programmes for a special announcement proclaiming yet another victory on land, on sea, or in the air. These triumphal communiqués, which marked the progress of the German forces in Norway, in France, in the Balkans, in North Africa, and in Russia, were introduced by a blare of trumpets, and followed by a martial song, each campaign having its special signature fanfare and its special chant of triumph. It was obvious that a lot of care had been bestowed on these

---

The Creighton Lecture in History delivered at the Senate House of the University of London on 10 November 1969.

dramatics, but the new Goebbels documents add telling details. When in June 1940, shortly after Dunkirk, the zealous German editor of an illustrated weekly published a feature about these special announcements which showed the record of victory fanfares being put on the turntable, Goebbels was furious. If such a disillusioning picture was ever published again he would not hesitate to send the editor to a concentration camp and to have the censor who passed it arrested.[4] Did he want people to think that a massed band of trumpeters really assembled and burst out in joyous music every time they heard of a victory? Certainly not. He did not want them to think at all. They should surrender themselves to the spell of the medium and be carried away by the elation of the moment without the disillusioning intrusion of reality.

For Goebbels, of course, looked upon propaganda as an art and he saw himself as a great artist capable of playing on the emotions of the nation. Like an artist he carefully distributed his climaxes and decreed in advance, for instance, that during the coming Balkan campaign there should be no more than two (or at the most three) of the maximal victory announcements with drum rolls and hymns to prevent the effect from wearing off.[5] I do not think myself that he need have worried. Such effect as there was, was surely due to the victories rather than the victory announcements. But the belief in the omnipotence of propaganda which pervaded the policy of the German wireless was not only due to Goebbels' inflated sense of self-importance. He had taken over this belief from his master, Adolf Hitler. It is plain how this myth arose if you read the many turgid pages of *Mein Kampf* in which he expounds his faith in the power of words. Hitler was convinced, or professed to be convinced, that the German army had never been defeated in an honest fight. The war was lost on the home front, because Germany's enemies had discovered the black magic of psychological warfare, against which the straight and decent Germans had no defence. It was this theme that sent Hitler to the then popular studies on the psychology of the masses, notably to Le Bon's famous book of 1896, from which he derived his conviction of the basic irrationality, emotionalism, and extremism of the crowd.[6] To make a lasting impression on its members propaganda must be restricted to a few themes and slogans, but these must, in Hitler's words, be perpetually repeated. 'Whatever change may be introduced for variety's sake, must never affect the content of the message but must always say the same thing in the end.'[7]

Not that Hitler's faith in the power of this method derived entirely from books. He had experienced it—or at least he thought so—in the political rallies in which he tried out the power of repetition by denouncing the Jews and the disgrace of Versailles and had unleashed those storms of emotion the theory had promised. It was the mass rally that carried Hitler and Goebbels from strength to strength and ultimately to victory through intrigue and intimidation. Small wonder that the novel instrument of radio was conceived by them first of all as a means to extend the range of listeners and thus to convert the whole of the nation into a super-monster rally which hung on the lips of the Fuehrer and at least vicariously joined in the cheering and the chanting of slogans.

I am not sure that German home broadcasts ever got away from this basic conception of the loudspeaker as an amplifier of the political meeting. Throughout the first years of war its professed highlights were the carefully managed relays of Hitler's or Goebbels' speeches, which were invariably held in front of responsive and well-drilled audiences. People were encouraged to listen in groups, in factories and barracks, for the idea of the hearer alone in the privacy of his room and even able to switch off was anathema to this theory. It has often been remarked how diametrically opposed to this fiction of an extended super rally was Roosevelt's conception of what he called a 'fireside chat'. Here the speaker pretended to visit the home, there the home was swept into the Sportspalast.

Hitler's speeches, especially after he had become chancellor, were of course built up as historic events, acts of state which determined the fate of the nation and of the world. I am not sure that the younger members of this audience can have an adequate conception of these occasions even though they may have heard snippets of recordings or seen extracts from newsreels. It is in the nature of things that these extracts concentrate on the emotional climaxes and thus have preserved the memory of Hitler's terrifying hysterical screams. But these frenzied outbursts were carefully prepared and set off by long dull passages delivered in a deep voice in which Hitler acted the statesman rendering account to the nation.

On the German wartime radio these two contrasted styles were initially allocated to two agencies. The German High Command used a terse and tight-lipped style which the propagandists extolled as soldierly reserve. The commentators in their turn provided not only the fanfares but also the screams of delight or injured innocence. For the war which Hitler started with his attack on Poland in the autumn of 1939 was to be the first war in which one of the newly developed mass media was harnessed to the purpose of making the whole nation vicarious participants of History with a Capital H—*Weltgeschichte*. The nine news bulletins of the day—not counting special announcements—the political commentaries given by such ace performers as Hans Fritzsche, the feature programmes of outside broadcasts from the Home Front and from the War, even the carefully dosed mixtures of serious and martial music and the occasional hours of uplift were all planned to make the listener feel that he or she was living through great times and stirring events, and that the radio provided him with the privilege of witnessing history in the making.[8]

Meanwhile, the mass media have made us familiar with this claim as all of us remember who watched the first moon landing, but in 1939 the cliché had not yet worn so thin. Indeed there were times, then as now, when the claim may not have been far from the truth. Action and propaganda, myth and reality, appeared to fuse particularly at the moment of that carefully staged historic melodrama when the surrender of the French army was arranged as a symbolic act specifically designed to reverse the result of the German surrender of 1918. As you know, the railway coach in which the first surrender had been negotiated was specially brought back to Compiègne from a Paris museum to this end and the world was treated to ecstatic descriptions of the ceremony in which the alleged shame of the past was wiped out by the genius of the Fuehrer. You will find a good account of the radio's treatment of this episode based on our monitored material in the book by my late friend Ernst Kris and Hans Speier on German Radio Propaganda published in 1944.[9] Let us remember that if England at that time had accepted Hitler's peace offer, this theatrical performance would have become a world historic event rather than an episode which we all prefer to forget.

World history as seen from Germany at the time was the fulfilment of a destiny, the redeeming of a promise. This promise lay implicit in the Nazi conquest of Germany, the *Kampfzeit* to which Hitler, Goebbels and the others would revert in good times and in bad; for just as their miraculous rise had triumphed over their corrupt opponents on the left and on the right, so the reborn nation would triumph over the envious and decadent warmongers in the West who were always referred to as the Plutocrats. For as you know, it was part of the Nazi myth that National Socialism was a revolutionary creed. There was no comparison possible, as Goebbels wrote, between the First World War and the Second, for now the German army carried the spell of invincibility, being preceded by the magic of a glorious revolution.[10] It was this rather than the more esoteric sides of National Socialist ideology that was kept in the foreground of propaganda. The cranky mystique of Rosenberg and of Himmler would obviously have alienated the mass of Christian listeners, and even too explicit an emphasis on the racial superiority of the Nordic *Herrenvolk* would have created diplomatic and psychological problems with Italy and with Japan. But the slogan of the young nations was sufficiently vague to be flexible and sufficiently emotional to be rousing, and so the German armies were made to march into France to the strains of the *Frankreich Lied* 'We come and smash their old and corrupt world to bits'.[11]

In this initial reading then, the war, which had of course been forced upon Germany, was no more than the regrettable friction that accompanied the birth of the new era and so obvious was the superiority of German morale and German equipment that the front line was little more than a demonstration piece of German courage and chivalry. In the middle of May the department of propaganda of the High Command had issued a directive that newsreels should avoid sights apt to arouse horror, revulsion, or disgust of war.[12] In the Front Reports of the radio, fighting seemed equally rarely to involve wounds or death. This makes the exception all the more telling and an example of death in battle may introduce you to the style in which the German myth was presented to the German people, as far as this is possible in translation.

When the German battleship *Bluecher* was sunk off the Norwegian coast in the spring of 1940 the High Command had announced, perhaps truthfully, that most of the crew and the soldiers on board had been saved. Still, this implied that some had died, and so the Front Reporter Heinz Laubenthal told the story of the ship's last moments as he had allegedly heard it from a Lieutenant-Colonel:

> Suddenly the stern reared up, seven to nine metres straight into the air, and we see it clearly, there stands a man, upright and erect, his arm lifted in the German salute. I have seen statues, medieval knights of shining metal, carved figureheads of legendary fame, but I shall never forget this living symbol of a German soldier standing like this in his hour of death ... we on our island were thrilled to the marrow, a German soldier who knows how to die, a hurrah broke loose, and our fervent hearts welled over in the song 'Deutschland, Deutschland über alles'.[13]

The death of an enemy soldier was a different matter; though when the reporter occasionally mentioned a fallen Norwegian, Frenchman or Englishman he rather tended to reflect on the poor dupe who had been sent to his fate by the irresponsible warmongers. But there was an exception even in these early months of the war—French colonial soldiers from Africa had always been singled out as an object of special hatred by German nationalists, and encountering their dead bodies after their position on the Somme had been wiped out by dive bombers, the same Heinz Laubenthal described how he saw them lying there in heaps with lacerated and distorted features:

> Animal is too honorific a name for these monsters in human shape, with their bloated lips, far-protruding teeth, flattened noses and matted hair.[14]

Such gloating over individuals remained an exception, but it was different with collectives when towns and even whole countries were described as receiving the heavy punishment that awaits those who challenge German might. Warsaw and Rotterdam had committed this crime, and soon it was to be the turn of London.

During the Battle of Britain the leading official of the Propaganda Ministry, Eugen Hadamovsky, took over the role of the star reporter recording his despatch directly from a bomber over London on 11 September 1940:

> We can see an endless chain of lights, in fact, it looks as if London were lit up by one gigantic system of illumination, but it is not an illumination ordered by Churchill. Unheard by us, without respite, the most ghastly scenes must be occurring down there, beneath our machine....
>
> We see the blazing metropolis of England, the centre of plutocrats and slave holders, the capital of world enemy number one.... Here go the bombs, they have found their mark but we still circle over the city a few times so that those below should hear that we are here ... (18.00).[15]

As you can imagine, I was not much inclined to believe German broadcasts, but I do remember the feeling of exhilaration when I visited London after this report and saw it still standing.

Goebbels was aware of this discrepancy. In fact he issued the directive that expressions such as 'London in flames' should be avoided[16] but, he hoped, not for long. On 7 September[17] he had explained to his team that the coming destruction of London would probably be the greatest catastrophe in the history of mankind, and this 'measure', as he called it, would somehow have to appear as justified in the eyes of the world. Recent British raids on Berlin had done too little damage to justify a proper outcry, but it was hoped—and these are his words—that other British raids would provide such an opportunity as soon as possible.

I do not know to what extent the R.A.F. obliged, but it appears that on 19 September the children's hospital of Bethel was hit and nine people killed. The directive was of course that this incident should be 'thoroughly exploited'[18] and here is what we heard.

> Murder upon murder is the pass-word of the British warmongers. Churchill is letting loose his airmen against the civilian population of Germany. With typical British brutality he makes them attack places marked with the Red Cross as sanctuaries of Christian love. The eyes of the German people have been opened once and for all. It is Churchill's aim to exterminate German women and children. Churchill, who pretends to fight for the interests of Europe, has plunged his European allies into misery. Chur-

chill, who once dared to pose as the protector of the German people, now shows his real feelings, he hates the German people from the depth of his soul.... This brutal hatred, which we once failed to understand, is now returned by us. The blood shed by Churchill's mercenaries in Germany, the blood of German mothers and children cries out for retribution and harsh retaliation, which so far is only in its initial stage. (20.9.40, 22.00)

I have had to shorten this tirade, for it lies in the nature of things that I cannot give you an adequate picture of the style which turned the news bulletins of the German Home Service into cataracts of abuse. Following Hitler's precepts of repetition and emotionalism they were of course intended to drown not only the still voice of reason but the louder voice of enemy broadcasts in what came to be known as the ether war. For the German propaganda machine had to adjust willy-nilly to the difference between a mass rally in a closed hall and the reality of an audience endowed with the capacity of twiddling knobs.

To listen to foreign broadcasts was naturally a crime in wartime Germany. But Goebbels' conferences show how this possibility or likelihood was constantly on his mind. Carefully dosed announcements had to be made every few weeks about heavy prison sentences imposed for black listening, dosed, because if all had been published the frequency of the offence itself would obviously have clashed with the myth. Most of all Goebbels was concerned from the outset that every line of enemy propaganda should be countered or rather smothered in the torrent of words that poured from German loudspeakers. As long as the war went well these polemics were actually grist to his mill. They provided so many pegs on which to hang the repetitive slogans in which he, no less than his master, believed.

The only variation open to the German newscaster in this programmatic and intentional monotony was a variation in tone between the sneer and the smear, the supercilious satire or the shrieks of abuse. Here is an example of the first of 11 May 1941:

The fugitive Duchess of Luxembourg talked on the English Radio on the occasion of the anniversary of German troops entering her country. Resorting to laughable excuses she called her own flight and that of her Government from Luxembourg a demand of duty and of honour.... Needless to say, this charming set of democratic émigrés would have been incomplete without Wilhelmina the Dutch. For good measure she made no less than two speeches on the English Radio, which were conspicuous by their mass of empty verbiage. (14.00)

You may notice two characteristics of this silly item, which I picked almost at random. The first is that it contains no overt lie. The Duchess surely did speak and I have no reason to doubt that she spoke of the demands of duty and honour. After all the purpose of this kind of item was to take the sting out of speeches which had been made, just in case anyone had heard them. The cheapness of the sarcasm is equally intentional. Hitler and Goebbels had nothing but contempt for those fastidious intellectuals who failed to see the need for crude vulgarity in effective propaganda. Here the smear comes into its own as you may see from a news item of 19 September 1941:

> A branch office of Roosevelt's gangsters in the Argentine: Judah's candidate for the throne of world domination, Herr Roosevelt, has hired a shady character for the pursuit of his sinister aims in the Argentine. An Argentinian deputy devoid of honour and dignity, by name of Taborda, has founded a crime club at Roosevelt's behest. The task of this criminal gang is to sling mud at the German Legation and other German institutions in the Argentine. By means of forged documents, infringement of diplomatic rights, and slander, Taborda and his evil associates pursue the plan which Herr Roosevelt has hatched.... Germany will not take it lying down if her official representatives are to be made the victims of Roosevelt's gangster conspiracy. (21.00)

Please remember that what I have just read was a news item in a news bulletin. Admittedly its news content was minute. One cannot imagine anybody in Germany in the autumn of 1941 when the fate of the Russian campaign hung in the balance to be interested in the alleged activities of Señor Taborda in favour of the Allied cause. But information was not part of the purpose. It was simply to hammer in the association Roosevelt–gangster till it became automatic. In the spring of 1942 Hitler had recommended in his table talk that in home broadcasts Roosevelt should invariably be called a criminal and Churchill a drunkard.[19] But by then he was perhaps a little out of touch. For clearly even in this technique there is a law of diminishing returns. However effective the shouts of 'criminal' may have been during the *Blitzkrieg*, listeners must have wearied of this artificial frenzy. In fact we monitors noticed a decrease in the volume of Billingsgate as the war dragged into its third year. At the end of 1942 we were startled to find the assassination of Darlan commented on in the following manner:

> The violent end of the French traitor-admiral Darlan continues to form a topic of conversation in the whole world. Concerning the attempt on the life of the French ex-admiral which had been ordered by Churchill the following reports are at hand: New York: the murderer of Darlan was

yesterday placed before a court-martial, Anglo-American Headquarters in North Africa: Darlan's murderer was sentenced to death ... his name is kept secret. (26.12.42, 12.30)

And so on with further brief quotations of datelines and agency reports.

To us this swing of the pendulum appeared as a sign that there must have been a profound crisis of confidence in Germany, which compelled the German service to imitate at least the form of Allied factual broadcasts. I have not seen any direct instructions demanding this switch, but we now know that Goebbels admitted in November after El Alamein when Stalingrad only just held out and North Africa had been invaded that the task of German propaganda was 'not easy', as he put it.[20] In particular he became incensed against the German High Command for having withheld the news of the fall of Tobruk. 'There was a danger of a very serious crisis of confidence at least in the field of news policy.'[21] It was this crisis which led to the sobering up of the style of German news bulletins which had been coming for some time.

But I think we must avoid falling into the trap of taking Hitler's and Goebbels' assertions about the essence of their propaganda at their face value. The repetitive style of news presentation could be safely dismantled without affecting the core of the technique and without jeopardizing the ultimate aim of Nazi propaganda. This was and remained to allot to every item of news and every event its proper place within that preconceived pattern of historical development which I have called the myth. Whether he shouts or instructs, the propagandist takes care to focus the listener's mind on this lesson. For example:

Roosevelt continues his systematic pillaging of the small South and Central American States. Reuter learns from Washington that, like other Central American States, Honduras, too, has now been forced to sign an agreement in Washington under which she has to sell her entire rubber output up to the year 1946 to the U.S.A. (5.8.42, 20.00)

Notice that by subordinating an event which can be of little interest to the German listener to the general idea of 'Roosevelt's systematic exploitation of helpless states' the propagandist has turned it into yet another incriminating incident. He then has merely to insert the word 'forced' into the text of the Reuter message and he has made this Allied report fit for inclusion in a German home news bulletin. Or:

It is symptomatic of the progressive Bolshevization of England that the following suggestion has been made by an English sociologist in a letter to *The Times*: he demands that the task of carrying out the social and economic changes in post-war England should be entrusted to an economic-political Soviet. (3.8.42, 17.00)

The key word in this last item is the opening word '*bezeichnend*', significant or symptomatic. The term provides the magic wand by which the most trivial story or incident can be turned into an important message.

In the course of listening to German broadcasts I gradually arrived at a formula which Goebbels to my knowledge never put into words: it is that whatever is reported of the home front should, if possible, be represented as a symbol of German strength and heroism like the saluting soldier on the sinking ship—while anything that is reported from the enemy camp should be interpreted as a symptom of his depravity and basic weakness.

There exists a mental condition which is prone to this type of reaction—I mean the way the paranoiac scans his surroundings for signs to confirm his ideas of persecution and wickedness. I should like to propose that what is characteristic of Nazi propaganda is less the lie than the imposition of a paranoiac pattern on world events. Not that Goebbels ever shunned the lie when it suited his purpose, but the most downright fabrications were generally reserved for the so-called black transmitters which posed as the voice of dissident Allied groups. These worked for such short-term effects as the spreading of panic during attacks; Goebbels knew very well that as a long-term strategy lies such as 'London in flames' might be found out. Whether he was fully conscious of the strategy of paranoia I would not know, but he cannot have been unaware of the basic technique, used year in year out to dissolve the news in propagandist comment, which was no less characteristic of German broadcasts at home than those for abroad. Take a relatively minor incident such as the Allied occupation of Madagascar in May 1942. German listeners were told:

... the cowardly attack on Madagascar pursued two intentions: to divert attention from the series of military defeats suffered during the last few days, which found its climax in the Japanese victory at Corregidor, which has just been announced, and also to create a base replacing the incomparably more valuable British bases which were surrendered to the U.S.A. in return for fifty old destroyers. (6.5.42, 12.40)

Brazilian listeners were given a slightly different interpretation:

The real reason for the occupation of Madagascar is that Britain wishes to secure a good naval base before she loses all her positions in India. (Zeesen, 9.5.42, 01.15)

A Spanish broadcast for Latin-America insinuated another motive:

> Do you believe that the prestige success in Madagascar will placate Comrade Stalin, i.e. meet his demand for the opening of a second front? (Zeesen, 6.5.42, 04.15)

and the same commentator two days later:

> ... in attacking this defenceless island Great Britain has shown that she suffers from a deep inferiority complex. (Zeesen, 8.5.42, 04.15)

What is interesting in this last quotation is, of course, the ease with which the propagandist makes use of the tools which modern psychology has developed for the interpretation of motives, I mean the psychoanalytic interpretation of human motivation. It would be interesting for the historian to try to trace the methods of real or pretended political analysis deriving from the two powerful trends of our time—psychoanalysis and Marxism. Both have been called methods of unveiling or unmasking,[22] and both clearly lend themselves to the misuse of imposing a particular reading on events. The history of the application of these techniques to psychological warfare would offer an interesting topic of research. Not that it would be an easy subject, for we are all so much influenced by these attitudes that we have come to take them for granted. I have just provided an example myself, for though I know nothing of psychiatry I have still ventured to diagnose the pattern of Nazi propaganda as paranoiac. Maybe it is I who impute such motives, where there was only honest interpretation?

I admit that Pilate's question 'what is truth?' is not easy to answer, least of all in the welter of war. But the historian also knows that there are straightforward techniques which can be employed to detect bias, for if the treatment of events and motivations is elusive and their interpretation subjective, the treatment of texts is a different matter. Let me give you an example which happened to interest me for obvious reasons: On 21 July 1943 the German home news bulletin reported:

> Berlin: on 6 July the *Daily Sketch* expressed itself in favour of the bombing of Rome. From the paper's argument it can be seen that the deliberate bombing of European cultural monuments is partly due to the feeling of inferiority on the part of the British and the Americans. The *Daily Sketch* says: 'We have always found that Rome with its huge buildings, gates, roads and triumphal arches oppresses us. If all these monuments were left unharmed the wish would always remain to restore them to their former significance. We in London would therefore welcome the disappearance

of these monuments from Rome.'—The British paper thus demands the destruction of the cultural monuments in Rome because London, New York and Washington do not possess anything of the kind. (14.00)

I was sufficiently startled by this report to look up the *Daily Sketch* of the relevant date. Needless to say the paper did not demand the destruction of Rome; but it did publish a letter by one E. G. Bisseker, who took issue with another correspondent who had evidently wanted Rome to be spared on account of its connection with civilization and culture.

> I have always found—says the letter—that Rome oppresses me with its bombast, its Forums, the King Emmanuel monument, the Triumphal Ways and Arches. If all the monuments to the conquering Caesars are to remain intact, there will be never ending desire in the future that they shall come to mean something again. We get on much better in London without these extravagant reminders of war, and it would be just as well for them to disappear from Rome. The real culture of Italy is in Sienna, Florence and such towns, and I should regret their bombing almost as much as I do that of Coventry.

I do not want to pretend that this was a sensible letter, but it clearly never demanded that cultural monuments in Italy should be destroyed because London, New York and Washington had none. But then it was not from this text that the propagandist derived his interpretation. It was from a speech by Goebbels made ten days before the letter ever appeared. Speaking at the opening of the Munich art exhibition on 26 June of that year he had said:

> It is a historic inferiority complex that runs amok, trying to destroy in our lands what the enemy himself cannot create and what he was never able to create in the past ... they lay waste the towns of Europe, because they are unable to equal such examples in Chicago or San Francisco...

Such a speech, of course, was tantamount to a directive. It was the task of the propagandist to hammer home its message throughout the subsequent campaign. In fact the letter in the *Daily Sketch* fits this campaign so neatly that one might almost wonder if it was not a plant. Goebbels did make use of this technique, particularly when he was short of quotes from the neutral press, but I do not think that we need suspect such an elaborate procedure here. The dutiful propagandist who scans the incoming messages for suitable material will always be likely to find something that can be accommodated to the required stereotype.

In this respect, too, the evil art of hate propaganda is not so far removed in technique from the mechanism of real art. In my book on *Art and Illusion*[23]

I have tried to show how the artist makes use of what I called schemata and how he scans the world around him for motifs which can be accommodated to this pre-existent vocabulary. Unconscious projection merges into conscious distortion. Sometimes the stereotype will automatically modify the motif he wishes to portray, another time the transformation becomes more conscious in the interest of an artistic aim, as happens in caricature and cartooning.

I have referred to the cartoon figures of the gangster Roosevelt and the drunkard Churchill. But like the cartoonist the propagandist must also know how to personalize groups or nations and to build up these images again and again out of almost any material.[24] Hans Fritzsche was particularly well versed in this trick. Thus when it had been announced in April 1942 that he would discontinue his talks and join the army, he pretended to be outraged by the surprise and speculation this news had allegedly caused in England. What a symptom of depravity:

> The British assertion that it is something quite new when men doing political work become soldiers . . . demonstrates with the utmost clarity the difference between the two philosophies . . . which clash in this war.

And soon he led up to a personification of Britain which showed that this astonishment was all of a piece with her well-known qualities:

> England, who for centuries always invested money in her wars but let mercenaries and auxiliaries do the fighting for her, entered this, her fateful struggle, once more in the part of the moralizing tea-drinking governess who faints if anyone treads on the tail of her lapdog, but would have thought the starving out of all the women and children of a whole nation—had it succeeded—as a deed particularly pleasing in the eyes of God and particularly humane, above all since no blood is shed in death by starvation. (28.4.42, 19.45)

You see how the propagandist effects the transition from the interpretation to personification of the enemy. He links his comment to the old and familiar stereotype of perfidious Albion as a cruel tea-drinking governess who cannot but act or react in this typically wicked way.

Thus when I chose as my title 'myth and reality' I was not only trying to find a more genteel formulation for the blunter title of 'lies and truth'. Just as the primitive myth studied by anthropologists tends to personalize the forces of the natural universe into beneficent or malign beings, so the Nazi propagandist transformed the political universe into a conflict of persons and personifications.

Seen from Germany, the war was a mythical drama of young Siegfried fighting manfully against the evil schemers who had tried to keep him down. Luckily the very wickedness of these cartoon figures contained the seeds of their ultimate undoing. For after all it sprang from the laws of their being that they would ultimately do each other in. The paranoiac projects his own paranoia on the world around him.

England, naturally, has always fought to the last Frenchman, Greek, Russian, or whatever the topical version of that old jibe may be. But the English have found their match in the Americans, who hope for their exhaustion so that they can inherit the earth; they in their turn are the mere tools of the Bolsheviks, who would be the real gainers if Germany were to lose the war, and by the Bolsheviks the initiate does not mean the Russian people, for these, finally, have been enslaved by the Jews. It is in the revelation of their evil plot that the Nazi technique culminates.

Let me just quote a few headlines of political commentaries given on the German radio by one Peter Aldag between April and July 1941 and which he collected in a pamphlet:[25]

> Does England fight America's battles? South America in the grip of Plutocracy; Plutocracy and Bolshevism meet in the murder of the defenceless; Smuts, the mercenary of Plutocracy and Jewry; Who financed the Bolshevik Revolution? Who drove the U.S.A. into the World War? Sidney Hillman, symbol of the Trinity of Plutocracy, Judaism and Bolshevism; The triad of Plutocracy, Judaism and Bolshevism; Churchill and the Bolsheviks . . .

Of course it was not the Nazis who had invented anti-Semitism. Even that notorious old forgery, the so-called protocols of the Elders of Zion who had worked out a secret blueprint for the enslavement of all peoples, was only taken over and disseminated by Hitler's propaganda.[26] And yet it may be argued that if the Jews had not existed, they would have had to be invented; the myth demanded for its consistency some cement that held it all together. The Jews had proved their usefulness as scapegoats in internal propaganda, for since some of them are poor and others rich, some conservative and some radical, any anti-Semitic movement can represent all other parties as 'Jew-ridden'. The same is true on the international plane, for since Jews are scattered over the globe they provided the unifying element that was still missing. Thus when Hitler attacked Russia without warning on 22 June 1941 he proclaimed, as you know, that he was 'foiling the plot of Jewish Anglo-Saxon warmongers and the equally Jewish overlords of the Bolshevik Headquarters in Moscow'.[27] It is this gigantic persecution mania, this paranoiac myth that holds the various strands of German propaganda together.

Now in speaking of paranoia I do not want to give the impression of proposing some wild and far-fetched hypothesis as if the Nazis had fomented a particular mental disease. Paranoia is not simply an illness like typhoid. In the sense in which I use it here it is rather the pathological magnification of a reaction to which we are unfortunately only too prone, because it is rooted in the given contrast between me and 'them'. I am, of course, good and right and I work as hard as I can, and if my wishes remain unfulfilled this must be due to 'them'. It is they who thwart me and do me down. Every frustration may produce such irrational reactions in all of us. If I have to wait long for a bus it would not take much to persuade me that London Transport just wants to make all decent people late, and if the bus, when it comes at last, does not take me I will brood on ways to expose the whole sinister establishment which is out to paralyse the life of London. If we can also laugh at our fantasies, this is due, I believe, to our knowledge that others would laugh at us. But remove this safeguard, forbid any expression of doubt in the paranoiac myth and you will automatically foster the tendency to what psychologists call regression, a back-sliding towards the more primitive habits of mind which Le Bon attributed to the crowd. The language we speak is imbued with myth, and so we return with ease to the animistic reaction of turning abstractions into living entities and classes or nations into mythical beings. Force everyone to chant the same slogans, wear the same badges and uniforms, and inflate their egos by flattery and community feeling, and the opponent will almost automatically increase in stature, for how else can you explain that the world does not acknowledge our superiority and our right? I say the opponent, for clearly in the regressive state the outside world which frustrates us is no longer a medley of unpleasant realities but a negative image of our own claims and aspirations. They are as much one as we are. And if we cannot see them as one, the reason must be precisely that they hide behind so many masks. Here indeed is another sign of superiority. We are not taken in. We know. Join us and be initiated into the secret that explains your and my sufferings.—You will notice that the years of contact with propaganda have turned me into a pessimist in these matters. The defence of sanity is never easy, since the world is not a pretty place and material for this kind of artificial psychosis is always at hand. Germany was not a pretty place when Hitler, the typical man with a grievance, set this mass psychosis in motion. It was a worse place when he had succeeded in bludgeoning critical reason at home and mobilizing the outside world against him. But at least he could offer a key to it all.

You remember the news item: 'Judah's candidate for the throne of world domination, Herr Roosevelt...' You believe that Roosevelt is the chosen representative of the American people? How naïve of you, he is really the tool of the hidden hand. You believe that Churchill is the Premier of England? He is really the Plutocrat who has sold out to the Bolsheviks. You think the Bolsheviks are the Russians? They are just being whipped into battle by the Jewish commissars. But are not the Americans capitalists and the Russians communists? Your naïveté again! All this is camouflage of course; they are all in league, their only aim is to hold down the young and vigorous nations, who must be enslaved and exterminated. But if all nations knew their true interest the world would soon be at peace again, for the war is only a war against the devil, the Jew.

I believe that in a paradoxical way this propaganda claim has not remained without effect. What has remained of this terrible war in the public memory and in the minds of the young is mainly that Hitler ran amok against the Jews. The unspeakable horror of the extermination camps with its six million Jewish victims has all but eclipsed the other horrors perpetrated by the Nazis against literally untold millions of Eastern slave labourers, Russian prisoners of war, and all their other opponents in the vast area they had occupied extending from the Atlantic coast to the Volga and from northern Norway to the gates of Egypt. You may want to know how much of this terrible reality was allowed to leak through to the German news media. In a way I have given the answer already. The myth excluded such blemishes. The only real exception I remember—and how could I ever forget it?—was the announcement that, as a reprisal for the killing of Heydrich, the whole male population of Lidice had been executed and the women and children sent to a concentration camp; but this announcement was confined to the regional wavelength of Bohemia. As far as I remember concentration camps were not mentioned on the Home Service except very late in the war when they were described in a talk as places of harsh corrective labour, presumably both to intimidate and to reassure the home population.[28] Nobody was expected to inquire what happened to the Jews who were deported to the east. When a fraction of the terrible news seeped through to the west, Goebbels had no advice to offer but the old boomerang technique of accusing the enemy of atrocities.[29] The more cruel the enemies were made out to be, after all, the more would the German people see the myth confirmed and the more desperately would they resist defeat.

For this, in a way, is the final horror of the myth. It becomes self-confirming. Once you are entrapped in this illusionary universe it will become reality, for if you fight everybody, everybody will fight you, and the less mercy you show, the more you commit your side to a fight to the finish. When you have been caught in this truly vicious circle there really is no escape. Compared with this effect the principle of advertising and mass suggestion in war propaganda may almost be called marginal. There are strict limits to what you can make people do or believe in this way, you certainly cannot repeat for long that defeats are victories without losing their confidence and you cannot tell them no bombs are falling when their cities are being laid waste. We have seen in fact that German propaganda was led to revise its advertising technique as Germany's fortunes changed in the third year of the war. But this change of style did not affect the basic pattern of paranoia. For the bombs which fall can still be a confirmation of the enemy's fiendishness, and the refusal of the Russian armies to accept defeat points to the mortal danger of Bolshevik terror. Hitler himself had already drawn this lesson in *Mein Kampf* from his reading of Allied propaganda in the first war, which he admired as 'psychologically correct'. In representing the Germans as barbarians and huns—he says—the Western allies had prepared their own soldiers for the horrors of war. The most terrible weapon they might encounter thus only appeared to confirm what they had been told.[30] From this point of view the propagandist can only welcome a development in which the mythical threat becomes increasingly real.

The minutes of Goebbels' conferences reflect this paradox. The optimistic forecasts which Hitler had permitted himself in the autumn of 1941 when he announced that the Russian enemy was prostrate and would never rise again, and once more in the autumn of 1942 when he was carried away to promise that Stalingrad would be taken, were naturally a terrible embarrassment to the propaganda machine. When the Russian ring round the Sixth Army before Stalingrad tightened and it became clear that no relief was possible, we find Goebbels returning from Hitler's headquarters with the good news that the Fuehrer had agreed to a policy of complete frankness.[31] He called it a liberation. At last our propaganda will again stand on firm ground. During the crisis of Dunkirk, he reminded his team, Winston Churchill had told the English people the absolute truth with admirable frankness. At that time they had failed to understand this, but it was through these tactics that Churchill had aroused the conservative forces of the nation. In thus trying to take a leaf out of British propaganda Goebbels of course still followed Hitler's old line that the British were past masters in psychological warfare. And thus he laid on the gloom and gave instructions that out of Stalingrad all German news media must create a myth that would form the most precious possession of the German people.[32] The media rose to the occasion and contrived with their radio silences, their solemn music, their uplift, and their professions of loyalty to transform the nightmare image of a frostbitten, broken and annihilated army into a symbol of patriotic self-sacrifice.[33] Goebbels hoped by this means not only to create the mood for total mobilization, but also to scare the rest of Europe into acquiescence in German domination.

It was the strategy which our propagandists at the time dubbed 'strength through fear'. In a way, as you realize, it was not a new departure, for fear is always present in the mind of the paranoiac. Even in the moment of victory the Nazis had to justify their aggression by insisting on the mythical plots of their enemy. But where, in this gloomy myth, is there an assurance that the world-wide plot can be overcome at all?

You remember that from the outset Nazi propaganda looked for this reassurance in the plot of history. Hitler was the man of destiny, the instrument of history chosen to lead the party to victory over its enemies at home, and he would perform the same miracle when Germany would triumph over the whole hostile world. True, as the war situation worsened the principle of vicarious participation in this world historic process had to yield to the realities of living through increasingly hard times,[34] but at least they were historic times, and as such they carried their promise within them.

It was no longer an unconditional promise, however. Goebbels told his team that one should never imply that Germany could not lose the war.[35] Of course she could, if the German people failed to respond to the challenge of the hour. But this lesson, too, could be drawn from the book of history. In particular it was Carlyle's *Life of Frederick the Great* which was almost raised to canonical stature in these times of adversity, for the way it showed the Prussian king during the Seven Years War doggedly holding out in a seemingly desperate situation till Russia's unexpected change of front under Catherine the Great came to his rescue.[36] Not that the Nazis were the first to look for patriotic inspiration in the history of their people. But in their reading history was more than a storehouse of great examples. Their philosophy derived from the German Romantic tradition which saw the history of mankind as an extension of cosmic evolution. We are unlikely to grasp the profound intellectual aberration that found its expression in the Nazi myth unless we take cognizance of their conception of history in which the great leaders must obey the laws of mankind's destiny but no other laws of God and men.[37] I am afraid you would find some food for thought if you read the book on Julius Caesar by Gundolf, who had been one of Goebbels' professors in Heidelberg.[38] Ernest K. Bramstedt, in his recent book on *Goebbels and National Socialist Propaganda*,[39] has conveniently assembled some of these characteristic appeals to historical providence. But neither he nor, as far as I can make out, anyone else has resuscitated the most dramatic of these appeals which Goebbels made in a broadcast to the German people on 28 February 1945 when parts of Germany both east and west were already under Allied occupation.[40] Having told of a German girl who had hurled defiance in the face of her American judges he turned her into a symbol of Germany's unbroken spirit and worked up to the following declaration:

> I declare that I firmly and unswervingly believe that ultimately our cause will be victorious, and that if this should not be the case, the Goddess of History would merely be a whore out for money and a cowardly worshipper of numbers; but that in such a case History herself would be devoid of a higher morality, and that the world she would allow to emerge from the terrible travails of this war would cease to possess any deeper justification for its existence, that life in such a world would be worse than hell, that I would no longer deem it worth living, neither for myself nor for my children, nor for all I have loved ... and that I personally would gladly throw such a life from me, because that would be the only thing it deserved....

But, Goebbels went on, History had never given man cause for such thoughts. She had always been just, if only the nations had given her the opportunity to be so. She had always most cruelly tested those she had destined for the highest call, but having driven them to the very brink of despair she had never failed to come down to them and graciously to hand them the palm of victory. She cannot be different now, for though ages, nations and people might change, History remained immutable in all eternity.

But this last refuge of the myth was also shattered by reality.[41] Two months later, when the Russians advanced into blazing Berlin, Goebbels and his wife followed Hitler into suicide after having their six children killed by lethal injections.

Die Göttin der Geschichte nur eine Hure ; I still hear the voice and the words ringing in my ears.

I believe that it behoves the Creighton Lecturer to defend History against this dismal verdict of her disappointed suitor.

History is neither a whore nor, indeed, a goddess. Clio can make no promises and take no bribes. She merely records modestly and reluctantly what crimes are committed in her name.

Research in the Humanities: Ideals and Idols

THE TERM 'research' is used indiscriminately to describe activities in the sciences and in the humanities. I can only speak with competence about the latter, but I believe that the role of research in science differs fundamentally from that with which I am more intimately concerned. The idea that science represents what used to be called 'a body of knowledge' has become obsolete. It is not the facts stored up in textbooks that constitute science, but the questions that are asked and the problems that demand solution.[1] Seen in this light, science is an activity, and research is of its essence. It can only continue to exist if it continues to advance. The scientist is like the rider on a bicycle; he could not remain in his seat if he had to stop.

Certainly the humanities should not remain stagnant either; and though I shall argue in this paper that the assumption that they should emulate the sciences in matters of research can lead to grave distortions, I should like to reassure my colleagues that I am not going to let the side down and argue for the curtailment of the small funds we have been getting. Still, the notion of a body of knowledge is less inapplicable to some of the humanities than it is to science. The humanists of the Renaissance were concerned with a group of texts and monuments which they wanted to recover, preserve, and correctly interpret. It was their aim to master the languages of these texts and to expand their references because they admired the civilization of the ancient world and wished to profit from its heritage. The range of texts and monuments which concern the humanist today has enormously widened, but his basic motivation is the same. His concern is still with languages—taking the term in its wider sense—and any vocabulary constitutes a 'body of knowledge'. The editor of this issue, presumably, still expects its readers to connect something with the name of *Daedalus* and to appreciate its association with the schematic labyrinth on its cover (see p. 122). It is this type of knowledge that is kept alive by the humanities without the benefit of research.

Take my own field, the history of art: without some knowledge of the Bible and of the principal stories from the classics, the work of Michelangelo or of Titian would become mute. If you do not connect the name of Moses with anybody in particular, Michelangelo's statue in S. Pietro in Vincoli

Reprinted from *Daedalus: Journal of the American Academy of Arts and Sciences*, Spring 1973, *The Search for Knowledge*.

would look odd indeed, and if you had never heard of the Loves of Zeus, Titian's *Europa on the Bull* would be even more puzzling. This is not a matter of doing research in iconography, simply of knowing the symbols current in a civilization. Admittedly it is all a matter of degree. Nobody can expand all these references, and part of scholarship consists in the knowledge of how to consult dictionaries—using the term in a slightly extended sense.

As long as a civilization feels sure of its values, the need to make contact with these canonic texts and monuments of the past need not be argued. I am old enough to remember the generation of doctors and lawyers, civil servants and bankers, who read the classics as a matter of course in the original language, and who could be described as genuine humanists though the idea of research may never have entered their minds. Even teachers at school or dons in the old universities saw it as their principal mission to pass on their knowledge, their enthusiasms, and indeed their veneration for this heritage, without feeling called upon to make fresh discoveries.

Admittedly this unquestioning acceptance had its dangers. The guardian of canonic texts can easily become the pedant whose concern with irrelevant trifles has been ridiculed for so many centuries. It has always been the justified charge against the pedant that he killed the texts he was meant to keep alive. Where lively minds are engaged with the heritage of the past, humanism will also remain lively. Even those educated laymen to whom I referred never regarded the texts of the classics on their shelves as dead matter. They were part of their intellectual universe, the objects of love or, maybe, of aversion; there were reputations to be questioned and interpretations to be challenged.[2] These people, also, were the natural public of the professional scholar whose editions they used and whose views they debated. What distinguished the professional academic was mainly that he had more leisure and more technical competence to engage in such constant revisions. It was the mark of the real scholar that he could not read a text or look at an image without being aware of the depth of his ignorance and of the need to find out more. Sometimes such a search would take him to a library, occasionally also to an archive; he might decide to wade through certain records for years in search of an answer, or just to store the problem away in his mind, hoping that the solution would turn up one day in an unexpected place. It was in this way, on the whole, that the scholars of the past conducted what we now call 'research'.

Indeed one would hardly use the term when describing the life style and activities of an archetypal scholar and humanist such as Jacob Burckhardt. His lectures and his books testify to the immense range of his systematic reading, and nothing he touched could remain inert. But his immense productivity lay in his capacity to illuminate and re-interpret the texts and sources rather than in the discovery of new ones. I believe we must distinguish such inspired productivity from the idea of 'output' or 'results' if we are to understand the peculiar problems of the humanities.

The contributors to this issue were asked, 'In what fields does the nineteenth-century model of the scholar working by himself still predominate? What confidence is shown in this model through the ways monies are appropriated and recognition awarded?'

I have expressed a certain nostalgia for the model of the nineteenth-century scholar, but I do not think that any ways of appropriating monies or of awarding recognition would be likely, by themselves, to bring back what was essentially a style of life. Take the life-work of Burckhardt's successor, Heinrich Wölfflin, the great interpreter of stylistic developments in art. It is hard indeed to imagine him receiving a research grant to study the compositional devices of Raphael or being influenced in his search by any thought of recognition. True, as the occupant of the Chair in the University of Basle he was free not only from financial worries, but very likely also from the many pressures which nowadays beset a department head.

When I was a student in Vienna old Wölfflin paid a visit to my teacher, the great scholar Julius von Schlosser. As they both emerged from the Professor's *sanctum* where they had been closeted, the host pointed to the rooms of his Institute where we were sitting and working and said with more candour than tact: *Also hier beginnt das Grauen* ('this is where the horror starts'). By the horror, he meant us—though these professors certainly knew how to keep their students at arm's length.

Much has been written about the authoritarianism of the old-fashioned German University Professor, and the abuses of the old system are too obvious to need labouring. What is relevant in our context is only that for all its faults the tradition was good for scholarship.[3] There are two diametrically opposed conceptions of a university which somehow got mixed up in our time. The first may be said (schematically) to be derived from the continental medieval system, in which the university provided a 'chair', a pulpit even, for the eminent man who can be persuaded to pass on his knowledge to those who are willing to 'sit at his feet'. If he disappoints them, they can go elsewhere (as I left Schlosser's lectures for a term to hear Wölfflin's in Berlin). There is nothing wrong, in the abstract, with this idea that a great man has the obligation to take some time off his work for the benefit of his disciples. Alas, there can never be enough great men to fill all the chairs and so we got the small men who had to assume the pose of eminence and were corrupted in the process.

In the English college system this danger was less acute; for the don was primarily a tutor to the young gentlemen who were to become lawyers and clergymen. While the loyalty of the continental professor was to his subject, that of the English university teacher was really to the students who stayed under his care unless they were 'sent down'. Morally and socially there is much to be said for this conception of teaching, but the attempt to marry the two systems may be responsible for the perplexities which are the topic I have been invited to discuss.

Our system of appointments and promotions in the Anglo-Saxon world is still based on what might be called the assumption of eminence. Indeed the letter of appointment used by my university quite properly includes among the duties of the recipient that he or she should 'advance the subject'. Yet we have also taken over from the college tutor the burdens and responsibilities of caring for the intellectual and spiritual welfare of our students. It is well known that the tensions and conflicts between these two responsibilities have resulted in much restlessness and unhappiness. It was bad enough for the German Professor to feel that he was expected to be a great man. It is much worse for the ordinary member of a university staff to know that his worth will be measured by the number of papers he has published and the symposia he is invited to attend. It is these pressures that result in what is often called the academic industry, an industry that only rarely 'advances the subject' and quite often impedes its growth.

It is easy to decry this industry, but less easy to remedy its shortcomings. After all, most of us are part of it. We live in a world that values results. The Annual Reports of our Departments and Institutes should present them as veritable beehives of activity; more offprints are sent round and received in return than any of us will ever have a chance of reading; we are on the boards of learned journals and are even guilty of writing books. Like most industries, ours finds itself confronted with the problems of overproduction and—if the truth is to be confessed—with the danger of polluting the environment. The 'fall out' of the academic industry is the pretentious jargon that seeps into language. More depressingly even, its overheated apparatus appears unable to adjust its output to the needs it was once designed to meet. There are too many areas where we fail to live up to our responsibility as humanists, which I defined as that of recovering, preserving and interpreting the cultural heritage of mankind. Today no less than in the past these obligations can only be met by those who have mastered the requisite body of knowledge, and we all know that even the knowledge of classical languages is declining at an alarming rate. An even more glaring instance of such a breakdown is the fate of the monuments and manuscripts of India. Many of them are disappearing through pillage and neglect before their existence has even been recorded.[4]

It is important to realize that scarcity of funds is only one element in situations of this kind. Money is neutral. It can aggravate the ills of overproduction as easily—or more easily—than it can be used to cure these serious malfunctions. What is needed in the humanities is not yet another lobby for more grants and research projects, but rather a forum for the exchange of views on what constitutes worthwhile research, and what dangers threaten to distort its progress.

Francis Bacon in his *Novum Organum* listed four groups of idols the worship of which he found detrimental to the progress of science. I know that his vision of science has been criticized as naïve, but he was still a great propagandist who knew how to put his ideas across.[5] I shall take a leaf out of his book and list four classes of idols which, in my opinion, divert the humanities from their course.

I propose to identify as my first group the *idola quantitatis*. These are in fact set up by the very conception of science with which the name of Francis Bacon is connected, the creed of 'inductivism', which claims that truth emerges in the form of generalizations based on the accumulation of data. This, as we know, is an idle dream. There are no neutral data; we can only collect evidence if we want to bring it to bear on a particular hypothesis, and in doing so we must never forget to ask whether the game is worth the candle.[6] Evidence for the proposition that 'all men are mortal' need not be sought by putting all birth and death registers preserved anywhere in the world through a super-computer.

Of course both in science and in the humanities there are collections of data which save a lot of trouble. I have referred to dictionaries as a case in point. The importance of other tools of research such as reference books, bibliographies or editions of texts need not to be laboured. But those who gratefully turn to these works also know that it would be quite pointless always to demand completeness. It is the insistence on this demand, the belief that the recording of all available data must precede all other research in the humanities that I associate with the cult of the *idola quantitatis*. Do we need a corpus of *all* doorknockers? I do not raise this question because I find doorknockers particularly uninteresting. On the contrary I have been interested in the frequency with which they show threatening masks, snakes or other apotropaic devices. The question is only whether we would gain a lot by a statistical survey of all doorknockers made, say, before 1700, to establish the exact distribution and relative frequency of these motifs. Even so, a project of this kind might easily find institutional support; teams could be organized and photographic archives established, though by the time the project approached completion the problem of magic survivals might interest nobody and the 'use' to which this campaign was to have been put might be entirely forgotten. What scholars might want to know by then might be the relation of doorknockers to the coming of the electric doorbell, and for this question the whole enterprise would have proven useless. 'It has to be done all over again'—or has it?

The worship of the *idola quantitatis* is not only sterile, it induces sterility in its devotees, especially the young. How many good ideas must remain still-born because the priests of the cult demand that they should be established by induction. It is this inductivism which produces the feeling among the young that they will never 'know enough', and which will ultimately prevent them from daring to ask any worthwhile question. It diverts them to the tiny plots of specialists who know 'more and more about less and less'.

My second group of idols may be known as the *idola novitatis*. Here, too, the emulation of the sciences leads to distortions of true productivity. If, as I have argued, the humanist remains to some extent a guardian of texts, novelty is not his prime concern. True, there is something exhilarating in discovering a fresh interpretation of a term, or a turn of phrase in a well-known text which has escaped countless commentators and which illuminates a forgotten meaning. But even the best of these conjectures or discoveries must take their modest place among the footnotes. The commentary remains subservient to the text. In this respect the humanist as an interpreter of our heritage has something in common with the performer who interprets a text on the stage or in the concert hall. We want him to be the faithful mediator rather than the purveyor of novelty for its own sake. It is easy to propose a fresh reading if we treat a text cavalierly and disregard the intentions of the creator, if, in other words, we prefer the new to the true. Unfortunately, such is the fabric of the academic industry that even an absurd reading will be accorded immortality in the footnotes. Anyone who can get a reputable journal to publish a learned paper purporting to prove that the Mona Lisa represents Cesare Borgia in disguise would at least be discussed in all sub-sequent treatments of the theme. Those who doubt it should remember that Marcel Duchamp's schoolboy prank of painting a moustache on a reproduction of that portrait still figures in survey courses—and in this paper.

Close by the *idola novitatis* in the temple of learning I find the *idola temporis*, the idols of the age. By this term I refer to the lure of newly developed intellectual and mechanical tools which seem to promise prestige to those who 'apply' them to the humanities. I am anxious not to be misunderstood here. It is not the tools and techniques I wish to question under this heading. I am no more concerned with the validity of such movements as Marxism, psycho-analysis, or structuralism than I am out to criticize the use of film cameras, tape recorders or computers in those fields where they yield relevant data. It may certainly be argued that the coming of these tools has placed the traditional humanities at a disadvantage. Who would not want to have a tape-recorded interview with Shakespeare or a film of the first performance of *Hamlet*? It is altogether characteristic of the humanities that our evidence is very fragmentary and that we have to make do with accidental scraps of information. We must resign ourselves to the fact that we know nothing about Shakespeare's sex life, eating habits, earnings, and politics, and that we therefore cannot put his life and work through the paces of any of the current theories of human behaviour. Sociologists, psychologists, anthropologists and linguists will naturally select a type of material where the evidence flows more abundantly. It is more rewarding, in many respects, to investigate monasticism in modern Ceylon by interviewing a large cross-section of monks about their beliefs[7] than to study the Cistercian monasteries of medieval Europe. But, though the records and monuments of this movement are far too incomplete to offer suitable material for any of the modern approaches, the humanist will not want to neglect them. After all these monks helped to shape the physical and intellectual landscape we now inhabit. We study them in our constant efforts to assess our own heritage.

Certainly, we try to learn from the results of any science, but we can only do so if we know our place, our strength, and our limitations. There is nothing more dreary than the mechanical application of any formula to one topic after another. Vulnerability to intellectual fashions is the most depressing effect of the pressures created by the academic industry. Here, too, the cult can be particularly harmful to the young, who are so easily impressed by a fresh and prestigious jargon. If the *idola novitatis* may at least encourage a somewhat hectic originality, the *idola temporis* merely promise originality to enmesh their worshippers in a predictable conformism.

If these warnings sound conservative, I hope to dispel this impression by identifying the last cluster of idols, the *idola academica*. They are the idols that have established themselves in academic life in the very process of teaching the humanities. For administrative reasons universities tend to be organized in departments which offer a syllabus leading to examinations. Alternatives have been tried, but I do not think there is much to be said against this system as long as it is applied to the acquisition of skills. Whether we want to learn to drive a car, play the flute, speak Chinese or read cuneiform, we must be guided through the various phases of proficiency which can be tested reasonably well. Even such traditional faculties as theology, medicine and jurisprudence require certain skills as qualifications and may well be suitably organized for their teaching and testing.

The so-called 'arts subjects' however, are certainly distorted through this division into 'disciplines' and 'departments'. It is true that I have argued that the humanities represent to some extent a 'body of knowledge', but bodies do not survive dissection. Shakespeare's sonnets are studied in the English department, Petrarch's in the Italian, the sonnet form in that of Comparative Literature, and Petrarch's Latin works in no department whatever. What is at issue is not the need for 'interdisciplinary' studies. I have argued elsewhere that this very monster of a term begs the question because it implies that there are 'disciplines'.[8] The alert reader of any text must inevitably ask questions which will take him into linguistics today, into history tomorrow and probably into social studies next week. Obvious though this is, a student of any syllabus would probably still be discouraged from doing 'research' on any topic that falls outside it, and if he persisted he would encounter what Aby Warburg called the frontier guards who would ask for his credentials. There is more of academic trade unionism in these demands than is often acknowledged. An alert and industrious scholar can acquire the skills to investigate nearly any question which arouses his curiosity. Thus, Aby Warburg learned enough of astrology and Rudolf Wittkower enough of the theory of music and proportion to transform, respectively, iconology and the history of architecture.

I fear that the insidious effects of the *idola academica* extend beyond this timid territorialism. Teaching a syllabus inevitably creates a bias that carries over into research. The course becomes the thing. It must be supplied with material, the machine must be fuelled, and topics will be scrutinized with this unconscious bias. The authors who figure in the syllabus must serve as pegs onto which to hang suitable classroom themes. The sabbatical leave of six months may just be long enough to carry out this little piece of research that will be useful also to colleagues teaching the same prescribed text. Where this is the attitude of the teacher, his students are likely to gain a similar conception of what is expected of the research worker. His efforts and his methods in turn should ultimately be geared to the teaching of the subject. The subject of his Ph.D. research on which he will agree with his teacher will naturally be marked by this bias.

The importance attached to this exercise, which has notoriously increased during the last few decades, has come in for much justified criticism. I do not think, however, that the institution is necessarily harmful, as long as it is regarded as genuine apprentice work. Those whose job it will be one day to supervise research can be expected to prove that they have mastered the basic techniques. But instead of being a kind of 'driving test', the Ph.D. thesis has come to resemble one of those terrible ordeals so frequently connected with rites of initiation. The priesthood of teachers sometimes seems bent on guarding the prestige of their order by making entry difficult and painful. Thus the formative years of a young scholar's life are frequently taken up by an effort which serves, in the official phrase, 'to satisfy the examiners'. By the time he has done so, the clay has hardened; he is committed to a line of research which he may find difficult to abandon. Hence that tendency to self-perpetuation and that overcrowding of certain fields which we have observed to be matched by the neglect of others. The humanistic subjects which must be taught in every culture for good educational reasons—Dante in Italy, Goethe in Germany, Shakespeare in English-speaking countries— are squeezed dry for research topics by those who seek academic employment. A type of periodical has sprung up listing 'research opportunities' in these overgrazed areas, while a few steps beyond their confines virgin land is crying out to be cultivated.

Nor is this unbalance the only negative effect of the *idola academica*. The very techniques of the classroom, the way students are inducted into the reading of an author or the appreciation of an artist, have come to influence the style and the aims of research. The extent to which the routines of teaching sometimes guide and distort the practice of research seems to me particularly characteristic of the humanities. The refusal of the German Professor to adapt his lectures to the capacity of his students may have been morally reprehensible, but the admirable effort of the devoted teacher may be more disastrous in the end. Pedagogic devices developed to engage the interest of beginners become elevated into methods of research. I am here thinking of the analysis of formal relationships in painting, of images in poetry, or of the meaning of words in philosophy. They may be indispensable for the teacher who wishes to fill an hour and to compel his class to attend to a text or to a picture, but they are unlikely to 'advance the subject'.

How, then, can this desirable aim be furthered? The wind bloweth where it listeth, and I do not think that the growth of good ideas can be organized; but it is not impossible that we can make a conscious effort to create a climate in which their growth will not be stunted. Much that is sterile in the academic industry of today springs from simple anxiety. The existence of academic primadonnas or super-stars, the publish-or-perish complex, the impossibility of 'keeping up' with the literature, the crowded schedules, and the increasing demands of a home life based on 'do-it-yourself', make one wonder how those admirable young scholars one still encounters managed to come through it all. But too many seek shelter in 'safe' topics, while others hide their insecurity behind the façade of aggressive novelty hunters. Those who want to cure these and related conditions must tackle them at the root and remove the anxiety. In this respect the creation of havens for eminent scholars is no remedy. It is a strain even on the elect to be cast into the role of the sage who merits a perpetual sabbath.

What is needed are mixed communities of scholars where younger and older people can freely mix and exchange ideas without being over-impressed or under-impressed. Communities where the members are not so totally exempted from ordinary chores and routines that they must ask themselves day and night whether they have lived up to their position, but where they are not ground down by the demands of teaching and administration either. In such a community there are no 'stars' who are regarded with false awe, nor need a beginner be afraid to air his views. Everyone should feel free to follow his hunches in any direction without the fear of being told that this is not his business. Only in this way can it happen that once in a while a fresh perspective is opened which suggests a new line of research in the humanities.

If this prescription sounds uncommonly like an idealized portrait of the Warburg Institute, this may be due to the fact that I am only familiar with my own parish. What I think I have learned in my 36 years of association with that group of scholars is that such an institution is comparatively inexpensive. I do not want to sound unappreciative of the University of London, which has provided and continues to provide the running cost of an institute the purpose of which is not easily explained in terms familiar to financial committees. I would not dream of suggesting either that an institute of this kind could not do with a larger annual budget. What I want to stress for the purpose of this issue is merely that in comparison with the cost of cyclotrons and computers even a first-class library in the humanities needs no exorbitant grants, particularly if the purchasing remains firmly in the hands of a very competent scholar-librarian who knows how to be selective. Admittedly, here my experience is perhaps a little misleading. The Warburg Institute Library is based on the stock of books collected by Aby Warburg and maintained for several years after his death by the Warburg family. Moreover, we happen to benefit from the proximity of the British Museum Library, with which we need not and cannot compete. But users of our library have found that it not only serves research, but also generates fresh ideas, as does our photographic collection. To follow up these ideas the handful of scholars who form the institute's academic staff certainly need time, but they are quite happy to teach both undergraduates and postgraduates as long as the pressure is bearable. Add a modest sum for travelling for which they can apply, and the provision of junior and senior research fellowships without which the continuity of the institute's work would be in danger, and the financial requirements of the institution will be satisfied.

I believe that in terms of cost benefit the contribution of such a place to the advancement of learning need not compare unfavourably to that of larger centres. It is true that any intellectual nonconformism must involve the adventurer in the risk of academic isolation, but there is no guarantee today that it is the overcrowded fields which offer the best chances of employment. I hope indeed that even on this practical score we need have no qualms in encouraging the young to exchange the cult of idols for the true religion of scholarship.

VALUES IN ART

Art and Self-Transcendence

A HUMANIST invited to address an audience largely composed of scientists may well be forgiven if he feels a little apologetic. The study of art certainly offers ground for apologies. Its systematic or philosophical branch, called 'aesthetics', has now been in existence for more than two centuries, but I, for one, share the scepticism about these endeavours which Father Vincent Turner S.J. summed up in an essay called 'The Desolation of Aesthetics'.[1] As historians we may feel a little more respectable, but even here our specific conclusions about styles and attributions are rarely testable and sometimes no better than anybody's guess. But on second thoughts I do not feel apologetic about the presence of a student of art in a conference concerned with values. Even though aesthetics may not have got far in pontificating about the Beautiful, the Sublime or the Expressive, even though the critics have shown their notorious fallibility in the face of masters past and present, the historian of art can at least tell you what artists thought about value and he, in his turn, may reflect about these thoughts.

Here we must first take cognizance of the Platonic tradition which paradoxically dominated Western philosophies of art—paradoxically because Plato, as we know, had banished the artist from the ideal Republic as a mere conjuror whose skill could never reach the intelligible world of ideas, which is also the world of values. And yet it was the faith in the existence of such a world which inspired the artist with an idea of transcendent perfection against which alone they wanted their art to be judged.

Before he describes the ascent to the *Paradiso*, Dante, whom these notions reached in their Aristotelian transformation, tells us that the intention of art is often frustrated by lack of responsiveness in matter.[2] The idea cannot be fully realized in the medium. The artist's hand, he says elsewhere, is never perfect, it will always tremble and thus fall short of reproducing the idea.[3] This, of course, is particularly true when the artist's aim is to describe or portray the perfection of beauty, where the highest flight will always fall short

Address to the 14th Nobel Symposium in Stockholm on 16 September 1969.

of reality and every artist must resign himself to giving up the pursuit of perfection.[4]

History tells how this philosophical conviction spread among the studios of the artists in the Renaissance[5] and became the academic doctrine which was formulated in its authentic Platonic form by Winckelmann's friend Anton Raphael Mengs in his *Reflections on Beauty* in 1762.

> Since perfection does not belong to mankind but only to God and since nothing can be conceived by man except what can be apprehended by the senses, the Almighty has impressed on man a visible idea of perfection and this is what we call Beauty... We might compare it with the idea of the geometrical point. Such a point being infinitely small is incomprehensible, but since we feel the need of forming a sensible notion of the point, we call a dot a point.
>
> I should like to suggest that perfection is like such a mathematical point. It comprises in itself all the most perfect qualities, and these cannot be found in any material object, for whatever is matter is imperfect. Thus we have to imagine a kind of perfection adapted to human understanding, and it is this image we call beauty, which is visible perfection in the way a dot is a visible point. True perfection is only in God, but beauty therefore reflects a divine reality.[6]

In our history books the fight against this academic doctrine is generally represented as a fight for liberation from an outmoded classicism. But I think we miss much of the real drama if we fail to understand the psychological trauma that resulted when this metaphysical prop was no longer holding up the artist's self-respect. The discovery that ideals of beauty varied according to time and place suggested that all norms in art were subjective and that the idea of an immutable world of perfection had been as much a dream in art as it was in religion. The only value left to the artist was fidelity to his own self. It is the creed so nobly expressed in a letter by Courbet in 1854:

> I hope to make an unprecedented miracle come true in my life, I hope to live all my life by my art, without departing by an inch from my principles, without ever having lied for a single moment to my conscience and without having covered even a stretch of canvas as large as my hand with paint to please anyone whoever it may be, to have it sold.[7]

You will notice that Courbet, who said he could not paint an angel because he had never seen one, believed as passionately in realizing a value as any academic artist. But the loss of a metaphysics had made it a more difficult creed, and if proof of this assertion were wanted I could refer you to many of the leading twentieth-century artists, artists such as Kandinsky, Klee or Mondrian, who tried to revert to some version of Platonizing mysticism by which to sanction or sanctify their artistic mission.[8]

I am afraid few of these efforts are even intellectually respectable and I would be the last to recommend them to you. But I wonder if we need this kind of metaphysics to justify a more than subjective theory of art, one that explains and accepts the demand for self-transcendence and some notion of perfection.

I should like here to refer you to two papers by my friend Sir Karl Popper in which he stresses the emergence of problems in nature and in history as the emergence of what he calls a 'third world which is neither the world of things or facts nor the world of subjective feelings'.[9] For problems allow of solutions, some better, some worse, some perhaps perfect.

Take an elementary artistic problem that may go back to the dawn of history: the decoration of a pot with an evenly spaced row of marks. Whether or not we postulate a subjective 'decorative urge' that drives the craftsman on, he must still submit himself to the objective realities of the situation and work out the number and the intervals of marks till they fit. A richer pattern, covering a wider area, would demand correspondingly more attention to the limiting factors involved. However, this attention is likely to be rewarded by the discovery of fresh relationships emerging unplanned between the decorative elements, and these might be exploited and adjusted in their turn. On this model it is easy to see how the craftsman's experience can crystallize in simple rules of procedure which can become embodied in the tradition, enabling the next generation to take certain problems in their stride and advance to the solution of fresh ones, which are always likely to emerge in their work.

I am quite aware of the fact that the type of problem I have chosen is too simple by half. It belongs at best to the problems of the craftsman rather than to that of the artist. What counts for the artist, it may be argued, is not the acquisition of skill but the expression of the self. The theory of 'abstract expressionism' concentrated indeed on the artist's mark as a graphological trace of his spontaneous and unique gesture, which thus became a means of 'self-discovery'. But as a historian I would reply that the problems and values of art—including even those of abstract expressionism—have emerged from the problems and values of the craft. It is a fact of history that most of the great artists of the Western tradition have felt involved with the solution of problems rather than with the expression of their personality.

Let me quote at least one more witness to illustrate what this feeling looks like from the inside, as it were.

Writing to his brother about the consolations and dangers of drink, van Gogh speaks of his demanding work:

> the mental effort of balancing the six essential colours, red, blue, yellow, orange, violet, green. This is work and cool calculation, when one's mind is utterly stretched like that of an actor on the stage in a difficult part, when one has to think of a thousand different things at a time within half an hour.

After that, van Gogh admits, he must relax and drink and smoke:

> but I'd like to see a drunkard before his canvas, or on the stage ... Don't think that I would ever artificially work myself into a feverish state. Rather remember that I am engrossed in a complicated calculus, which leads to the quick production of one rapidly painted canvas after the other, which has, however, been calculated at length *beforehand*. And so, if they tell you that it is done too quickly, you can reply that they have looked too quickly.[10]

What is this calculus, this balancing act of which van Gogh speaks with such conviction as his mental work? It is precisely the desolation of aesthetics that we cannot formulate it with the same precision we can formulate the problems of science or the rules of a game. Even if we had the artist here to explain his aim of fitting colours or shapes into some complex configuration of contrasts or consonances, there would be nothing but your sense of courtesy to prevent you from saying 'so what?—We can see that it is hard to do and to get it all as you want it, but is it worth it, is it a value, is it art?'

Remember that in asking this question you would only ask what young artists have so often asked their teachers when they rejected one problem in favour of another, which seemed to them more worth pursuing. And yet I think we would be wrong to conclude from this that the values pursued by van Gogh or any other master were therefore totally subjective and illusory.

The problem he had set himself was not only his personal whim. It had emerged in the context of art, he had learned about it in his contacts with fellow artists whom he admired or rejected, whom he wished to emulate or even to surpass. If anyone, van Gogh happens to be an example of this aspect of self-transcendence, of this feeling that artists are engaged or ought to be engaged in a common pursuit.

Though art differs very much from science, what he and we mean by art still has in common with the scientific quest for truth that it is felt to be cumulative. No problem is ever solved without new ones emerging.[11] It is true that in this process values appear to change, beauty may be felt to be less important than tension, or feeling less artistic than cold purity. The tremendous Rembrandt in the National Gallery in Stockholm—which alone makes it worth coming here—embodies different values from the gem of a Watteau in the same gallery.

In recent times the undeniable fact that different styles and periods have pursued different problems and values has led to impatient questions about the relevance of past values. Why should we bother to concern ourselves with an art that embodies values different from our own? Rumour has it that here in Sweden the demand has even been raised that the teaching of art history should be confined to the art of the last hundred years, because this alone could conceivably be relevant to our own age.

You will not be surprised to hear me say that this parrot cry of relevance seems to me total nonsense. If there is one thing about which, in my view, the teachers in faculties of the humanities should not feel apologetic it is their interest in a variety of values and value systems. The egocentric provincialism of people who so lack the capacity for self-transcendence that they can only listen to what touches their own individual problems threatens us with such intellectual impoverishment that we must resist at all costs.

The first thing we have to learn is that people have different values and pursue different problems. Perhaps we can only learn about values at all in considering this range and diversity. In all civilizations men have set themselves problems of skill and daring that demand outstanding qualities for their solution. The mastery of games and feats of prowess show men submitting to some kind of value and we can all admire these achievements even if we do not want to join in the game. True, there is the story of the Chinese mandarin who wondered at the exertions of foreign diplomats in their daily games of tennis: 'Even if, for some obscure reasons, these balls had to be tossed around, could not this strenuous chore be left to the servants?'

Our modern mandarins who look at the arts of the past with similar incomprehension are less excusable. For art has come to embody even higher values than has the game of tennis: in games it is skill which counts, and the skill is measurable through the institution of matches and tournaments. He is master who has come out on top. No doubt there is an element of this standard in art. There certainly was a time when mastery in building, carving, bronze casting or painting was mainly seen in terms of such skill. Only that this skill was at that time rarely pursued for its own sake. It was harnessed to other values, the values of religion, of power or of love.[12] The art with which a temple or palace was adorned with rich, intricate and precious decoration, the marvels of goldsmithwork with which the wealthy bridegroom may have wooed his bride, all this showed art in the service of ulterior aims, but these did not preclude the commission for such important displays of skill going to the most consummate master of the craft.

Maybe it was precisely in this context that the concept of art began to transcend the concept of mere skill. You remember Dante stressing the gap that must of necessity separate the poet's craft from the description of heavenly perfection. This feeling, which is no doubt of religious origin, has become enshrined in the tradition of art where it has been emancipated from religion. Once this tradition had emerged, art could no longer be seen, like games, as a contest of skills. Indeed it is the paradox of this tradition that the virtuoso is almost seen as the negation of the artist. For the virtuoso, who knows all the rules and all the tricks, has failed to see that his contest is not with other artists, past or present, but with the Platonic idea of perfection, which always demands higher and higher exertions in the pursuit of the problem. It is the humility and dedication demanded by this outlook which has made the great artist the successor, in popular estimation, of the Saint, even where his life and personality may have been far from saintly.

The religion of aestheticism, the religion of Oscar Wilde, of Bernard Shaw's Dubedat in *The Doctor's Dilemma*, or of Hermann Hesse's *Glasperlenspiel*, does not appeal to me very much. It lacks that awareness of distance that his religion gave to Dante. The value that has emerged in the Western tradition of art is precisely that feeling of an infinite pursuit that precludes the self-satisfaction of the aesthete.

I once happened to meet a member of a famous string quartet and asked 'how long they had played together'. 'Never yet,' he replied, 'but we have tried for twenty-nine years.'

The performing artist has, as his standard, the masterpieces he wishes to realize and which, in the nature of things, cannot emerge absolutely flawless, because he is only human and his hand, like that of Dante's craftsman, always trembles. But his attitude towards the masterpiece is mirrored, on a higher level, by the creative artist's feeling of the existence of values which will always transcend his skill. He senses the challenge of the problems which his tradition and his task present to him. He feels, and rightly feels, that his own powers alone would never suffice to bring the shapes, sounds and meanings into perfect harmony, and that it is never the self, but something outside himself, call it luck, inspiration or divine grace, that helps to bring about that miracle of the poem, the painting, the symphony he could not have willed.

Before you dismiss this feeling as metaphysical sentimentalism, let me remind you of the theme of this conference, the place of value in the world of facts. Most of the participants of this meeting have rightly decided to confront the pressing problems of the world of facts which they have come here to discuss. But even the greatest optimist would not be disposed to deny that many of these problems are not capable of solution. You need only look into the papers to read of intractable conflicts of interest and of that dreadful power of mass emotions which must indeed make the hand of the reformer tremble. The problems in the realm of art, in the world of values of which I have spoken, may also be recalcitrant. Yet there is no intrinsic reason here why the solution should always elude the artist bent on ordering a large but limited number of elements which may and do fall into place and come right, as do the tones in one of the great fugues by Bach.[13] Such an artist, as I have said, works within a medium that is pre-shaped by tradition. He has before him the benefit of countless experiments in creating orders of a similar kind and value. Moreover, in setting out to create another such ordered and meaningful arrangement of tones, he will, during the process of creation, discover new and unintended relationships which his watchful mind can exploit and follow up, till the richness and complexity of the work transcends in fact any configuration that could be planned from scratch.

In this respect the pressures and bonuses of a continuous period of evolution in art may have something in common with those evolutionary processes which culminated in the complex beauty of a shell or a spider's web.[14] In the past such works of nature were considered by theologians to prove the existence of a conscious creator, in what was called 'the argument from design'.

Strangely enough our age, which has rejected this argument, has yet fallen for a conception of creativity in art which sees only the individual creator and his state of mind. It forgets that even Bach, great as he was, could not have invented that marvellous medium that is the Western system of music— or if it does not forget it, it tends to regret such traditionalism and to imply that every artist should invent his own system. Even where the creative agent is not believed to be the conscious self it is somehow personalized as the spirit of the age, the class situation or the unconscious.[15] But taken by themselves none of these explanations is ever sufficient to account for the coming into being of such meaningful complex orders as a fugue by Bach.

I believe that this failure has not been without effect on prevalent conceptions about the meaning of art to the individual. The emphasis on objective problem solutions which I have presented has as its corollary the idea that we can strive to understand a work of art. Such understanding may never be exhaustive, but it will always demand a thorough familiarity with the traditions and the problems within which the work took shape. Not that this understanding, this grasp of the problem which the work attempts to solve, is the same as approval. We may understand the problem but reject the values it embodies, for we remain free agents and have a right to say that even a masterpiece that rests on a long tradition strikes us as evil rather than good. There is such a thing as refined cruelty, and there may also be refined depravity embodied in art. But both the effort freely undertaken in search of understanding, and the freedom to submit or to reject, have suffered neglect through the emphasis on subjective response which is conceived to be largely automatic. In its vulgarized form it demands nothing more of the work of art than that it should 'switch us on' or 'send us', like a drug. Small wonder that we have seen the emergence of a new term, the term of 'escapism', to censure those who seek refuge from the world of facts in the opiates of art.

I do not want to deny that there can be some moral force in this disapproval. But I should like to argue that there is a greater moral force in the belief that in freely submitting to a great work of art and exploring its infinite richness we can discover the reality of self-transcending values.

I realize of course that this conception of art has an old-fashioned ring. The Victorian cult of uplift which offered art as a noncommittal substitute for religion has understandably repelled many genuine lovers of art. Thus the young find it hard to share the feeling of awe with which former generations responded to the classic masterpieces of poetry, painting or music because they held out the promise and the solace of a realm where values had been realized.

Ladies and Gentlemen, the title of this symposium, 'The Place of Value in a World of Facts', is of course taken from a book by the great pioneer of Gestalt Psychology, the late Wolfgang Koehler. I had the privilege of attending Koehler's lectures in Berlin in 1932, shortly before the catastrophe which threatened to extinguish the sense of all values from Western Civilization. I hope it is still remembered how courageously Koehler opposed this disaster. In the first months of Nazi rule, while he still held his chair in Berlin, he dared to write a newspaper article against the purges of the Universities. When I was fortunate to meet him again in Princeton, shortly before his death, conversation fell on this episode, and he told how after the publication of this protest he and his friends spent the night waiting for the fatal knock on the door, which luckily did not come. They were playing chamber music all night long. I cannot think of a better illustration of the place of value in a world of facts.

Art History and the Social Sciences

PREFACE

THIS IS an expanded version of the text I read at the Sheldonian Theatre at Oxford on 22 November 1973 and deposited in the Bodleian Library under the terms of the endowment. It might be more correct, however, to describe the lecture as a telescoped version of the fuller presentation which is here published after further reworking. It would have been both impracticable and inconsiderate to inflict a lengthy discussion on a captive audience. It would be inconsiderate as well as unwise to withhold from my readers and critics all the supporting arguments I consider relevant to my case. As in the publication of my Philip Maurice Deneke Lecture of 1967, *In Search of Cultural History*, Oxford, 1969, which presented me with the same problem, I have introduced subheadings as guide-posts to the reader. As in the previous case, also, I have referred in the Notes to other writings of my own, whenever I felt that this enabled me to make a point without going over the whole ground again. But I have refrained from footnotes for footnotes' sake, and have rather inserted references in the text than asked the reader to look for them elsewhere.

IT IS a very great honour to be invited to give the Romanes Lecture; it is an equal privilege for an art historian to be asked to lecture in this building, the first work of the future architect of St. Paul's. We art historians are used to talking in blacked-out interiors to display our slides, but while denying me this facility the Vice-Chancellor might have quoted the famous inscription over the door of Wren's masterpiece, 'Si exemplum requiris, circumspice'. If you need an example, just look around you (Figs. 1, 2).

Not that I have made any fresh discoveries about this building, or that I would be entitled to act as your cicerone. At other times two pamphlets by true masters of English architectural history, published by the Oxford University Press in 1964, are here on sale: a lecture by Sir John Summerson on *The Sheldonian in its Time*, and an illustrated booklet by Mr. H. M. Colvin

---

The Romanes Lecture for 1973 delivered at the Sheldonian Theatre, Oxford, on 22 November 1973.

on *The Sheldonian Theatre and the Divinity School.* Maybe it is fortunate for my purpose that these authorities have absolved me from devoting too large a portion of my lecture to my *exemplum*, for as you may have gathered from the title, my purpose is to illustrate a problem of method. I have called it *Art History and the Social Sciences*, and I can perhaps best explain this choice of a topical subject by suggesting that some of my younger colleagues would find that title somewhat puzzling. Why art history *and* the social sciences? In their view, if I understand it correctly, art history is simply one of the social sciences, or at best a handmaiden of sociology, an *ancilla sociologiae*, and the same would apply to the other activities usually grouped together under the name of arts subjects or the humanities.

Now rivalries between the Arts and wrangles about their pecking order have accompanied the life of learning from time immemorial, and I must disclaim any wish to join in the slanging match that is going on in the academic world about the barbarous jargon of sociology or the irrelevance of the humanities. I am a peace-loving person, and I shall be quite content to lead you gently to the conclusion that all the social sciences from economics to psychology should be ready to serve as handmaidens of Art History. Only, I have no faith in settling such matters in the abstract. Whenever I read disquisitions about the method proper to one of the disciplines my reaction tends to be pragmatic: Go ahead and do it, and we shall be able to judge.

I. ART HISTORY AND HISTORY

What is it an art historian would do after he had looked round in this building? If you had brought him here blindfold he would first try to classify the elements of this interior. He would not have to be a great master of his craft to conclude that he is not in China but in a region of the world which adopted for its buildings the classical tradition, with columns, capitals, and friezes. The building could not date from before the sixteenth century, and is unlikely to have been erected in the last thirty years, for then there would be less gilded decoration and more plain surfaces. Certain idiosyncrasies of the design would make him suspect that he is not in Italy but somewhere in the North, where the classical idiom was an acquired language, and the sight of the large ceiling painting would remind him of the fact that this type of decoration went out of fashion in the course of the eighteenth century. It is easy to produce this kind of reasoning from hindsight, but I am sure that if our art historian were a master of the class of Summerson, Colvin, or Pevsner, this game of twenty questions would soon bring him close to the documented date of the building, which was erected between 1664 and 1667 and opened in 1669. This is the basic skill of what we call art history: the ability to assign a date, place, and, if possible, a name on the evidence of style. I know no art historian who is not aware of the fact that this skill could not be practised in splendid isolation. The historian of art must be a historian, for without the ability also to assess the historical evidence, inscriptions, documents, chronicles, and other primary sources the geographical and chronological distribution of styles could never have been mapped out in the first place. It is this map the art historian keeps before his mind whenever he pronounces a hypothesis about the date or attribution of an individual work.

Beyond this need it may be a question of taste and temperament how far the individual art historian allows himself to be tempted to read in these sources and to build up in his mind the circumstances which gave rise to any particular work of art. I think it is part of the mental make-up of the engaged historian that he should be interested in the life of the past, and even in what journalists call a human interest story. Take the situation that gave rise to this building. The sources tell us that the ceremonies of this University, notably the Encaenia, were traditionally performed in the Church of St. Mary, but that a good deal of profanity had crept into these occasions through the presence of the jester, the *terrae filius*. It was to rid the church of this scandal, we read, that Archbishop Sheldon offered to pay for a separate building, which was commissioned from the young Professor of Astronomy, Christopher Wren, then barely thirty and almost unpractised in architecture. Hearing this story, I for one would like to leave art history on the side for a moment and learn more about the *terrae filius* or about the training of astronomers that enabled Wren to accept this commission. Others, maybe, would like to know how the Archbishop came to possess the £12,000 it cost to erect this structure, or whether William Byrd the stone-cutter and Richard Cleer the carver were adequately paid for their magnificent labour.

I have mentioned these questions at random to illustrate the obvious point that we cannot and need not put any theoretical limits to the historian's curiosity. I speak of curiosity because I do not think this is a question of method. Method is concerned with theory, not with motivation. If you ask the historian—why do you want to know?—he has every right to reply—because the question interests me. If you insist on probing further you may again find a welter of factors, some rooted in the historian's personal psychology, others in his schooling. There are the pressures of intellectual fashions and the influence of the problems of his own time which naturally draw attention to new aspects of the past. There is also the more immediate context and purpose of his research. A museum official will become interested in the attri-

bution of works under his care, teachers will want to put the work in a wider
setting for the benefit of their students. In this respect the relation between
art history and social history is not really so much a theoretical as a practical
problem, a problem of policy, as it were, which admittedly has affected the
fortune of my subject within the academic syllabus. In the past the more
austere among historians were rather suspicious of a type of study that offered
to the practitioner such varied temptations to go off on a tangent. More recently this possibility has endeared the subject to anti-specialists who look
for attractive points of entry into the problems of the past. I am all for history
without tears, or at least without too many yawns, but when we recommend
the introduction of art history into the syllabus, because works of art so perfectly reflect their age, we should also add that like mirrors they will reflect
different facts about the age according to the way we turn them, or the stand-
point we adopt, not to mention the tiresome tendency of mirrors to throw
back our own image.[1]

We have had antiquarians who used the monuments of the past mainly
for the study of such *realia* as costumes or tools; we have had philosophical
art historians who searched works of art for the manifestations of world views
or *Geistesgeschichte*; others more recently were captivated by the traditions
of symbolism; now the tide of interest appears to turn towards the use of
monuments as mirrors to reflect the social structure of their time. The motivation behind these fluctuations is not very hard to diagnose, nor do I think
that one should be too solemn about it. The herd instinct is a potent force
and often results in academic overgrazing. There is considerable merit in
finding new pastures and we must genuinely applaud those who will fill the
gaps in our knowledge about social conditions, workshop organizations, or
the motivations of patronage. The history of art is one strand in the seamless
garment of life which cannot be isolated from the strands of economic, social,
religious, or institutional history without leaving any number of loose threads.
Where he makes these cuts and how he constructs his narrative will depend
for the art historian as for any other historian both on what he wants to know
and on what he thinks he can find out. For though I have spoken of a seamless
garment, what has come down to us is rather a rag-bag of miscellaneous information. However much I should like to know the profane joke by the *terrae
filius* to which we may owe this building, it is most unlikely that it can be
retrieved from the files.

But have I not been begging the question in any case when I remarked
that we owe this building to that joke? Surely we owe it to Sheldon? Or do
we owe it to Wren, or to the masons who put it up? It is here that we come
to the need to clarify the way the historian will construct his narrative. It

is easy to agree on the trivial point that historical events are the result of many determinants. It is less easy to resist the temptation of regarding some of these as more essential than others. Alas, I belong to the school of thought which does not think it makes much sense to ask whether the warp or the woof is more essential to the cloth. The warp may here correspond to the threads of tradition, to what linguists nowadays call the diachronic study of language. There is no element in this hall, whether column, frieze, or decorative flourish, that could not be traced back by a conscientious historian over hundreds or even thousands of years, for the language of decoration exhibits an astounding tenacity, and the acanthus leaf which you see all around you may well be connected with the motif of the lotus used in ancient Egypt some five thousand years ago. But the existence of such traditions does not absolve us from studying what is called the synchronic structure of a style, the way the design responded to the pressures of the moment. Both these elements are relevant to our description, but neither constitutes an explanation in the sense in which science uses this term.

II. EXPLANATION AND INTERPRETATION IN HISTORY

I am afraid we are here approaching a scarred battlefield, churned up by many a fight about the status of history and about the role of explanation in social studies. I shall cause no surprise if I try to pick my way between these craters, keeping close to my predecessor as a Romanes lecturer, Sir Karl Popper, who has written amply on this topic and whose views seem to me totally convincing.[2] Popper has denied the claim frequently made that the logical structure of explanation used in science differs from that used by the historian or for that matter by the man in the street. What is different every time is precisely the direction of our interest, in other words, the question we ask. The scientist, including the social scientist, is interested in general theories about regularities or the so-called laws of his subject. His aim will usually be to test these theories against his observations to find out whether they really hold. The historian will be interested in the individual event which will exemplify any number of such laws. In so far as he makes use of explanation it will also consist in an appeal to general theories, some trivial, some less so. I have just formulated such a general theory when I mentioned the power of tradition, that is, of style, in the formation of this building. Put in theoretical terms my assertion would be that this building exhibits a recognizable style because there exists a law according to which nothing can come of nothing and all cultural products have precedents. Those who feel incredulous may well be stimulated to look for what is called a counter-example and refute my law by pointing to something that really was created from scratch. But for the historian the awareness of these and other presumed regularities is only background knowledge. Looking at this interior we do not wish to test the theory that all buildings have a style; we want to know as much as possible about its particular individual appearance. Now it seems to me clear from a logical point of view that this appearance could never be caught in the network of general concepts. It could never even be exhaustively described because descriptive language makes use of universals such as the names of shapes and colours, and you could always want me to specify more and more without ever coming to an end. The scholastics who were impressed by the fact that the individual eludes language coined the famous phrase that *individuum est ineffabile*. I think it follows from this that *individuum est inexplicabile*.

It so happens that at the very time when this building was going up, that is probably in 1666, Newton saw the famous apple fall which, if we can trust William Stukeley, led him to the theory of gravitation. But what constituted the achievement of this explanation was of course his inspired question why the moon, which is so much like an apple, does not fall. The explanation presupposed a classification and a general law governing this class. Not even Newton could have fully explained the unsurprising fact that the apple fell, if he had gone on to ask why it fell at that very instant. There are too many variables—the weight of the fruit, the strength of the stalk, the intensity of the wind, the elasticity of the bough—each of which would have to be subsumed under a general law of which this was an instance. Outside the laboratory, this would be a hopeless enterprise. But though total explanation in history is a will-o'-the-wisp, this need not drive us to total scepticism. We can always try to make sense of an event. What I have read about this building offers a perfect example.

When the young Professor of Astronomy received the commission to provide an alternative to the church of St. Mary for the Encaenia, he decided that what was needed was a type of building more suited to secular or even profane displays: in other words, a theatre. There were precedents for universities erecting theatres for other purposes where spectators had to be admitted, notably anatomical theatres, but here he had to look for something more festive. The ceremony for which he designed the building was enacted in Latin, as it still is, and no one questioned the prestige and the model character of classical antiquity. Accordingly, Wren consulted such architectural handbooks as an edition of Vitruvius and a treatise by Scamozzi and based his design on these precedents. If we are to believe his son, the building would have been 'executed in a greater and better Style, with a View to the ancient

1. The interior of the Sheldonian Theatre, Oxford, looking south

2. The interior of the Sheldonian Theatre, Oxford, looking north

3. Robert Streeter: The ceiling of the Sheldonian Theatre

4. *Theology* imploring the assistance of *Truth* (detail of Fig. 3)

5. One of the Proctors' rostra (see also Fig. 2)

Roman Grandeur discernible in the Theatre of Marcellus at Rome but he was obliged to put a Stop to the bolder Strokes of his Pencil, and confine the Expense within the Limits of a private Purse'[3]—as useful a reminder as we can hope for of the economic realities within which the architect had to work. But there were other realities which demanded adjustments of his plan. Roman theatres were open to the sky, and you could not transfer this feature to our clime without the risk of the academic senate and the honorary graduands being drenched. The building had to be covered.

Note that in taking over this account from my authorities I have made use, as they also have, of what Popper calls the rationality principle or the logic of situations. I have tried to reconstruct the situation in which the designer found himself and have asserted that, given his aims and his means, his action was rational and therefore makes sense. But such an interpretation should not be confused with an explanation. It always implies a number of assumptions which may or may not be correct. After all, if Wren had been asked to build an assembly hall for a sect that believed in the cleansing power of water from heaven, it would have been rational for him to omit the roof. As it was, the logic of his situation presented him with a more than trivial problem. He had no beams of sufficient length at his disposal to bridge the whole width of this hall because—and here we can say because—trees do not grow to seventy feet in this country. He had to use a system of struts and mutual supports, which caused the writer of a Pindaric ode on the building to devote a special stanza to this feat of engineering that made the loving trees embrace in mutual trust:

O quam justa fides nectit amantes arbores.[4]

I have learned from Sir John Summerson's lucid account why this construction was hailed with so much applause. It appears that the problem of what he calls the 'geometrical flat floor' built from timbers of insufficient length had been as much debated since the Renaissance as that of perpetual motion, but unlike the latter it had a solution. Wren was not the first to adopt it here in Oxford, but no one had done so on anything like this scale.

There is no cause for alarm, however; it is no longer Wren's roof which covers this hall. Even so, I have reason to be grateful for its part in my story. For it allows me to say without fear of contradiction that it was a good solution.

III. ENDS, MEANS, AND VALUES

Next to the problem of explanation, no issue has proved as controversial and intractable as the problem which is so awkwardly described as that of value judgements in history and in the social sciences. The historian is traditionally enjoined to write without fear or favour, *sine ira et studio*, and the scientist is believed to be even more committed to objectivity. It is this demand which we shall find to be of central importance to the relation between art history and the social sciences, but maybe it is best approached from the side of technology first. If there is any branch of history that cannot do without a yardstick of success or failure it is the history of technology.

Naturally the description of a solution as successful does not imply an approval of the purpose for which it was designed. Detective stories and films have made us familiar with the rather revolting notion of the perfect crime, the ingenious circumvention of the law or of moral values, and we also know only too well that such crimes are sometimes defended in the name of an overriding value or purpose, be it patriotism or party allegiance. Wren could have used his mastery of mechanics to build his roof as a trap made to collapse at the very moment when an enemy came in, and our verdict on this use of his technological devices might depend in its turn on our sympathies.

When we call a solution successful, in other words, we do not therefore commit ourselves to an approval of the values it was made to serve. The first is an objective verdict, relating to means and ends, the second inevitably depends on our own value systems. We need not even think of crime or war to find successful solutions which can conflict with our values. Indeed the whole question of the relation between art and society was first broached in such a context. I am referring to John Ruskin, who condemned the style and tradition in which Wren worked because he saw in it a forerunner of industrial tyranny. In his opinion the Gothic craftsman was bound to enjoy his work because he had scope for the exercise of his fancy; with the coming of the Renaissance and its cult of regularity the workmen were degraded into mere executants of another man's design. Thus the whole of post-medieval architecture exemplified to Ruskin the sin of pride, the pride of the architect whose glory rested on the enslavement of his workmen.

Now the issues which Ruskin raised have surely lost nothing in topicality, though it may be less easy than he thought to draw up the correct balance sheet between the advantages of job satisfaction and the needs of organizational efficiency. There may indeed be many cases from the time of the pyramids to the present day when pride in the display of successful solutions disregarded their cost in human suffering. In our case, I hope, we are entitled to acknowledge the element of pride without serious moral scruples. Sir John Summerson reminds us rightly of the intellectual climate in which Wren's solution of the flat floor problem was put forward and applauded. Wren, of course, was one of the founding members of the Royal Society, which encouraged such experimentation. In fact this element is so important in the historical constellation that we disregard it at our peril. Was there really no other way to provide a shelter for the Encaenia? Did Wren not also want to meet the challenge to his skill and ingenuity? If this is pride, we may concede that it had a share in this building as in many successful problem solutions, including the ceiling painting by Robert Streeter (or Streater) which once screened the roof (Fig. 3).

We know from contemporary accounts that this painting was designed to fit in with the conception of the building as a classical theatre. Though it rains rarely in the South, the sun can burn mercilessly, and the illustration which Wren consulted includes a remedy against this contingency, a veil or *velarium* which could be pulled over a net of ropes to protect the audience. What could not be done in reality for climatic reasons could at least be done within that realm of fiction we call art. Hence the network of beams simulating twisted ropes, while crowds of winged little children support a heavy curtain just in case it gets too hot. They have really opened these awnings to allow us a glimpse into a world of radiance in which spiritual beings disport themselves on the clouds, except for some nasty intruders who are cast down, unworthy of those seats of glory.

Here my law of precedent certainly holds. The *velarium* is only one element in the story, for the idea of converting the vault into a picture of heaven also looks back to a long tradition. It was hardly a far-fetched idea to give the visitor to a church this vision of God and His Saints in the heavens above, though here as always certain technical conditions had to be fulfilled before it could be put into practice. Painters had to develop the skills of foreshortening, the suggestion of light, and other illusionistic devices to conjure up a vista of heaven for those who craned their necks and looked up to the vault. No doubt these devices in their turn owe a great deal to certain demands made on the visual image in a given social and historical setting, when the painter was asked to conjure up an imaginary reality as an aid to religious experience. Maybe it was Raphael who first solved the problem of suggesting the radiance of the divine setting in some of his altar paintings, but it was Correggio who used these means to transform the dark cupola of Parma Cathedral into a vision of the heavenly host receiving the Virgin into the eternal light. There was an interesting time lag before the solution caught on in the seventeenth century, but by then the device had become so effective and so popular that it was also adapted to secular usage. After all, the classical tradition of a ruler's apotheosis, of his Olympic glorification, gave a kind of spurious sanction to this transfer. There was an example of such an apotheosis near at hand, Rubens's ceiling in Whitehall Palace eulogizing James I.

But how could even this secularized heaven be adapted to the novel function of Wren's or Sheldon's theatre? Who was to be glorified here? We can see the answer if we look up and strain our eyes a little; I think it was a noble answer. The personification whom we see enthroned on the upmost cloud, her head bathed in the light of the sun she holds in her right hand, her legs uncomfortably drawn up, is Truth, naked, shining Truth descending from on High brandishing the palm of Victory. Below—in the words of the contemporary description[5]—'the Arts and Sciences ... are congregated together in a Circle of Clouds, to whose Assembly Truth descends on being solicited and implored by most of them.' It is to her that these various disciplines taught at the University are looking up—Logic, Law, Botany, Mathematics, Astronomy and the rest have donned the attire laid down in the tradition of Ripa's convenient handbook of personifications. They are all paying tribute to Truth, including Theology, who, with her book with seven seals, 'implores the Assistance of Truth for the unveiling of it' (Fig. 4). Even Religion does not claim to be in the possession of truth; she, like the others, is striving for it.

We are again reminded of the historical situation to which I have alluded, the foundation of the Royal Society in 1662, whose motto was and is *nullius in verba* (by nobody's words). Though rooted in the religious tradition, the painting illustrates a new faith, not anti-religious but independent of the Church and Authority, one which was about to give birth to a rival cosmology which depopulated the heavens for good and all.

Thus we may well invite the social historian to describe for us some of the concrete context of this momentous development. He might make us aware of the tremendous tensions of the Restoration period, not least of all here in Oxford. In his *History of the Royal Society*, published in 1667, the very year the painting took shape, Thomas Sprat specifically refers to this situation. Tracing the foundation of the Society back to meetings in Dr. Wilkins's lodgings in Wadham College, after the end of the Civil War, he mentions that 'The University had, at that time, many members of its own who had begun a free way of reasoning ... their first purpose was no more, then onely the satisfaction of breathing a freer air, and of conversing in quiet one with another, without being ingag'd in the passions, and madness of that dismal Age.' These men, Sprat claims, were 'invincibly arm'd against all the inchantments of *Enthusiasm* ... it was in good measure by the influence, which these Gentlemen had over the rest, that the University itself, or at least, any part of its Discipline and Order, was sav'd from ruine. And from hence we may conclude, that the same Men have now no intention of sweeping away all the honor of Antiquity in this their new Design: seeing they imploy'd so much of their labor, and prudence, in preserving that most venerable Seat of antient Learning, when their shrinking from its defence, would have been the speedist way to have destroy'd it.' Sprat goes on to emphasize to what extent the study of Nature is the best antidote to that religious fanaticism that had torn the fabric of society apart. 'There is but one better charm in the world, then Real Philosophy, to allay the impulse of the false spirit; and that is the blessed presence and assistance of the *True*.'[6]

For contemporaries, therefore, who entered this building designed by the most prominent member of the Royal Society, the combination of a classical idiom and an expression of a universal allegiance to Truth would certainly have had many more resonances than it has for us if we come as casual visitors. Surely we are entitled to admire this solution, doing justice, as it did, to so many requirements of a complex political and social situation. But can we also admire it for its own sake? Has it any value for us, who live in very different times?

There will be many who will wonder whether this question makes sense. Is not the fact that values are so demonstrably bound up with social situations proof enough that they must change as the situation changes? Are not all values, therefore, relative?

The author of the libretto for Streeter's ceiling obviously did not think so. He thought of Truth as an absolute, an aim that was common to all disciplines and one that would unite all men. Whoever it was who asked the painter to celebrate this faith could hardly have thought that this belief would ever be called in question and that he would therefore provide me with the text for my sermon—if sermon it should be called. For I need hardly mention that the faith of the Royal Society, the faith of the Enlightenment, strikes many today as naïve, precisely because it took it for granted that there are universally valid standards. There are some who even wish to deprive science of the claim to serve Truth; even scientific truth has been described as relative to the society that practises it, so that the history of science should really be written not as a story of discoveries and problem solutions but merely as the account of the changing behaviour of those members of society who call themselves scientists. By a legitimate extension we can describe the history of art as an account of people who play the role of artists in a given society.

IV. LIMITS OF SOCIAL DETERMINISM

Every historian of art no less than every historian of science has reason to be grateful for this challenge because it compels him to reflect on his own attitude to social determinism.

In its most extreme and perhaps also in its most popular form the challenge originates from that school of social science that calls itself Marxist. If I understand it at all, Marxism postulates the existence of a universal law according to which all cultural activities are the consequence, or more precisely the 'superstructure', of changes in the system of primary production. I know that there are as many interpretations of this formula as there are Marxists, and I have little competence, and luckily no need here, to enter into the dark maze of the dialectic. Certainly, the organization of production with its attendant social consequences will be part of the situation within which the work of art takes shape. That it cannot alone and uniquely determine this shape seems to me equally clear, for we had ample opportunity to confirm what might be called the law of continuity, the law of traditions which tend to be modified and adjusted to new situations but maintain their own momentum. I cannot imagine that Marxists can have overlooked the fact that man is a creature who learns and hands on knowledge and ideas, but it is not only Marxists who sometimes speak as if they wanted to forget this.

It may be all the more useful, therefore, to look at the consequence of this human ability in contrast to the situation in the Animal Kingdom, which so interested George Romanes. The student of animal behaviour, investigating the dance of the bees, the song of birds, the social behaviour of apes, will start from the assumption that all the features he observes are the result of selective pressures due to the struggle for survival. Even he, therefore, acknowledges the role played by the history of the species, even he thinks in terms of a warp and a woof. Evolution is the natural selection of properties which are useful or at least not harmful to the organism, as it adapts to its ecological niche. But here this process is confined to the genetic sequence. Both spiders and beavers are splendid architects, but beavers do not learn from spiders, for unlike man they cannot select their models.

Even the brief glimpse I have given of the history of this building reveals a very different situation. Some of the decorative elements are survivals from the theocratic society of ancient Egypt, while the shape of the building adapts of course the Roman theatre built for gladiatorial games. Can we do better than say that these formal elements survived because they were useful or at any rate not harmful? I do not think we always can, but in this case we know that the later society selected certain features from the storehouse of the past to draw on the prestige of 'ancient Roman grandeur'. We have another somewhat bizarre example here in the two Proctors' rostra flanking the hall (Fig. 5). The lion masks which appear to be smoking cigars are really holding the *fasces*, the grim instruments of execution carried by the lictors who accompanied the Roman Consul, just in case there was a head to be cut off. They are made to stick out like beaks because the rostrum on the Roman Forum was studded in some such way with the prows of warships captured at Antium. I do not claim that the combination of these features with the age-old tradition of terminal lion masks used as supports of rings or handles[7] is perfect, but it perfectly illustrates the transformation of cultural memories into a symbol of authority. The symbol, not the reality; for not even in 1669 were Proctors really entitled to use hatchets. The stark reality of one society survived as a mere symbol in another institution.

But there is another form of survival that must interest us even more. I mean that of discoveries. Let me hark back to the example of the perfect geometrical floor which was once applied to our roof by Wren. The roof has gone, but the solution has not. I gather that geometrically speaking it is still correct; it belongs to what Sir Karl Popper in his Romanes Lecture 1972, 'On the Problem of Body and Mind', called World 3, the world of objective problem solutions as distinct from the world of matter and the subjective world of experiences.[8] We can admire it for its intellectual elegance even if we do not need it at all. Whatever the forces and pressures that gave rise to it, it can be offered up by the personification of Mathematics on our ceiling to the Platonic Goddess of Truth.

V. HISTORY AND THE STANDARDS OF ART

And what of art? Is the undoubted fact that social elements play their part in the coming into being of styles and monuments reason enough to question their objective value? It is known that Marx himself was puzzled by this question. There is a passage in one of his manuscript drafts which shows him to have been somewhat less than a good Marxist:

> The difficulty does not lie in understanding the fact that Greek art and Greek epic poetry are linked with certain forms of social evolution, it lies in explaining the fact that they still offer us artistic pleasure and are to some extent recognized by us as a norm and an unattainable model.[9]

Less consistent than usual, he suggested that our reaction to Greek art was grounded in our nostalgia for the childhood of mankind. While other nations were like naughty or precocious children, the Greeks embodied the ideal of 'normal' childhood in all its eternal charm. He did not stop to explain in what respect men such as Thucydides or Euripides could be described as child-like, and even less what social determinants accounted for this strange interpretation, which he obviously took over from Schiller. After all, he had other concerns, and left the question of artistic norms in mid-air. We cannot afford to leave it there.

For however much we may be interested in the situations that help us to account for the character of a building or a painting, we should acknowledge the fact that our interest arises from the value we attribute to the particular work. If you are cynical you may say that this value may be expressed in monetary terms. I am not cynical. The Sheldonian is not yet for sale. I have said that I admire the way Streeter's painting is adapted to the ideas and purpose of our building; but is it also a good painting, a great work of art?

We happen to know that the question was debated before the painting was even *in situ*. On 1 February 1668 Samuel Pepys went to visit Streeter's studio, which was in Whitehall because he was the sergeant painter.

> I found him and Dr. Wren and several Virtuosos looking upon the paint-ings which he is making for the new Theatre at Oxford; and, indeed, they look as if they would be very fine, and the rest think better than those of Rubens, in the Banqueting-House at White Hall, but I do not fully think so. But they will certainly be very noble.

Pepys, we see, was not afraid of value judgements; he weighed the claims of the paintings, he applied the touchstone of Rubens, and he pronounced against the opinion of the other virtuosos. It would have been better if the matter had rested there. Alas, when the ceiling was finally unveiled, one Robert Whitehall, Fellow of Merton College, who had, incidentally, been the *terrae filius* in the Encaenia of 1655, published a rhymed description of the painting[10] ending in a notorious couplet which poor Streeter never lived down:

> That future ages must confess they owe
> To Streeter more than Michael Angelo.

My main purpose here is to propose the daring hypothesis that Robert Whitehall was wrong, just as Pepys was right. I know that nobody will be found to disagree, and yet I am not being ironical in describing my hypothesis as daring. It is risky to challenge relativism in matters of artistic value and to assert that even in the elusive region of aesthetic judgement there are statements which are true and others which are false.

Note that this hypothesis does not conflict with Robert Whitehall's real or pretended convictions. He was not out to question the valuation of Michel-angelo, only to predict that Streeter would be found to be better still. My point is not, therefore, that his prediction has not come true—not yet at any rate—but that his valuation is objectively wrong.

It was Michelangelo's own contemporaries who had set him up as the standard of perfection. Moreover they were not plagued by doubts about the way to explain and discuss perfection. Writing about the 'Last Judgement' less than ten years after it had been unveiled, Vasari uses the language of Christian Platonism:

> And in our art this is the great exemplar and that great painting sent by God to men on earth, so that they can perceive what Fortune decrees, when Intellects imbued with the Grace and Divinity of Knowledge descend from the highest realms down to earth.[11]

This is the metaphysics of absolutes which is still implied in our ceiling and which underlies the creed of the Academies.[12] Even though this faith had been somewhat diluted by empiricism by the time Sir Joshua Reynolds delivered his valedictory Discourse, he speaks of Michelangelo's genius with equal awe.

> Were I now to begin the world again, I would tread in the steps of that great master: to kiss the hem of his garment, to catch the slightest of his perfections, would be glory and distinction enough for an ambitious man ... and I should desire that the last words which I should pronounce in this Academy and from this place, might be the name of—MICHAEL ANGELO.

It so happens that in these very days a contemporary master has touched on his estimate of Michelangelo. Henry Moore naturally speaks in different tones, but his feeling of gratitude for Michelangelo's achievement is no less apparent.

> I think the world has gained enormously through the Pope making Michelangelo do the Sistine Chapel paintings: Michelangelo was doing in one day, with a painting—really the same as a drawing—a sculptural idea that he might have been spending a year on, so that we have two thousand or three thousand more sculpture ideas from Michelangelo than ... if he hadn't painted the Sistine Chapel.[13]

I do not claim that this consensus among artists of renown disposes of the spectre of relativism. Granted that we could now go through the somewhat tedious exercise of comparing Streeter's figures with those of the Sistine ceiling and establish without fear of contradiction that Michelangelo's grasp of anatomy was firmer and his repertory larger, we could not prevent anyone from getting up and asking why it was a good thing for an artist to know anatomy. After all, artists appear to have got on very well before the Sistine Chapel was ever painted. In any case the glories of Chinese art, of Byzantine mosaics, of medieval cathedral sculpture, or, for that matter, of twentieth-century painting, can be quoted as counter-examples to prove that it cannot be Streeter's relative inferiority in anatomical skill that ranks him below the admired Florentine master. No doubt he was different from Michelangelo; but why should this earn him bad marks?

VI. STYLISTIC RELATIVISM

This relativist argument has indeed won the day ever since the collapse of Academic absolutism at the time of the Romantics. And yet we art historians generally attempt to mitigate or avoid the most radical relativist conclusions. The word of power which is to keep these subversive thoughts at bay is the term 'style'. It is behind this concept that we like to shelter from the cool blast of the philosophical question. We grade a work of art within a style, but we refrain from pronouncing about the values of different styles. It may be worth while to illustrate this approach of stylistic relativism as it has been applied to our *exemplum*.

Professor Ellis Waterhouse, in his standard work on *Painting in Britain 1530–1790, Pelican History of Art*, 1953, concludes the description of our ceiling with these words:

> ... the whole is disposed with at least the science of the painters of the Italian or French baroque. The execution may be unselect and the whole ceiling be a very minor example of a form common enough in the rest of Europe, but it is not in the least amateurish in compositional resource.

The terms 'science of the painters' and 'a form common enough' imply the standards that are here applied. Streeter's ceiling is measured against other performances of the same kind and found 'unselect' but not un-professional. Waterhouse, in other words, approaches the problem of value from the side from which I approached it here, from that of technology. Streeter produced a workmanlike ceiling of the kind expected of him—and why drag in Michelangelo?

Dr. Margaret Whinney and Sir Oliver Millar, the authors of the relevant volume of the *Oxford History of English Art*, published in 1957, are a little less willing to give our artist good marks for skill.

> The execution is reasonably competent, but the ceiling is cold in colour, there is no real ability to convey unified movement and although the steep

perspective of the circle of figures seated on the clouds is not unsuccessfully realized, the foreshortenings in the figures that tumble from the heights are largely misunderstood.

Edward Croft Murray in the first volume (1962) of his work on *Decorative Painting in England* (1537–1837) apparently wanted to contest this negative verdict:

> ... there is no doubt that from the point of view of mere technical skill the Sheldonian ceiling far surpasses anything that had ever been attempted before by an English-born painter: the composition, though rather thinly spread, has unity—no mean feat on such a vast surface—the figures are firmly drawn, the draperies crisp, the foreshortening competent enough ... it is a Baroque recipe without the Baroque leaven.

Clearly then Mr. Croft Murray also measures the ceiling by the standard of similar works, though he also wants to remind his readers that Streeter was working in a tradition freshly imported from abroad and could not be expected to have the lightness of touch peculiar to Italian virtuosi.

As a keen student of the English decorative tradition Mr. Croft Murray makes another observation which confirms the fruitfulness of the technological approach.

> It must be confessed, however, that at first sight it is somewhat difficult to take in this erudite *trompe l'œil*. The cordage, being gilded and in high relief, distracts the eye from the painting itself which, now at least, is too dark and lacking in colour to show up effectively behind it; and the first impression is rather that of looking at an antiquated ribbed and panelled ceiling harking back to Tudor times, an effect emphasised by the rosettes which cover the intersection of the ropes.

Perhaps, we may add, the solution of the *velarium* was a bit too clever, too cerebral to work completely. The network of golden ropes suggests a decorated ceiling rather than an open heaven, the tradition of decoration and of illusionistic painting are only imperfectly harmonized in this ambitious work.

I hope these few texts from the works of distinguished contemporary art historians may have helped to confirm the usefulness of what I have called the technological approach to the problems of art history, and also to point at its inherent limitations. All the writers quoted appear to have some ideal image in their mind of what a baroque ceiling painting should look like, and it is against this ideal of the 'style' that Streeter's work is measured. The

procedure is even more explicit in the critical discussions of Wren's design
of the Sheldonian. Sir John Summerson's beautiful analysis, which is easily
available and too long for quotation, measures Wren's early work by the yardstick of his mature masterpiece, St. Paul's. He notes how far it falls short
of this standard but how many of the solutions triumphantly successful in
the later work can already be observed in 'chrysalis' state in the Sheldonian.

There certainly is an affinity between this method and the approach I have
derived from Popper's 'logic of situations'. It is always illuminating to explore
the situation in which the artist found himself, the options he had, and the
decisions he made within the tradition in which he was bound to work. The
art historian, therefore, is likely to use this method with more profit than
if he were trying to blame Streeter for not being Michelangelo or a historian
of science to blame Newton for not being Einstein. But there is a difference
between art on the one hand and technology and science on the other. The
artist works in a less tightly structured situation. There may be one or two
ways of constructing a geometric flat floor, but there are any number of ways
of painting a ceiling, and it is much less obvious which one is successful by
any objective standard. Hence our experts cannot even quite agree on what
Streeter has done. One concedes that 'the composition has unity and the
figures are firmly drawn . . . the foreshortening competent enough', the other
denies that there is 'real ability to convey unified movement' and finds some
of the foreshortenings 'largely misunderstood'. Frankly, I would not know
how to arbitrate between these contradictory statements. To judge a foreshortening we must know for which viewing point—if any—the figure is
designed; and as to the concept of 'unity', we may all know what it means,
but it is far from clear how it is to be applied to a composition of this kind.

Criticism is not a science. It cannot be, as we have seen, because *Individuum
est ineffabile*. There can never be enough well-defined terms in which to
discuss individual works of art, and even less can there be an exhaustive formulation of the precise problem a given work of art was created to solve.
It is here that the notion of style has proved inadequate to stem the tide of
relativism. It seemed such a splendid liberation from academic dogmatism
to insist, as the Romantics did, that a Gothic cathedral served such different
social and artistic ends from those of a Greek temple that the two could never
be measured by the same yardstick. But then different temples in their turn
also serve different ends and we have it on the authority of Vitruvius (Book
I, ch. 2) that a temple dedicated to Mars should conform to different standards
from one built to Venus. Surely one on a hill should also differ from another
in the plains, and marble should be treated differently from timber. Where
do we stop this fragmentation? Any work of art may be said on this reasoning

to be *sui generis*, and in the end we are left, at best, with some moral demand for authenticity which can never be verified in any case. It is a road that leads to the abdication of criticism, for the most blatant infringement of standards may be just what the artist was after. Why should not Streeter have disregarded correct foreshortening and intentionally created that conflict between the golden cordage and the illusionistic effect which Mr. Croft Murray noted? Why should we not like this dissonance and lack of unity better than the standards of harmony implicitly demanded by the writers I have quoted? Small wonder that radical relativism still looks like the most defensible position in aesthetic matters; it is the tradition of another scholastic tag: *De gustibus non est disputandum.*

If art were only a matter of 'liking' this would be the end of the matter. But it is precisely here that the approach through the social sciences can serve as an important corrective. It can help the art historian to reflect on the social role or roles of the various activities we bundle together under the word 'art'.

VII. THE MULTIPLE MEANINGS OF 'ART'

There is a railway station in the West of England with a large poster proclaiming that this is the town 'where the cider maker's art is still recognized'. The social scientist would not infer from this that everybody likes cider. It is enough that some people do care about distinctions between kinds of cider. In these social conditions a local craft can develop such pride in its traditional skills that it claims, and even receives, the recognition of being an 'art'. It is something that not anybody can learn overnight, because the maker like the taster must have a feeling for nuance. There are few social activities which do not partly or wholly conform to this model. We generally recognize degrees of excellence, ranging from the merely utilitarian to the product for the connoisseur. We have seen that even Wren's ceiling may have been made partly with the aim of displaying his skill in ingenious constructions. Surely neither a functionalist nor a merely subjectivist approach to art can ever be realistic. Human beings have any number of needs, practical, symbolic, and aesthetic, and those activities which yield the greatest range of different satisfactions are most likely to become established in traditions. Activities in which the aesthetic function develops into a firm tradition we call 'art forms'. Despite the advertiser's claim cider-making is not quite a recognized art form, but in the eighteenth century in England gardening came close to this status. Much ink tends to be wasted on such questions as whether photography or the film is 'an art'. It would in any case be safer to ask whether they are

art forms—activities or techniques meeting a variety of demands and sometimes aspiring to be loved and admired for the delight they can give. *Can
give*. No art can 'please' everybody or be forced down anybody's throat. It
is enough that they are the source of potential pleasure and enjoyment among
those who have 'acquired the taste'.

The student of architecture has always been compelled by the nature of
his subject to reckon with this multiplicity of social needs. A difference is
traditionally made between the builder, whose work is practical, and the
architect whose contribution adds another dimension to the design. Wren,
as we know, did not see it as his task simply to erect a shelter for the Encaenia.
The building had to aspire to certain criteria of decorum, it had to proclaim
its own significance; even though he had to curb his ambition for yet more
grandeur, he saw to it that the interior was worthy of the occasion and conveyed its social function through the repertory of forms he employed. This
function in its turn naturally merged with the aim of providing pleasure for
the eye. The eighteenth century in England also produced a type of architecture devoid of practical function, the so-called 'folly', erected merely or
mainly for its associations of grandeur. What is more interesting from the
social point of view is, however, that the very existence of these aesthetic
aspirations could also confer meaning on their explicit denial. In Wren's time
the plain chapel or assembly rooms presented an affirmation of puritanical
allegiance, and something similar happened on a larger scale when the creed
of functionalism in twentieth-century architecture rejected decoration.
Today one could easily imagine an anti-Sheldonian of aggressive red brick
and plate glass that proclaimed its own sense of anti-decorum.

It is merely an accident of language that no distinction has grown up in
the craft of image-making that fully corresponds to the distinction between
building and architecture. It is clear that painting and sculpture are art forms,
but we have come to refer to these and germane activities simply as 'art'.
We speak of 'child art' or 'art therapy', irrespective of the degree to which
the outcome gives delight to anyone. There is one other field of study where
all patterns and images are treated on a par with all buildings and all technological products: I refer to archaeology. A future archaeologist excavating this
city would have to give equal attention to any remnants of the Proctors' rostra
and a fragment of Uccello's *Hunt* happily surviving on the site of the Ashmolean.

Why cannot the art historian emulate him and treat all images simply as
artefacts of a given culture? I think the answer is simple. Such pretended
scientific objectivity would rapidly lead to the suicide of our subject. On a
purely practical level the archaeologist is saved from the agony of selection

by the relative scarcity of his evidence. We are in a very different position. Once we really decided not to make any distinctions between painted ceilings or, for that matter, assembly halls, we would be so swamped with material that Michelangelo's or Wren's creations would be lost in an ever-swelling card index. We could only tame it by computerization and statistics, the random sample and the graph, showing, maybe, the correlation—negative or positive—between areas of paint and educational expenditure. The result might be interesting to the social scientist, but it would not be what we mean by the History of Art. We are reminded of the famous speech by Ulysses in Shakespeare's *Troilus and Cressida*: 'Take but degree away, untune that string, and, hark, what discord follows.' It is, I know, a reactionary speech, and it may well be argued that it is the achievement of the modern age to have done away with the belief in all-pervading hierarchies. Science has taken degree away, and no discord follows. Those students of animals to whom I have referred no longer speak of the Animal Kingdom; they deal with the proverbial guinea-pig, the maze-running rat, or, if they are geneticists, with the lowly fruitfly, and advance our knowledge. But then their choice of evidence is related to the theories they wish to test and develop. In other words, they have their own criteria of selection which they could always justify in rational terms. We are still far from having reached this stage in the study of images.

I very much hope this study will come into its own and will become more scientific. Once you have a hypothesis you wish to test, any image can indeed be grist to your mill: inn-signs and samplers, posters, comic strips, or that dreadful fall-out of the tourist industry, the horrors we see in the souvenir shops all over the world which really do not belong into the history of art. I wish social scientists would take more note of this vast range of material which is almost totally neglected, and that historians of art may assist them in spotting the equivalent of the fruitfly and other test cases for theories. I have myself tried my hand at such an enterprise in *Art and Illusion*, where I investigated illusionistic devices in images and speculated on the social pressures which gave rise to their development. Inevitably the comparative novelty of this approach also resulted in misunderstandings. I never wished to equate illusionistic devices with art in the laudatory sense of the term. They can be used by the souvenir industry, but they have also offered opportunities to great artists such as Constable to create potential sources of wonder and delight.

It so happens that I have also written a book, albeit for a different audience, which I called *The Story of Art*; I was careful not to tie myself down to a rigid definition of this elusive term, but tried then, as I do now, to stress the multiplicity of functions in image-making. 'It is the secret of the artist,' I claimed (p. 473 of the 12th edition), 'that he does his work so superlatively well that we all but forget to ask what his work was supposed to be, for sheer admiration of the way he did it.' The history of art, in this light, is rightly considered to be the history of masterpieces and of the 'old masters'—an excellent term, when you come to think of it.

It looks as if the multiple social functions of the crafts of building and image-making also demand a different focus for the social scientist who wants to help in their elucidation. For this dimension of mastery which can be claimed for both sculpture and cider-making is surely a phenomenon which must concern him.

VIII. SOCIETY AND MASTERY

Social anthropologists certainly could tell us a great deal about the various ways in which man's desire to excel and to admire finds expression in different societies. Johan Huizinga in his book *Homo ludens*[14] has surveyed such instances, from war games to contests in riddles, to show that deep urge to establish degree, an urge which of course is also exemplified in this very building and the Institution it serves. What must interest us here is the very problem which I left unsolved, the problem of objective criteria of mastery. It is easy to see who has won a race. But even contests are not always one-dimensional. In the ancient pentathlon you had to prove your mastery in five events, but here you can still add up the score mechanically, as it were. Needless to say, even in sport we may come to different methods of assessment when points are accorded to various aspects of the performance, as they are in our university examinations. As soon as these aspects become a matter of debate, perhaps in criticizing the umpire's decision, you get connoisseurs, looking out for what are called the finer points, and this process of refinement in its turn may make the concept of mastery more esoteric but not necessarily more subjective. What may be a matter of bias is the emphasis placed by some judges on one point rather than another. You may get partisans and fans extolling one champion over all others. I think there is no culture or subculture where you could not watch this emergence of standards and the social atmosphere that develops, whether you think of *aficionados* of bull-fights, or balletomanes, or jazz enthusiasts.

Some of these phenomena are ephemeral, the hero of the hour disappears into limbo after a time, but some, as we know , are remembered, with the result that the elders plague their children with the remark—'if only you had seen so-and-so, he could have taken on the lot of them'. It is in this way, if I may be schematic, that achievements become legendary and enter the realm of myth: the prowess of Achilles, the cunning of Ulysses, the skill of Daedalus, are embodiments of standards, touchstones as it were. It is left to anybody to imagine their degree of excellence, which must certainly have been superhuman, far beyond what any one of us could even dream of achieving. There is only a small step from here to the true immortals who are seen as embodiments of diverse human qualities raised to mythical proportions, Apollonian or Dionysiac.

This is what I have been driving at. From an anthropological point of view the old masters are something like culture heroes, but heroes whose achievements are not only remembered in legend, but preserved by society as a continuous challenge to those who come after. Remember how the Virtuosi in Streeter's studio arranged in their mind a match between their contemporary and the great Rubens, convinced he was going to win—with only Pepys having his doubts. Remember also the boast of Robert Whitehall that the new champion would outclass Michelangelo, a hyperbole that must almost have smacked of blasphemy.

It may also be a little easier for us to explain why the umpire's decisions look authoritarian and dogmatic. The way a great artist collects his points is not susceptible to quantification. Roger de Piles's brave attempt at the beginning of the eighteenth century to do precisely this should have established this impossibility for good and all.[15] For mastery is not only multidimensional, it is also infinitely supple and resourceful, both in the development of technical solutions and in the compensation for technical shortcomings through novel and unexpected moves in other directions. Small wonder that such richness could never be achieved if the master had to create his miraculous configuration from scratch. Those who stress the importance of style are right in so far as they remind us of the prefabricated elements out of which alone a more complex masterpiece can be built. What makes Robert Whitehall's fatal comment so unfair is precisely that Streeter clearly lacked this advantage. He was bound to lack it in a society which had just emerged from iconoclastic rejection of religious images and puritanical hostility to luxury. The needs of connoisseurs were satisfied by foreign imports and the demand for portraits largely by foreign immigrants. It is a measure of his talents that he was able to overcome such a formidable handicap to the extent he did; it is a measure of Wren's genius that he surmounted a similar lack of training and tradition in such a triumphant way, going to France to learn the rules of the game.

Art is not merely a game, but it may be the advantage of this approach through the aspect of mastery that we can use the comparison without compunction. For games, like art, need a social atmosphere and tradition to reach that high level of cultivation that goes with true mastery. In a champion, be it of tennis or chess, certain skills and expectations have to become automatic. For this to happen it needs the kind of atmosphere to which I have alluded, the eager interest of whole groups, the debates about standards. So much, indeed, is valid in what I have called 'stylistic relativism': that different styles resemble different games which have their own yardsticks of success. Grinling Gibbons, for instance, became the acknowledged champion of carved decorations in his age, and we may regret that, being born in 1648, he had not quite come into his own at the time when the Sheldonian was fitted out, for Wren to enlist his services as he later liked to do. It would obviously be foolish, on the other hand, to bemoan the fact that Gibbons was not asked to decorate the Alhambra. But does it follow from this that we can only compare performances within the same game or style? We have seen that this widely accepted position leads ineluctably to radical relativism, precisely, perhaps, because art is not a game with fixed rules but makes up the rules as it goes along.

The skills in which Grinling Gibbons excelled, and the taste he displayed in their exercise, are certainly worthy of admiration; we may also grant that they are incommensurable with the skills developed by the tradition of Moorish decorators, and yet I do not see why we should be debarred from making a 'value judgement' even here. The great decorative styles of Anglo-Irish interlace or of the Arabesque are among the great achievements of mankind, they are closer to the idea of 'art' in a laudatory sense than is the decorative craft of Restoration England. Even in games there are hierarchies, after all. Tiddlywinks may demand a good deal of skill, but chess is accorded more general esteem.

The Olympus of art, like its mythological counterpart, has room for all grades of divinities, from humble sprites to awe-inspiring powers. Grinling Gibbons will find his place here on the foot-hills and even Streeter might be accommodated on its slopes, but Rubens and Michelangelo belong to the true immortals: the first may be worshipped as the God of sensuous exuberance, the latter as the embodiment of sublime power. We need not frequent their shrines to acknowledge their divine status.

Now the social scientist could certainly contribute greatly to a description of these cults in our civilization. He could study their manifestations and fluctuations in the record of auction prices, in the spread of reproductions and the organization of pilgrimages by tourist agencies. He might notice the development of exclusive sects and even of heresies. He would spot culture heroes who remained, as we say, a 'minority cult' and correlate the rise and fall of such reputations with other social movements.[16] He might also have much of interest to say about the social conditions which favour reverence for old masters and the atmosphere that induces pride in contemporary achievements in art. After all, even games do not flourish in isolation from other social trends.

The atmosphere in which Michelangelo spent his formative years in the household of Lorenzo de' Medici is certainly an element in the growth of his mastery that no biographer would want to neglect. It was a commonplace in Michelangelo's own time that fame was the spur to artists, and fame demands opportunities and communication. Vasari, in his life of Perugino, gives a fully sociological analysis of conditions in Florence; he tries to account for the excellence of its tradition by the spirit of competition, and for Perugino's decline by his withdrawal from this bracing climate.[17] But here as always we must be on our guard lest the logic of social situations leads us to take for a law what is merely an interpretation of a particular development. It was not this spirit that declined in the subsequent generations of Florentine artists and patrons. On the contrary, if anything it increased: Benvenuto Cellini, Baccio Bandinelli, even Vasari himself were eager enough to compete and to display their skills. Why, then, do we assign them a lower place on Olympus? Why has all the interest in the style of Mannerism and the new appreciation of these sophisticated artists not led anyone yet to claim that we owe to Baccio more than Michelangelo?

It is when we come to these questions concerning value, questions which are and will remain vital to the art historian, that the social scientist would, I think, have to refuse to be drawn. He is not used to being asked whether any of the religious beliefs he studies are true or false, and he would be equally unable to say whether the admiration for one style or master is more justified than that for another. As a social scientist he must confine himself to social evidence, and this evidence can, in the nature of things, have no bearing on values. To put the matter epigrammatically: the social scientist can always tell us which are the top ten; he cannot commit himself to picking a first eleven. The top ten, as we know, are based on real or pretended statistics of sale; the choice of a first eleven is a matter of past performance—and of faith.

IX. THE VALIDATION OF THE CANON

Being no more a sports' fan than I am a pop addict, I took over this metaphor from a newspaper critic who reviewed a recent Arts Council Exhibition and wrote that Salvator Rosa did not quite belong to the first eleven. He was right, for though Rosa's name had become proverbial in the late eighteenth century, his œuvre cannot quite stand comparison with the great masters of his time, a Claude Lorrain let alone a Rembrandt. What we usually say of these towering masters is that they belong to the 'canon'. It is this canon, in fact, which is implicit in the critical procedure I have described as that of critical relativism. The discussions of Streeter I have quoted presuppose an unspoken awareness of the canon. When Mr. Croft Murray speaks of 'the baroque recipe without the baroque leaven' he is probably using the touchstone of Pietro da Cortona or—less fairly—of Tiepolo. When Sir John Summerson weighs the claims of the Sheldonian he is thinking of Wren's personal canon, especially St. Paul's.

This term canon was coined by the schoolmasters of antiquity who drew up lists of prescribed texts which students should emulate, and so a faint aura of academic orthodoxy clings to the word. The feeling has grown up that the canon was set up by pedantic critics, but this view vastly overrates the power of professors. There is no developed culture which lacks a canon of achievements handed down in tradition as a touchstone of excellence, though cultures differ in the kind of mastery they value. The critics of antiquity concentrated on poetry and oratory, though painters and sculptors could serve as useful illustrations of various forms of mastery. For what the critics did in antiquity, and what they have done ever since, was to analyse and subdivide the grounds for admiration and to articulate the multiplicity of human experience embodied in the canon.

To quote an example from Cicero for its convenient brevity: 'Isocrates has sweetness, Lysias subtlety, Hyperides acumen, Aeschines sonority, Demosthenes force' (*De Oratore*, iii. 28). The fact that these descriptions ultimately refer to human rather than to supernatural experience distinguishes the study of the canon from the study of mythologies. It makes no sense to ask whether Apollo was really vindictive, but we can try and find out whether Isocrates really has sweetness. We can, that is, if we know enough Greek to respond to those nuances of mastery cultivated and appreciated in the tradition of Greek oratory.

I am afraid we are once again approaching an area where the sound of gun-fire is heard in the distance and the smell of powder is in the air. What has art to do with knowledge, what sense is there in speaking of understanding a masterpiece? We can never know what it meant to its creator, for even if he had told us he might not have known himself. The work of art means what it means to us, there is no other criterion.[18]

This argument, of course, is the ultimate refuge of aesthetic relativism, for if all our reactions are equally subjective there are no standards left, and the idea of a canon would collapse by itself. I confess that whenever I get involved in this argument I have a curious feeling of unreality. I feel as if I had to convey to a visitor from Mars who lacked the gift of hearing what meaning music has for me. To him the performance of a Beethoven quartet would present a most puzzling spectacle: four people rubbing catgut with horsehair to make the air vibrate in given frequencies. I would have a hard time to explain to him that I so much liked having my ear tickled in this way that I even paid for the pleasure, and that I shared with others a reverence for the man who wrote down the instructions for this air-shaking. I grant that my visitor could still write a learned survey of the role concerts play in our society, but he could never come to grasp what distinguishes a concert from a magic ritual.

Let us assume for argument's sake that the concert included a performance of Beethoven's String Quartet op. 132 in A minor with its slow movement entitled *Heiliger Dankgesang eines Genesenen an die Gottheit, in der lydischen Tonart* (Sacred hymn of thanksgiving to the divinity after recovery from illness, in the Lydian mode); after all, this might be a ritualistic sequence of sounds composed and performed in obedience to a superstitious formula. Moreover you do not have to be an imaginary visitor from Mars to find a late Beethoven Quartet hard to understand. Not only members of foreign cultures, even the vast majority of our own may remain unresponsive. It will never belong to the top ten. But it does belong to the canon, and rightly so, because those who are interested and persevere will slowly be able to authenticate the deep emotions embodied in this sequence of sounds and will understand in what way the Andante section of this movement is meant to express its title *neue Kraft fühlend* (feeling new strength). If they are conversant with the idiom of classical music they will ultimately also come to appreciate the choice of the unusual and archaic Lydian mode for this unique composition.

The reason, no doubt, why this kind of assertion meets with a certain amount of scepticism, not to mention hostility, is not hard to discern. To enthuse about a work which another cannot appreciate lays one open to the suspicion of that worst sin in this year's calendar, the sin of 'élitism'. In other words, the faith in the objective validity of the canon is confused with a claim of being a 'superior person'. In fact there is no such claim, for the conviction entails the belief that there are innumerable masterpieces in many styles and modes to which we have no access.

Take Chinese calligraphy, which plays a part in Chinese culture that may well bear comparison with that of music in our own. There is no better way, therefore, to illustrate the implications of aesthetic objectivism than to consider an art so far removed from our own experience.

Professor Chiang Yee, in his enlightening introduction to that art, rightly remarks:

> To those who lack the sense of abstract visual beauty, or are unable to experience it from Chinese characters, the enthusiasm of those Chinese connoisseurs who lose their heads over a single line or group of lines that have no apparent logical meaning, will seem little short of madness; but such enthusiasm is not misplaced, and it is my aim in this book to explain whence this joy is derived.[19]

It is a tribute to the author's insight and skill that he can indeed keep this promise and leave us with the conviction that the connoisseurs are far from mad. We may even be able to glimpse from afar what one of them meant when he listed various faults.

> Reserved persons exhibit a stiff and stilted manner. Undisciplined natures violate alike the rules which can and those which cannot be violated. Unrelieved gentleness ultimately proves effeminate; untempered courage produces stridence.[20]

And yet, reading this catalogue of sins one can also appreciate why Arthur Waley, when asked by a lady at a party how long it would take to learn and savour the form of Chinese cursive known as Grass Writing, replied 'Hm—five hundred years.' Note that it is not a relativist reply. He, if anyone, knew that there was something there to be learned, but he also implied that he himself was not one of the elect.

Relativism grew out of the reaction against the belief of eighteenth-century aesthetics that our response to art is rooted in human nature and must therefore be universal.[21] The reasons why it cannot be are almost trivial. And yet there may be something in this eighteenth-century view that deserves consideration. Surely one is entitled to say that there is something universally human in psychological states we have seen embodied in the arts, states like gratitude for recovery from illness, the feeling of new strength, undiscipline, or effeminacy. To insist on this universality is not to ignore the surprising plasticity of 'human nature', the possibility of different attitudes to illness, discipline, or effeminacy. Suffice it that the ultimate elements that go into these art forms belong to the common experience of humanity. Not that art should therefore be equated with the expression of feelings. Feeling alone will never result in a masterpiece any more than will manual dexterity alone. But all the arts, whether music, calligraphy, dancing, poetry, painting, or architecture, send their roots deep down into the common ground of universally human response.[22]

It is time to return to our *exemplum* to test this assertion. The official description of Streeter's ceiling published at the time contains as good an illustration as any.

> For joy of Festival the other Genii sport about the clouds with their festoons of flowers and laurels and prepare their Garlands of Laurels, viz. Honour and Pleasure for the great lovers and Studiers of those Arts.

Naturally we must be conversant with the conventions of our culture to know that laurels are connected with fame; the 'meaning' of roses as signifying pleasure is less fixed, but it is not hard to understand why these flowers rather than thistles were chosen for that purpose.[23] Naturally, also, the notions of fame, of honour, and of pleasure to be gained by study are culture-bound, and might not be immediately intelligible to members of different cultures who value rather ascetic withdrawal, prowess in war, or a lotus-eating existence. But I would be surprised if social scientists could produce a tribe where the idea of children 'sporting about' for 'Joy of Festival' would be totally unintelligible, though there must be plenty who would be puzzled by the act of levitation permitting the Genii to cavort in the clouds.

It can never be emphasized enough that in art, as in life, 'understanding' is always a matter of degree, and that neither our share in what is universally human nor our intellectual preparation makes us safe from misunderstanding.[24] For even our correct emotional interpretation of a human reaction will ultimately be determined by that same 'logic of situations' which has to guide our assessment of social events. But while we understand human actions on the basis of the rationality principle, on what was seen as the best way to a particular goal, the touchstone of understanding human reactions is our own response to comparable situations.

Take another motif of our ceiling, now obscured by the organ, but described with relish in Whitehall's poem:

> With grinning teeth, sharp fangs and fiery eyes
> Besmeared with blood of friends and enemies
> Rapine appears: a flambeau and dagger are
> His weapons of delight with arms stript bare
> Wolf-like devouring, lying still in wait,
> Unseen 'till now (except in 48)
> He Magistracy hates, abhors the Gown
> But a Herculean Genius strikes him down.

It seems to me that we have a right to claim that we understand the basic meaning of the monster without benefit from tradition. I doubt whether many human beings could be found anywhere who would call it lovable, though admittedly some people today might describe it as funny. But within this general reaction that the creature is surely up to no good, there are still any number of degrees in understanding the exact import of that symbol of evil.

I for one was alerted only by Whitehall's allusion to 1648 to the personal memories which must have been aroused by this personification twenty years after Cromwell's triumph. We have seen that an awareness of this historical situation will certainly help us to understand the choice and import of the whole subject of Streeter's ceiling. What matters even more in the present context is that a fuller understanding also depends on an awareness of the situation in art itself. The expected move hardly registers. We become blunted to the cliché in art and in life and discount its original emotional meaning. It so happens that the group in question is such a cliché, a formula almost indispensable to Baroque ceiling compositions. Where there is an apotheosis there must be the hostile or hellish forces over which the Good is seen to triumph. It may be impossible for us to tell what impact the composition made on the first visitors to the Sheldonian. After all, the scheme was new to Oxford, and so they may have responded more keenly than did the more travelled virtuosi among whom we must also count ourselves.

Here we come back from another angle to the role which style plays in the History of Art. For style has this in common with language or other means of expression, that it determines the level of our expectations and thereby also our response to deviations from the norm. Without this framework of convention we cannot really assess the significant surprise. The style within which the artist works is therefore part of the situation which we instinctively try to reconstruct. How far we succeed will depend on our familiarity with the idiom.

Architectural styles lend themselves even better to the illustration of this important point than styles in painting. By the standards of 1669 the interior of the Sheldonian must have made a considerable impact by the richness of its decoration. How far it exceeded the norm only a specialist could tell us, but we all know that the degree of ornamentation can become a sensitive issue and therefore acquire special expressive significance. I am old enough to have witnessed such a shift in calibration. In the days of my youth the absence of decoration in a functional interior was certainly more telling and therefore more impressive than it has become since. It appears to me that this absence is no longer registered at all as a positive expressive quality by the generation who grew up in this type of surrounding. It is quite likely that as with language, so with art, our responsiveness to nuance is most sensitive in idioms we have absorbed early in life. I have reason to believe, for instance, that my own reaction to the architectural style of Christopher Wren is slightly distorted by my early habituation to the decorative exuberance of the Austrian baroque. I would therefore trust Sir John Summerson's judgement more than my own. I would not do so if I were a relativist and believed that one reaction was as valid as another.

This influence of early conditioning on our automatic expectations and responses certainly accounts for the phenomenon which is so frequently quoted in support of aesthetic relativism—the hostility or indifference which in their time greeted some works of art now generally acknowledged to be masterpieces. It certainly needs time to build up that set of expectations that permits us to understand and evaluate the moves of a master. I do not think, in fact, that there are short cuts to this state of readiness. At any rate it seems to me that the 'sales talks' used by critics to effect this change of heart are more likely to create sales resistance than a true response. Not that this difficulty can constitute an argument against innovation in art. New conditions, new problems, new media, and new topics are bound to disrupt the old skills and demand new habituation both on the part of the creators and on that of their public. We must hope that opportunities for mastery will always arise, but we cannot be sure, and we must let the future look after itself.[25]

I cannot see how this uncertainty can undermine our conviction that there have been great masters in the past. But have not these masters also been subject to radical changes in evaluation? Has not the canon changed almost from generation to generation?

I think to insist too much on these changes is to confuse popularity with appreciation, the top ten with the first eleven. One is a matter of taste, the other is not. Whether anyone likes or dislikes a game is a purely subjective matter, though he may have been influenced in his attitude by a hundred and one different factors. There are people who dislike opera, others who are bored by sculpture; there are whole genres which have fallen under a kind of social taboo, such as didactic poetry or anecdotal painting; there are others which are rediscovered by an élite, such as emblematics or the Japanese Haiku. Apologists for certain kinds of art often plead that if we only understood it, we would also like it. By and large, I think, the sequence is inverted. Without first liking a game, a style, a genre, or a medium we are hardly able to absorb its conventions well enough to discriminate and understand. Those who object to Rubens because he painted such fat women will not usually notice how well he painted them.

There are and always have been prejudices of such a kind which have barred access to whole periods and styles. Those who expected a degree of illusionism from painting were blind to the excellences of medieval art, those who attached importance to decorum were uneasy about Rembrandt. It is certainly interesting and important to study the shifts in value systems which underlie such movements of taste. They are often due to extraneous factors. A teetotaller is unsuited to appreciate the 'cider maker's art'. Since Ruskin thought that the Renaissance style demanded the enslavement of the craftsman he was 'put off', and hardly allowed himself to yield to the natural pleasure we receive from order and precision.

What must interest the social scientist in this connection is perhaps rather the isolation in which Ruskin found himself. The values of mastery have become all but autonomous in our society, and it is considered inappropriate to apply moral criteria in such a context. Indeed the plea of 'artistic merit' has become enshrined in the laws of many countries in defence of the infringement of ethical values. It would be interesting to trace the history of this special licence which has never ceased to worry the upholders of moral standards. I happen to have no more sympathy for moral relativism than I have for the aesthetic variety.[26] I think it right that bullfights are not permitted in this country, though I readily grant that a great matador may display mastery in the skill of elegantly dispatching a raging bull. Alas, there are examples of more evil mastery in art and literature involving the vicarious enjoyment of cruelty and degradation which we may acknowledge and yet reject. Where, in every case, we draw the line, is a matter of personal decision, for it would certainly be a real impoverishment if we demanded of all masterpieces that they should coincide with our own value system. It would be an impoverishment precisely because art is not life, and can help us to extend our sympathies and our understanding of basic human reactions, which transcend the limits of any one culture or value system.

Marx was troubled by the fact that the art of a slave-owning society like that of the Greeks could retain its value, and looked for the solution of this problem in our longing for the paradise of childhood. But maybe he was as mistaken in his interpretation of that longing as he was in that of Greek art. Why deny that there is much cruelty in Homer and worse in the institution of those Roman arenas which Wren selected as a basis for our building? However much art is invariably rooted in the life and value system of its age and society, it will transcend these situations when, as we say, it 'stands the test of time'. Not, to be sure, by making us forget the human condition from which it grew, but precisely by making accessible to our imaginative response experiences which no longer form part of our practical lives. It is in this way that the masterpieces of religious art continue to speak even to non-believers.

They stand the test of time not as formal exercises but as an embodiment of a value system which they teach us to recognize. Michelangelo's vision of the act of creation on the Sistine ceiling is a case in point. Its continued resonance in our culture is second only to that of the book of Genesis it illustrates.

Maybe if our ceiling here had been an equally transcending masterpiece it would also still embody man's quest for Truth in ever memorable images. It was this perhaps which Robert Whitehall hoped for when—to quote a few more lines of his notorious poem—he concluded his description:

> These to the life are drawn so curiously
> That the Beholder would become all Eye
> Or at the least an Argus, so sublime
> A phant'sie makes essayes to Heaven to climb
> That future ages must confess they owe
> To STREETER more than Michael Angelo.

If there really had been beholders over the ages who had been seized by such raptures, the rumour of this addition to the canon would have spread from the few to the many and this interior, God forbid, would be as crowded with pilgrims and tourists from all parts of the world as the Sistine Chapel always is. It would be more than one of the sights of Oxford that is so rich in sights, more even than a landmark in the history of English art; it would be a towering feature in our mental landscape, a peak by which to orient ourselves in our civilization.

For this, I believe, is the real role the canon plays in any culture. It offers points of reference, standards of excellence which we cannot level down without losing direction. Which particular peaks, or which individual achievements we select for this role may be a matter of choice, but we could not make such a choice if there really were no peaks but only shifting dunes.

There are teachers today who feel the need to convince their students of the reality of these peaks; they want them to learn how to measure these heights and to make reliable 'value judgements'. I would not want to discourage the discussion of values, but ultimately, I believe, the values of the canon are too deeply embedded in the totality of our civilization for them to be discussed in isolation. Civilization, one hopes, can be transmitted; it cannot be taught in courses leading to an examination. Our attitude to the peaks of art can best be conveyed through the way we speak about them, perhaps through our very reluctance to spoil the experience by too much talk. What we call civilization may be interpreted as a web of value judgements which are implicit rather than explicit. Bernard Shaw remarked somewhere that he had never read *Die Jungfrau von Orleans*, but that the tone of voice in which people spoke about Schiller made him sure he would be bored. I think he may have talked to the wrong people; but the observation is acute enough. To grow up in a culture is to hear people talk of foods we have never tasted, natural wonders we have never visited, enjoyments that still await us, and encounters we hope to avoid. We learn to enter these rumours on our intellectual map with which we embark on the way through life.[27] True, we will not want to use it uncritically. We want to test the warnings and promises we have received and absorbed. But we could not do so at all if we distrusted any map from the outset. Maybe the canon of beauty-spots lets us down. Maybe we find that a famous sight is not all it has been cracked up to be. But even in such a case it might be rash to jump to the conclusion that all our enthusiastic fellow tourists had been brainwashed by clever travel agents. We must also be critical of our own reactions. The fault may lie with us, because we are not in the right mood. As soon as we even consider this possibility, we have ceased to be complete relativists and subjectivists. We have sided with tradition against our own reactions. In fact we may feel that as far as the peaks of art are concerned, it is not so much we who test the masterpiece, but the masterpiece which tests us.

Early in November I read in the colour magazine of the *Observer* that Michelangelo is 'out'. Those of us who believe in the objectivity of artistic values will be sorry to hear that, for if it were true the loss would be ours. He was not called great because he was famous. He was famous because he was great. Whether we like or dislike him, his greatness is an element in the story we are appointed to tell. It forms part of that logic of situations without which history would sink into chaos.

Now a committed sociologist might easily interpret such faith in tradition as a symptom of political conformism and perhaps of an 'authoritarian personality'. He may be right or he may be wrong in his diagnosis, but as an opponent of relativism I am still entitled to ask him whether I have been right or wrong in stressing the objective component in the experience of artistic mastery.

What we can learn from the scientist, including the true social scientist, is not relativism but modesty. I myself would gladly give whole volumes on art appreciation for the following passage from the conclusion of R. H. Tawney's beautiful lecture (1949) on *Social History and Literature*.[28]

The truth is that, apart from a few commonplaces, we know at present next to nothing of the relations, if such exist, between the artistic achievements of an epoch and the character of its economic life, and that the only candid course is to confess our ignorance.

I submit however, that it is precisely at this point that the art historian can discover where his contribution must lie. Tawney would have liked to see a bridge built between the facts of economic life on one side of the gulf and the artistic achievements of the epoch on the other. Who would not want to join in such a venture? But surely such a bridge can never become a reality before either of us has decided at what point of the bank a bridge-head can most profitably be established. In surveying the land neither of us can and will start from scratch. The social scientist has his own problem situation, his own theories he wishes to test and investigate. What he cannot tell unaided is what the land is like on our side. He has no instrument in his tool-kit to spot those 'artistic achievements' which are worth examining in the light of Tawney's problem. Whether he knows it or not, he will have to rely on the art historian who is the keeper of the canon. The canon is our starting point, our guiding theory about that aspect of image-making we call mastery. It may be no more infallible than other theories can ever be, but neither we nor the social scientist can ever ignore it. The psychologist interested in the processes of creativity, the economist studying the correlation of investment and enlightened patronage, the sociologist plotting the fluctuations of taste, they all cannot begin their work before they have decided what evidence to use and what is their *explicandum*. It is this I had in mind when I suggested at the outset that, while the social scientist can assist the art historian, he cannot replace him.

Years ago my late friend Ernst Kris, who combined with distinction the roles of keeper at the *Kunsthistorische Museum* in Vienna and of practising psychoanalyst, invited me to join him in investigating the rise of caricature, an eminently psychological and sociological problem. I remember my elder colleague returning from a trip to Italy and my asking him eagerly what new insights about the psychology of art he had brought back. 'I have made a discovery,' he said gravely. 'It is the great masters who are the great masters.'

From my student days I have always hoped to show that the study of art can be conducted in a rational way, and I have no wish to recant. For I am sure it is rational for human beings to acknowledge human values and to talk about them in human terms. Whatever the true origins of the term 'the humanities' may be, it may serve us as a reminder that we are merely impoverishing ourselves when trying to discuss people as if they were insects or computers. Yet this is what we are forced to do if we surrender the only yardstick we have, the yardstick of our civilization validated by our own experience.

We cannot but start from the hypothesis that values have been realized in history and that there is not only good technology, good science, and good art, but that there are even good languages, good *mores*, and good societies. The inscription on the façade of this building proclaims in bold letters that it was dedicated by Gilbert Sheldon *Academiae Oxoniensi Bonisque Literis.*[29] If the moment should ever come when the teachers and students of this *Academia* question the meaning of *bonis* it will be time to close this building as a temple to an extinct creed. That would be a pity. It is a fine temple to a good creed.

Canons and Values in the Visual Arts: A Correspondence with Quentin Bell

IN MY Romanes Lecture on *Art History and the Social Sciences* [pp. 131–66] I defended the traditional notion of a canon of excellence in the arts. These lectures are given in the Sheldonian Theatre at Oxford, and I therefore used that building by Sir Christopher Wren with its ambitious ceiling painting by Streeter to remind my audience of the light which the social sciences can throw on the origins and the significance of such works. Yet, I argued, no 'value-free' scientific discipline can deal with the claim made at the time 'that future ages must confess they owe to Streeter more than Michael Angelo'. Not only does this boast make use of the canon of excellence, it cannot be refuted without reference to it. It would be insufficient to demonstrate by means of statistics that the prediction did not come true because Michelangelo remained more famous than Streeter. We cannot evade the problem of the reasons for Michelangelo's greater fame, in other words, his greatness. Thus while the history of building and of image-making is properly the domain of the social sciences, the history of art as a history of mastery remains inextricably linked with the values acknowledged by civilization. Any social scientist interested in exploring and explaining the history and sociology of art must sooner or later consult the existing canon, if only to select the data against which he wishes to test his theories.

---

12 May 1975

DEAR ERNST,

I should have written before to thank you for the Romanes Lecture, but I had to read it not once but twice and am indeed inclined to think that I ought to read it a third time before trying to measure the generosity of your gift. What did indeed strike me at first reading, and again at second, and is clear as daylight is the sheer triumphant elegance of your essay—the ingenuity, the clarity, the speed with which you so enviably do it; and this does indeed make it a delight. But with the pleasure of reading you and enjoying your

Reprinted from *Critical Inquiry*, Spring 1976.

ingenuity and your fun there goes a feeling of worry about your main argument, or what I take to be your main argument.

In this question of relativism I feel as Dr. Johnson did about determinism, 'all human reason is in favour of it, all human experience against it' (probably I have misquoted). In other words I sit on the fence, and when I see anyone descending in too decided a fashion on either side, I utter shrill cries of alarm.

'The history of art, in this light, is rightly considered to be the history of masterpieces and of the old masters . . .' Yes, certainly, but of how much else. I wish I knew more about Egypt but little as I know I do get the impression that, from the Old Kingdom to the Ptolemies, with only one notable deviation, there is a steady and equal flow of talent and achievement—no mountains, no foothills, no genius, no epigones. Perhaps if I knew more the ground might look less equal, but was there in Egypt the kind of variation that distinguishes Streeter from Michelangelo? Surely not and, if not, are we to say that really there is no history of Egyptian art? I suppose we may, but after all this didn't prevent you from writing an excellent and illuminating chapter in *The Story of Art* devoted to Egypt. But supposing I am completely wrong about Egypt, suppose there are really vast differences of excellence, does this—the extent of our valuation—make history possible?

I am putting this badly. Let me try another tack. You have a good deal to say about Michelangelo and, if I understand you rightly, you say that we have to place him within a canon based not on reputation but on absolute unquestionable value. If we are to make sense of art history, it is not enough that we should say that Michelangelo is better than Streeter in the eyes of the world but that he is in some absolute sense better—and this I find hard to take. Supposing by some appalling catastrophe everything that Michelangelo ever made were destroyed, or worse still, supposing nothing remained but those horrible presentation drawings. Let us suppose that this catastrophe had occurred about a century ago so that one had to take Michelangelo as one takes Apelles, on trust. Could one in any real sense say that one felt his supreme merits. With only the *Fall of Phaëthon* to judge by, the words would stick in my throat, they would be insincere. But I could always sincerely say that Michelangelo had been one of the great art historical events—something which having happened, changed the world for ever—and I could do this without liking his work or being in a position to make any judgement about it.

About seventy years ago my father and my mother were dining in Kensington. The talk turned to Rubens and Van Dyck. Of the large and highly cultivated party at that table only my parents doubted the superiority of Van

Dyck. To everyone else it seemed self-evident that Van Dyck was more refined, more sensitive, more civilized, more clearly 'of the company' than his master. There was something coarse, something brutal about Rubens. If these people could have known that by the third quarter of the twentieth century it would be generally accepted that Rubens was the greater man, I think they might have said: 'So much the worse for the twentieth century. Clearly if this happens it will mean that you have lost some of our culture, our refinement, our powers of discerning certain shades of feeling.' And can we say that they would have been altogether wrong? What they saw and admired in Van Dyck is to us much less important than what we can find in Rubens. In terms of objective truth we can say that both Van Dyck and Rubens exert a vast influence upon their contemporaries and their followers. Does it really help us to include or to exclude Van Dyck from the canon? And surely it is this consideration—I mean the magnitude of the artist as an art historical event—which saves us from the need for the random sample and the graph. If one compares Whistler with all his many British imitators of the last decade of the nineteenth century, it is quite clear who is imitating whom, even though it may not always be clear who is painting the best paintings.

I suppose this business of valuation, or at least the association of values with art historical judgements, is one of the bees in my bonnet. There is another which you also fluttered when you refer to the value that may be expressed in monetary terms. This you call cynicism, but I am not sure that this is quite fair. The Sheldonian is not yet for sale, neither is Chardin's *Retour du Marché*, unless the Louvre has changed its policy very much. Nevertheless I don't think that I am guilty of a completely absurd statement when I say that I feel that, despite its 'bourgeois' subject and the fact that everything has no doubt been 'paid for', this picture is only remotely concerned with money, whereas Quentin de La Tour's portrait of Mme de Pompadour is— that is to say that it reflects a certain expensive life style, it is intended for an élite which is either rich or has to pretend to be rich, and in this it resembles a great deal of courtly painting, furniture, and architecture. To go back to the Egyptians, surely it is not pure cynicism to say that there is a vulgar, an ostentatious quality about their work, an apparent belief that one can buy one's way into a future life which is wholly civilized and which we recognize in ourselves, the ancients, and the Chinese.

Well I must not get started on another page having written far too much already. It is impossible though not to look at any argument presented by you with attention and admiration, even when one finds oneself in disagreement. My only real regret is that I have nothing positive to offer in return.

I do hope you are well, as I am almost, and as we are I believe the same age, looking forward as I do to a busy retirement with a minimum of committee meetings.

Yours ever
QUENTIN

Cobbe Place
Beddingham

———————

13.V.1975

DEAR QUENTIN,

Thank you very much indeed for your kind and interesting response to my Romanes Lect. I don't know if you realize how rarely I get a real reaction to the stuff I send out. The majority of recipients don't acknowledge at all, and I don't blame them, for I frequently don't either. The rest mostly write a word of thanks, but give no evidence of having read the thing. You have read it twice, as you say, and that alone makes me proud. I did not write the thing for everybody to agree and to sign on the dotted line; on the contrary, I knew that it was controversial and rather explosive. Moreover, though the lecture is too long, it may not be long enough, and I may have failed in the end to put down what I wanted to say with sufficient clarity because I tried to answer beforehand such objections as I could think of.

I wonder if I could persuade you to engage in a kind of public discussion with me about these important issues—though I realize that we both may not have enough time and leisure to follow up this wild idea. I have been much urged by the journal *Critical Inquiry* to write something for them, and this might be a suitable topic—though to retract right away, I *must* first get the *Ornament* book into shape. How would the idea strike you in principle?

I fear I won't be able now to answer in full detail; let me try to start at the end. There are people who don't believe art historians should be concerned with value at all. I think neither you nor I belong in that category. There are others (Michael Levey, I think, wanted to make that point at the Association of Art Historians) who think that the responsibility for our critical judgement rests entirely and solely with each one of us, and we have to make up our mind alone and unaided in our confrontation with every work of art of the past. I don't happen to believe that either; it sounds grand, but it is not only unrealistic, but also vainglorious.[2] We never start from scratch, we have not invented our civilization and our values in any case, and we should not pretend we have. If we tried we would find that we could not possibly justify our predilections because these likes and dislikes are indeed largely subjective. So I believe, first as a matter of sheer observation, that our civilization transmits to us a canon of great poets, composers, artists and that we are in fact appointed to pass it on to future generations. Not, to be sure, uncritically, but with a certain humility.

The canon is not the same as a ranking order. I am sure the kind of discussion you tell about, whether Van Dyck or Rubens is greater, is also part of civilization, and I don't think it speaks against my proposition. There are followers of various Gods and divinities in every religion; I am sure these were both great masters, and one can empathize with those who find Rubens too robust.

The main point I really wanted to make is that we cannot start from scratch and that anybody who wants to know about the history of art, whether social scientist or amateur, really uses these 'guidelines' (ominous words!). Freud wrote on Leonardo and on Michelangelo's *Moses* because he wanted (rather unhappily, as it turned out) to test his psychological theory. I have no doubt, by the way, that Apelles was a great master. I take this on trust, as I take so many things on trust, for instance that Miltiades was a good general. How do I know? I don't. We cannot examine everything all at once; as little (and this was part of my argument) as the scientist can or does. But though I know I cannot prove Michelangelo's greatness in the way de Piles tried, by the awarding of points, I can select him for my canon on the grounds (as I wrote) of faith and hope. I am sorry you find the presentation drawings so horrible. I find the portrait of Quaratesi ravishing. Of course there is something almost repulsive in Michelangelo's mastery, but my awe is not much connected with my 'likes'.

Now about those Egyptians—I would be prepared to bet that their craftsmen were not all equally good (or bad) and that there were renowned masters among them, much like the 'cunning' craftsmen Solomon engaged from Phoenicia for his temple. In the Middle Ages Nicholas of Verdun was such a one in the twelfth century. I am sure even we can tell differences in quality there: but I have to concede that it is unlikely that the Egyptians had an 'art' in the sense the Greeks had it. In *The Story of Art*, to which you so kindly refer, I start with my doubts about the universal validity of that term (to which I return in the Lecture), and I also say, somewhere near the fourth page of the 25th chapter, that 'it is obvious that an Egyptian artist had little opportunity of expressing his personality. The rules and conventions of his style were so strict that there was very little scope for choice. It really comes to this— where there is no choice, there is no expression' etc. etc.

On the other hand it is true that Egyptian art as such belongs to our mental universe, to the furniture of our mind, and long may that be the case. Whether we 'understand' it may be a different matter. Few people share my faith in the possibility of understanding a work of art or even think it makes sense to talk about it. This might also be a topic we might debate if it ever came to it.

You see, I realize that in calling in the canon I am advocating something like a retrograde step towards an 'Academic' interpretation of art, but I am less worried by this consequence than many people would be. Have you not also argued for something like a canon when you pleaded that the Pre-Raphaelites should not be ignored?[1] I may 'like' them less than you do, but I don't find this all that important. I once shocked an American student of mine whom I had sent to look at the Raphael cartoons and who came back complaining she did not like them at all. I told her coolly that I was not interested. It was perhaps cruel, but it did the trick.

I recently was invited to talk about 'Art' at the Institute of Education of our University. There was a well-intentioned teacher there who put forward the view that we had no right whatever to influence the likes and dislikes of our pupils because every generation had a different outlook and we could not possibly tell what theirs would be. It is the same extreme relativism which has invaded our art schools and resulted in the doctrine (which I have read in print) that art could not possibly be taught because only what has been done already can be taught, and since art is creativity (they used to call it originality) it is not possible to teach it. Q.E.D.—I recently asked my history finalists what 'Quod erat demonstrandum' means and they did not know....

Sorry, I am starting to ramble, and I must close.

Many many thanks, once more,

Yours ever
ERNST

19 Briardale Gardens
London, NW3

May 15 1975

DEAR ERNST,

Your letter arrived this morning and has had a most demoralizing effect. For today is a free day, by which I mean that I have no teaching or committee work and am therefore 'free' to sit down and mark 25 scripts. I long for the A.U.T. to tell me I must not* but so far they have not done so, and I was fully determined this morning to get the odious task done. I will not attempt to describe my own motives, but I'm afraid that they are purely self-indulgent and lead me to sit down instead and attempt not an answer but a what do they call it?—*accusation de reception?*—acknowledgement of yours.

I think it might be very interesting and a valuable mental exercise if we were in some way to publicize our differences, or at least in some kind of joint pamphlet to discover what those differences are, for I must confess that I have not any settled convictions. The only drawback that I can see is that from an editor's point of view it might seem dull. What the public wants I imagine is a gladiatorial display, and we are both of us much too sensible to be gladiators. Still, shall we mention the possibility, making it clear that this is in fact no more than a possibility, to *Critical Inquiry* or some other journal and see how they react? Obviously you will want to deal with *Ornament*, obviously I can hardly think of such things until term is over.

But I think that there is a good deal more to discuss. Although I don't think that words like 'retrograde' or 'reactionary' have very much meaning within this kind of context, I must say that I am a little worried to find that you accept Apelles like that as it were. I find a good deal of difficulty in accepting Miltiades, accepting him, that is, as I accept a general like Sherman or even like Caesar. One knows so little of what the general actually did, what actually happened, that to me it seems that what one really does take on trust is Marathon. This is the military masterpiece that makes the fate of the world. And in the same way (but I know far too little about Greek painting) I think there may have been a kind of Marathon of the arts to which names like Apelles, Zeuxis (can't spell) etc. have been attached, but perhaps wrongly attached. And just as it is to me pleasing and poetical and somehow tremendously appropriate that Rembrandt should have painted a chaotic military conversation piece in the depths of the night, it is after all quite wrong, and my fine feelings rest upon error. Nor need I be too much ashamed of such a blunder. Did not Mme de Staël say that the very essence of British literary art was to be found in Ossian, and were not all the painters and poets of Europe in love with that spurious genius for a generation? What I am getting at I think is that in the end surely your canon must be alterable by the historian. I had not really meant to involve us in further argument but only to say that there is more to be said (on both sides no doubt) and it might be a good plan if we could find a way to say it publicly.

* The Association of University Teachers threatened at this time to call its members out on strike.

I must however take up one point. Your teacher at the Institute, is he really a relativist? Isn't he a kind of religious zealot? I used to teach school-children. With me there was a much better teacher (better in that she could interest and control a class and organize things and was in fact a very admirable and sensible person). One day she came into the room where I had been teaching and found a series of (to my mind) the most surprising and beautiful water colours. 'What are these?' said she. I explained that they were copies of Raphael made by eleven- and twelve-year-old children. I would have gone on to explain how interested I was by their resemblance, not to Raphael but rather to Simone Martini, for they had all the shapes beautifully right but none of the internal drawing or the sentiment, but I was checked by her look of horror.

'You've made them copy from Raphael?' she said. Her expression was exactly that of someone who had been casually informed that I had committed a series of indecent assaults upon the brats. And in fact in subsequent conversation it appeared that this was very nearly what she did feel. For her, what she called 'self expression' was as precious as virginity.

The irony of the thing was that these creative virgins were coming to school with traced drawings of mickey mouse and pictures from the lids of cereal packets and had indeed been violated 1,000 times over before I ever introduced them to the forbidden delights of the Divine Urbinate, as Claude Phillips used to call him. I wander and I must stop. I simply must deal with those waiting scripts. 'Take but degree away, untune that string.' It may be naughty, but I wish I could. In another six weeks I shall, and then let us think of a joint effort. (I should be enormously proud.)

Yours ever
QUENTIN

Cobbe Place
Beddingham

19th May 1975

DEAR QUENTIN,

I am sorry about those scripts. I have wriggled out of mass marking. I, too, must not allow myself to be tempted away from the straight and narrow path, however. But I am 'seduced' by your story of copying Raphael: (a) to ask you whether you know the charming book on children in the Brera[3] which reproduces a good many delightful copies of this kind; (b) your story has brought it home to me once more (I had made this 'discovery' once and forgotten it again) that autobiographically and so-to-say psychoanalytically *Art and Illusion* may partly have sprung from my reaction to this prejudice. In contrast to an elder sister who was and is very imaginative and produced very imaginative drawings much admired by my parents, I had taken to copying pictures of animals in a favourite animal book. I was quite proud of my efforts and somewhat mortified when I discovered from the tone of voice in which these drawings were duly 'praised' that my parents disapproved of copying. Those were the days of Cižek in Vienna ... As you see, I never got over this grievance. To work!

Yours ever
ERNST

*19 Briardale Gardens
London, NW3*

———————

Lucca*
July 30 1975

MY DEAR ERNST,

I think that I owe you a letter but, even if I do not, I now feel ready to try and get this correspondence restarted. It so happens that I have been seeing things which have a bearing on our previous letters. The 'things' were not in this delightful neighbourhood but in London. You will remember that I had said that: 'really there is no history of Egyptian art' and you, while conceding that it is unlikely that the Egyptians had an 'art' in the sense the Greeks had it, would 'be prepared to bet that their craftsmen were not all equally good (or bad)'.

It was not, let me assure you, in the hope of laying long odds on a 'cert' that I visited the Egyptian galleries of the B.M. In fact it would, as I now see, be rather hard to know who *had* 'won' the bet; it is possible, as one passes from one smart glossy mummy case to another, to fancy at all events that some of their skilful sign writers and decorators had a little more address than their neighbours, although I still think that, so far as finished works go—I mean the properly finished 'morticians'' goods—one is never startled, never shocked until one passes through all those thousands of years to the Ptolemies and the quite different, high spirited, downright 'amusing' vulgarities of

———
* (This at least was where I began writing; I make the point because I had no works of reference with which to check my statements.)

Roman Egypt. Of the monumental work it is harder to speak fairly, so much of the British Museum collection seems to be taken from the 25th Dynasty; but, recollecting the sculptures in Paris and elsewhere (I have never been to Egypt) one does get an impression of overwhelming sameness, greater because more precisely skilful than, for instance, the vast collection of almost identical funerary urns at Volterra. The Egyptian sculptor does seem to have taken his completed images from an inflexible and eternal mould, the same original block of stone pointed out in exactly the same way to give exactly the same effect, the same inane stare, the same reticent smile. 'And all you hold,' I muttered to myself, as I stood for, heaven knows—perhaps the thirtieth time—staring at those frozen poker faces, 'all you hold is a pair of threes.'

And in this I was entirely wrong.

The staggering thing is that, if only the Egyptians could be persuaded to show their hands, they were, I am convinced, almost unbeatable.

Do you know—but I'm sure you do—those little drawings which they made when they were off duty? The museum has gathered a number of them together in one case, and the effect, on me at all events, was staggering. They are rapid, expressive, sensitive drawings, drawings by men who could disregard outline and convey all that was needful by the use of accent, scribbles that remind one of Rembrandt—perhaps that's going too far—but of Tiepolo, of the freest, most perfectly adroit of European hands. The effect, when one sees it surrounded by all that pompous, polished gravity, is not unlike that which one sometimes finds when one can compare a rapidly finished sinopia with a completed work; but, much much stronger, for here the contrast is between something that is intensely alive and something which is more than half dead.

Perhaps this individual and imaginative art was, as it were, an underground accompaniment to the official art of the Pharaohs, never finding its way into public monuments except during one brief revolutionary epoch during the 18th Dynasty. How profoundly shocking that revolutionary period must have seemed, how grossly the artists then violated the canons of their art.

Perhaps it is not quite fair, in this context, to speak of 'canons'. But there was surely a generally respected custom which tied all public and presentable art to a set of unbreakable rules, and this, I suppose, is almost bound to be the case where art is so much a part of religion. What is unusual, I fancy, is to find two such very different notions of art within one society. In most societies one is a traditionalist because it doesn't occur to one to be anything else; in Egypt the tradition must have been adhered to as the result of something like a conscious choice.

I don't know that this 'proves' anything; but it does help me to explain (to myself at all events) some of my misgivings about any form of 'academic' authority. At the risk of being tiresomely autobiographical, I should perhaps add to the list of circumstances which make it difficult for me to accept the idea of a canon as something desirable. As you know, I am not an art historian in the sense in which you are, and I suspect therefore that, for me, the painting of the High Renaissance has not the central importance that it surely has for you. I was born into an artistic milieu which was, or had been, very much concerned to challenge the existing cultural establishment; my own efforts as an artist have been largely concerned with the making of earthenware; my first attempt to write about an aesthetic subject took the form of a theoretical work on fashion.

These last two points need to be expanded a little.

Of all the 'useful' arts ceramics stands nearest to the 'fine arts'. Indeed the work of the potter extends very naturally into that of the painter and the sculptor. It can carry almost as heavy an emotional charge. It was the chosen form and indeed a most capacious vehicle for the delicate and staggering aesthetic burdens of the celestial artist. In fine, the potter is or can be a creator of the highest genius. And yet, we have only to glance at the history of ceramic art in order to see how rare, how unusual a being he is *as an individual*. The individual studio potter is in fact a modern invention; in most epochs he is merged in the factory, the workshop, or indeed the entire culture in which he labours. Wedgwood, Spode, and Worcester are entities quite as distinct as Leach or Morgan or Palissy, and a word like T'ang is used to describe the very different artistic personality shared by heaven knows how many thousands of artists over a vast area for a matter of—what is it?—250 years.*

With these facts in mind it is not easy to see art history as a history of 'masterpieces and of the old masters' without wishing to make certain additions and qualifications.

This does not mean that I reject the idea of a canon as applied to the history of ceramics. In fact I think that there are examples which come to mind when one is trying to throw or to decorate a pot and which are at once an inspiration and a threat—an inspiration because there are qualities like honesty, elegance, and so on which are all the better for being exemplified; a threat, and in the case of pottery a very real threat, because it is so very easy to end by making a pastiche. But the canon here is of course composed not of the work of great individuals but of great collective achievements. Moreover, even more remarkably than in painting, we have during the past

---

* August 19. Only about 50 years out.

century and a half set our canon topsy-turvy. In our grandfathers' time the triumphs of the potters' art began in antiquity with red figure ware; in China it was the modern work of the Ch'ing dynasty, famille rose, etc. which provided the canon which was imitated by the great European factories. The earlier dynasties were hardly known, and our modern admiration for peasant wares, the geometric style, hispano mauresque, and all the rude, crude, deeply expressive wares of the older cultures would have seemed very strange. Indeed I think that we have gone too far in this direction and undervalue the frivolous, delicate, and highly decorative pottery of the eighteenth century.

All is flux—this brings me to my other interest which I tried to discuss in my first book: *On Human Finery*. One must no doubt be careful in attempting to apply the generalizations which one can draw from the history of clothes (unlike ceramics, a shallow container of aesthetic feeling) to the history of art in general. I have recently been rewriting this book and, in an appendix, trying to see how far such a proceeding is justifiable, so I won't attempt to enter into any detail; but I would say that the phenomena of dress have obliged me to think in terms of classes and class relationships rather than of individuals and that I have learnt a good deal both from Plekhanov and from Veblen, despite the fact that they both talk a great deal of nonsense. Status, expense, and all the various sublimations of expense do seem to me to exert a profound influence on the aesthetics of dress in a relatively static society while, in a dynamic society, one in which there is competition between classes, the first principles of taste are governed by fashion. As fashions change, our conceptions of value change, that which was good becomes bad and vice versa; and these revolutions of feeling result, so it seems to me, from the evolution of conflicting classes. This, I have argued, does not force us to accept a complete relativism; but it does mean, I think, that we see the fashions of our own day and even, to some extent, those of the past, through a distorting glass, a distorting glass which is for ever moving in front of our eyes.

This letter threatens to become inexcusably long. What I have been trying to do is to formulate my difficulties in accepting a canon but, as you will have observed, I have already implicitly admitted that I can accept the idea. Thus I do accept the highly academic notion of a hierarchy of the arts; I believe that the art of the modiste will not carry as high an aesthetic voltage as the art of the potter. More importantly when you oblige me to ask myself the question: 'Could not Streeter, in certain historical circumstances, become a greater artist than Michelangelo?' I have to answer 'no', whereas it seems to me that a consistent relativist must answer 'yes'.

As I said in my first letter: I sit on the fence. If you will bear with me, I will try to say what kind of a fence it is and in so doing find out how far I can agree with you.

You are right in saying that we both disagree with those who say that 'art historians should not be concerned with value at all'. It is almost true to say that art history is concerned with nothing else for it is the devaluation of old values and the discovery of new forms of excellence which concerns us; this surely is the very stuff of art history. Nevertheless I think I understand the point of view of those who do say this; they have been afflicted, as I have been afflicted, by a kind of art history which might more properly be called 'art appreciation' and which consists in a kind of aesthetic exhortation: the student is to be told what is good and what is bad, and 'history' becomes a kind of apology for the good. I have taught students who have received this kind of instruction (it is common enough both in schools of general education and in schools of art) and who were genuinely puzzled when, for instance, I have insisted that no account of painting in England in the eighteenth century could be complete without a discussion of the portrait painters. The boys and girls had been taught that Reynolds and Gainsborough were 'academic', pretty, and élitist; they could therefore be neglected and forgotten. This in fact was the kind of pseudo-history that I had in mind when, in my Leslie Stephen Lecture, I blamed those historians who, on much the same principle, omitted the Pre-Raphaelites. Like them or not, the Pre-Raphaelites are a part of art history: they existed, they were influential, they cannot be dismissed. You suggest that, in urging this, I am in fact 'advocating something like a canon'. And it is here, and again when you say of Michelangelo: 'my awe is not much connected with my likes' or again, when you point to the irrelevance of a student who announced that she didn't like the Raphael Cartoons, that we enter a territory where we can agree.

On these terms I can accept the canon. Take a concrete instance and, returning to Michelangelo, let me admit that, not only do I *not* like the presentation drawings, I suffer from still worse deficiencies. I am staggered by his power, but I never have and never will love any work by him as I love the School of Athens; worse still I find a comparatively minor figure such as Giovanni da Bologna much more sympathetic, much more congenial. But if I were trying to form a canon, obviously Michelangelo would have to be a centrepiece thereof; I might even be obliged to allow that Raphael was a shade less tremendous, and certainly I could not claim a place for Giovanni amongst the giants.

I think that it boils down to this: what does one mean by a canon, and what does one do with it when one has it?

To my mind the canon is a fact of intellectual life. As you say one cannot start from scratch. One is bound to inherit some kind of body of opinion, and this must provide one's starting point even when one is going to dispute its validity. The canon, you suggest, may be large enough to contain some internal contradictions. It allows the admirers of Rubens to coexist with the admirers of Van Dyck. We may treat it with scepticism and accept it only with strong reservations; but it remains a part of our cultural impedimenta— useful even to a person born blind, inevitable by anyone born in our kind of society—but by no means immutable in its character. Seventy years ago it would not have included Cézanne or even Piero della Francesca; today their position seems secure, more secure than say Carlo Maratti or Guido Reni.

If this be the nature of our canon, then indeed I can take Apelles on trust, for by this reckoning it is only his reputation that matters. It does not matter that, if we find a picture by him, I might be disappointed. It doesn't really matter if he didn't really exist at all.

The trouble is that by making the canon acceptable to myself I may have made it unacceptable to you. To the true canonist the canon is the ark of the covenant; I have turned it into a public convenience, which is not quite the same thing.

In the 'ark of the covenant' values must, I suppose, be constant. The meaning of 'bonus' must be clear beyond all peradventure and that being clear one can, if one is a true academician, know the correct value of everything.

But I'm quite sure that you can't claim to know the correct value of every-thing, and I rather wonder whether anyone ever had made such large claims. Poor old de Piles always gets remembered for his unlucky 'Balance des Peintres', but de Piles was in fact anti-academic, a Rubenist of liberal views.*
And although I suppose there have been hard and fast, cut and dry academic theorists, I believe that they have been few and that we imagine a dogmatism which had little existence in fact. Probably you can correct me on this. What I am really driving at is that a canon, taken in the sense of 'the ark of the covenant', is too rigid, too absolute a structure to be accommodated to the catholicity of human taste. We must have an entity which will serve as a guide, but we cannot altogether accept it. In short, we sit on the fence. I believe that it is the only possible position for me and I suspect that your own position is not so very different from mine.

* August 19, 1975. I cannot resist transcribing, now that I am home again, de Piles' actual remarks about his 'Balance des Peintres': 'J'ai fait cet essai plutôt pour me divertir que pour attirer les autres dans mon sentiment. Les jugements sont trop différents sur cette matiere, pour croire qu'on ait tout seul raison.'

Intellectually a fence does not make a very comfortable seat; but it affords a wonderful view of the scenery. I hope we may meet there.

Yours ever
QUENTIN

Castel Giuliano
11 August 1975

14th November 1975

DEAR QUENTIN,

Your letter raises so many questions that it would need several books to do justice to it, and it is you who would have to write these books. In any case it is a pleasure to welcome you sitting on the fence of my garden—and since you mention the 'ark of the covenant', let me assure you that I do not regard my garden as a sacred and closed precinct. I often like to stroll beyond its fence, though when I feel I am losing my way, I am glad to return to my familiar grounds. I would not even consider the fence immovable. We can all go and test a post here and there, and even move it a little, if we find that it 'gives'. My point remains simply that we must acknowledge that by ourselves we could never have staked out the area, planted the garden, and built the fence, nor could the greatest critic have done so on his own. We were born into our civilization and we owe our orientation to that tradition, which happens to be in bad odour just now. Of course we should be critical of what we are told, but informed criticism means focusing on one point, and you can't focus on every point at the same time either in science or in the humanities or—for that matter—in criticism. The historian who investigates the re-liability of a chronicle cannot doubt all accounts of the past without giving up his trade. One of the traditions not even the most radical revolutionary can dispense with is language. Up to a point what I have called the 'canon' is an element in our language.

An Italian barber in Cambridge (Mass.) once told me, while he cut my hair, that he had lost all pride in his craft. When he had arrived from Tuscany he did his work with care and deliberation only to be upbraided by his boss: 'Who do you think you are—Michelangelo?' I don't know whether either of them could have named many of Michelangelo's works, but they still knew what they were talking about. You and I have followed the rumour of that greatness to its origins and have tried to come to terms with it, but neither of us would have discovered Michelangelo in a civilization without memory, without a tradition—without a canon.

Of course every generation tries to revise it. Berenson so disliked the meticulous style of the 'presentation drawings' (which make you uncomfortable) that he deleted them from the canon, and only Wilde reinstated them, without convincing everyone. Which brings me to your remarks about ancient Egyptian art and your preference for the spontaneous sketches over the official monuments. I need not tell you that this reaction has its own history which goes back at least to the cult of genius and of Platonic frenzy (Vasari's comparison between Luca della Robbia's highly finished *Cantoria* reliefs and Donatello's inspired sketchiness is a *locus classicus*). The Romantics went to town over this, and Ruskin introduced a new element, his hatred of the dead precision of the machine killing the spontaneity of life. But I know that you have read through the whole of Ruskin's Collected Works which I have not, so I'd better steer clear of him. No doubt there is a real shift in our system of values here. There is a story in an ancient author (Diodorus Siculus I. 98) of two Greek sculptors who had mastered the Egyptian system of proportions so perfectly that each of them could carve half of a colossal statue in his own town and make them fit without flaw. It is not a test of excellence we would find very convincing, although technicians might be impressed. But has not the shift away from rational perfection gone a little too far? Are the sinopie really better than the frescoes, are the sketches by Rubens and Constable always superior to their finished works? We need not come to an agreement here, for the very fact that we can pose the question in this way demonstrates at any rate the usefulness of the canon as part of our language.

I fully agree with you that this frame of reference, these landmarks in my ground also include anonymous achievements. The canon may have arisen from the notion of famous inventors, but there were not only the Seven Sages but also the Seven Wonders of the World. There have always been centres of renowned excellence in the crafts, honey from Hymettus, blades from Damascus, Cremona violins. These names stand for something, so does the canonic name of Stradivarius. We shall not want to quarrel over definitions here.

There is one word, though, which I should perhaps have used with more care. My revered friend George Boas has objected to my use of the term 'relativism' because I do not wish to deny the relatedness of things and values. Maybe I should have used the term 'radical subjectivism' for the attitude I find untenable in criticism. Imagine that an undeniably authentic painting by Apelles turned up tomorrow and would look strange to us at first sight. I think we would think twice before we proclaimed to the world that 'Apelles was much overrated'. The cheap joys of debunking are neither to your taste nor to mine. We would probably rather try by an act of historical empathy to find out what the Greeks saw in his work.

May I here trail my coat properly in conclusion of this letter, which got longer than I intended it to be? Old Winckelmann in his *Geschichte* (part I, ch. 4) denies that we should approach Greek art without prejudice. On the contrary, he says, 'Those who are confident that they will find much beauty will look for it, and some of it will reveal itself to them. Let them come back again and again until they have found it, for it is there.' Brainwashing? Yes and no—but more no than yes. We are still free to tell him that it is his confidence which deceived him—as it certainly did in the notorious case when he fell for a cruel hoax and went into raptures over the fake antique paintings Mengs had concocted to show him up. But, as you know, I have taken the line in 'The Logic of Vanity Fair', which I wrote for the volume on K. R. Popper,[4] that we must expect such mishaps since trust is a necessary ingredient in any experience of art. Those who cannot lower their guards can never surrender to any spell. Not that we must therefore fall victim to any impostor. What was said of astrology may also apply to the canon: 'The stars incline, but they do not compel.'

May I write: 'to be continued'?

Yours ever
ERNST

19 Briardale Gardens
London, NW3

A Plea for Pluralism

IN HIS well-known book on *The Structure of Scientific Revolutions*[1] Prof. Thomas Kuhn introduced a terminology that has been the subject of much searching discussion. He wants us to distinguish what he calls 'normal science' from 'revolutionary science'. Most practitioners of any science in most periods (if I may condense his argument even at the risk of over-simplification) are not out to question the foundations of their discipline. Instead they apply what he calls a 'paradigm' in order to extend knowledge of a particular field. To be a research chemist means in our day mainly to apply techniques of analysis that have proved successful in the solution of certain puzzles to compounds that have not yet been subjected to this procedure. Professor Kuhn's critics do not deny that such an outlook exists, but unlike him they find the picture depressing.[2] Granted that there is a case to be made for applied science where such routines may yield desirable results—as for instance in the pharmaceutical industry—they express the hope that anybody who considers himself a scientist will never forget that it is critical thought that keeps science going. Indeed in the field of pure science the application of a ready-made paradigm to a problem seems to them to describe nothing more 'normal' than the bandwagon effect of intellectual fashions.

I have found this discussion engendered by Thomas Kuhn's book illuminating in thinking about the situation in the field of art history. Clearly there is such a thing as 'applied' art history that has arisen in answer to a social need. As long as there are public and private collections of art they will have to be manned by competent practitioners who can label the objects under their care by answering the routine questions of where, when, and if possible by whom the objects were made. Nobody needs doubt that the techniques for answering such normal questions are highly developed. To master them requires years of specialized study, first-hand acquaintance with many collections, a retentive memory and what is somewhat misleadingly called a 'good eye', a sensitivity to subtle differences that comes only with practice. It is a commonplace that in the last analysis all art history rests on the efforts of connoisseurs, for clearly it is no good pontificating about Raphael unless we know what Raphael painted.

But it is precisely because connoisseurship is so fundamental that one may

Reprinted from *The American Art Journal*, Spring 1971. In reply to a question on *The State of Art History*.

follow Kuhn's critics in questioning the value of any unchallenged paradigm. However refined the procedures of dating and attribution may be that result in the labels of our museums, they can but rest on hypotheses. This is not the place to ask what is generally meant even by a 'documented' work, for there may be many a slip between the cup and the lip, but whatever the circumstantial evidence, no serious historian will be inclined to deny that our ideas about the past are at least as fallible as are the theories of scientists which have so often been overthrown. Unfortunately in applied science or art history this conviction conflicts with the social demand. We do not much like to hear that the laws of statics used in building skyscrapers are rules of thumb that must be applied with a hefty safety margin; nor would we enjoy visiting collections in which every label is liberally sprinkled with question marks. Not only would they look distracting, they would lower the financial value of a painting or object out of all proportion. As far as I can see this situation has led to a somewhat undesirable polarization. The demand for certainty has tended to produce the mystique of the connoisseur whose 'good eye' is almost equated with second sight. On the other hand the awareness of the financial implications of attributions has sometimes resulted in an inverted snobbery that attaches greater prestige to scepticism than to faith. There are still laurels to be collected by a future art historian who will deny that Michelangelo painted more than two panels of the Sistine ceiling himself. After all, the implication of such a claim would be that his eye is so good that he can see distinctions that had been overlooked by all previous critics.

A case could therefore be made for removing even the routines of connoisseurship, the making of catalogues and the discussion of attributions, from the safe precincts of a 'normal' science and to expose them to the constant probings of fundamental criticism. Nothing would be easier, one should think, than to test the methods applied, by asking the connoisseur questions of which the answer is known on independent grounds. Are there volunteers for such experiments and how would they best be devised?[3]

But whatever the outcome of such investigations, there are other social needs that the study of art is expected to answer. One concerns the question that is more easily asked than answered—why is this good? There was a time when some kind of paradigm existed for answering this question. I refer to the technical interpretation of the history of art as a steady progress towards the achievement of certain ends. In this interpretation, which Vasari inherited from classical antiquity, the greatness of a master was equated with the contribution he had made to the progress of artistic skills. We can still write the history of aviation in some such terms, and thus assign their place to Montgolfier or the brothers Wright, but we have lost the confidence of writing the history of art in terms of problem solutions. Indeed some students are more attracted by the negative possibility of giving marks to artists for rejecting skills, but neither paradigm will do for real criticism[4] and, since nature abhors a vacuum, description of what happened, particularly in twentieth-century art, too often takes the place of a critical valuation of achievements.

True, such description can be dressed up as interpretation by the application of the Hegelian paradigm that enjoins us to look for the symptomatic significance of stylistic change. This paradigm has certainly contributed to the popularity of art historical studies in the context of liberal education. It holds out the promise of a history without tears, a survey course in which the Parthenon can be diagnosed as an expression of the Greek spirit and a view of Chartres Cathedral save the student the trouble of reading the tangled arguments of the scholastics. It is sometimes difficult, as Juvenal said, not to be satirical, but though I am very critical of this approach I must admit that any access to the past is better than that collective loss of memory with which we are threatened. After all some of those who first heard about the Greeks or the scholastics in such survey courses may really be stimulated to find out more and may even come to question the paradigm they had been taught.

But if these paradigms can be seen as a direct response to the questions naturally raised by art, and can be criticized in relation to the degree to which they satisfy these needs, there are others that are more subtly related to the intellectual climate of the day. I refer to the link that undoubtedly exists between the fashions in our field and the fluctuations of taste among artists and critics. Some of the movements of art history can be seen as rationalizations of these fashions, which owed their attraction to their original polemical stance. Seen in retrospect, it is not difficult, for instance, to trace the connection between Wölfflin's 'formal analysis' and the depreciation of subject-matter in art. 'Where you see a Madonna, I see an equilateral triangle, and that is what you ought to see, or attend to.' Meanwhile, of course, we have experienced the inevitable swing of the pendulum, not unconnected, perhaps, with the rise of surrealism: 'Where you see an equilateral triangle I see a wealth of symbolic references into which I am ready to initiate you.' Soon, one may venture to predict, the preoccupation of the young with sociology will lead to the formula: 'Where you see symbolic references I see the interplay of economic forces.' In all probability the learned footnotes referring to mythographic handbooks will give way to statistical tables correlating the size of paintings with fluctuations in investments—all backed by computers, of course.

I would not assert that these shifts of interest are necessarily harmful in themselves. Indeed it would ill become me to do so, for I have experienced the impact of intellectual trends and fashions as much as anyone else. While I was a schoolboy in Vienna I was deeply impressed by Max Dvořák's writings and if I have been critical of *Geistesgeschichte* in later years this was a reaction to an early enthusiasm.[5] I have mentioned elsewhere that I heard Heinrich Wölfflin in Berlin and arrogantly skipped his lectures,[6] but I certainly succumbed to the fashions of the day when, in my doctoral thesis, I applied 'formal analysis' to the mannerist architecture of Giulio Romano.[7] Having entered the orbit of the Warburg Institute, I was entranced by the new paradigm of iconology, which led me to interpret Botticelli's mythology in the light of Neo-Platonism.[8] Nor would I assert that my later work was not subject to similar influences. After all, this very paper derived its framework from the present debate stirred up by Thomas Kuhn while its heading echoes the title of a paper by Kuhn's principal opponent, my friend Sir Karl Popper.[9] In fact, it seems to me quite inevitable that a scholar will react to the traditions of his field, that he may fall under the spell of a great book or a great personality, and also that he may be attracted to problems that are being debated in his circle. By itself this sway of intellectual fashions may be no more harmful than the changing fashions in the hair styles of our students, provided we do not take either too seriously. One might argue, in fact, that a certain sensitivity to the issues that come to us from outside may even be beneficial if it alerts us to the multiplicity of questions that we can ask of the past.

It is precisely for this reason, however, that I cannot but agree with Thomas Kuhn's opponent who regards the existence of 'normal science', the application of an existing and ready-made paradigm, as a threat to the health of our search and research. This health, as we all know, has anyhow become precarious through the rise of what one can only call the 'academic industry'. It is an industry that demands 'research', not from a craving for truth, but quite openly as a qualification for degrees and promotions. Who can blame the victims of such pressure if they look for the nearest paradigm and apply it to whatever œuvre or work comes to hand? I am sometimes reminded of certain provisions in Austrian law that constitute extenuating circumstances. One is if the crime was attempted with unsuitable means (*Versuch mit untauglichen Mitteln*) such as an attempt at murdering someone by incantation, the other an attempt on an unsuitable object (*Versuch am untauglichen Objekt*), such as an effort to shoot a ghost. Everybody must know papers that fall into either of these categories, applying the methods developed for the critical study of Michelangelo to some fifth-rater or using a hopelessly inadequate apparatus for the analysis of a great work of art.

Of course we have all used incantations, and we have all fired at nonexistent ghosts. But at least we should train ourselves and our students in that spirit of criticism and self-criticism that alone makes intellectual pursuits worthwhile. One of the least desirable consequences of the academic industry seems to me a certain atrophy of discussion, as if vigorous criticism might endanger a colleague's chances of promotion. We cannot and must not evade the demand of constantly probing the foundations on which the various paradigms are based. We should not write about 'space' without stopping to inquire about the nature of three-dimensional representation, we should not talk about 'levels of meaning' without probing the implications of this search.[10]

It is precisely in the course of such probings— if I may again draw on my own experience—that we are likely to stumble across fresh problems of research that stand in need of new paradigms. If my own doubts have prompted me to acquaint myself a little more closely with the problems and results of contemporary psychology,[11] others may feel the need to inquire into economics or anthropology. Not that we can become experts in any of these fields, but we may learn enough to be able to talk to experts without being overawed. Indeed if there is one single cause that may impede the advance of learning it is the timidity that is inculcated by bad teaching, a teaching that harps on the quantity of knowledge to be acquired.

Knowledge is stored in books and periodicals where it can be activated any time by those who know how to use them. It is this we must persuade our students to learn; it implies learning languages and, if necessary, different terminologies. Once we have done this it should be easy to convince them of the intellectual impoverishment that a facile application of ready-made paradigms brings about. We can encourage them instead to look for questions that have not yet been asked and that may need new paradigms for their answer. Obviously there will be failures as well as successes, but if reasoned criticism of fundamentals will again be encouraged the process of trial and error should result in a real advance. Instead of cultivating 'normal science' we shall enter into that interesting state of ferment Thomas Kuhn describes as revolutionary science, and keep it on the boil. True, if that happens it will no longer make sense to ask about 'the present state of art history'. There will be not one art history, but many different lines of inquiry freely crossing the boundaries of any number of so-called 'disciplines' that owe their existence merely to administrative convenience, not to say inertia. Only in this way can our studies recapture what Erwin Panofsky so beautifully described as 'the joyful and instructive experience that comes from a common venture into the unexplored'.[12]

The Museum: Past, Present and Future

Under the sponsorship of the British Museum and the American Assembly a group of museum directors, curators, trustees and other interested parties from the United States, Canada, Great Britain and continental Europe met at Ditchley Park, Oxfordshire, England, in October 1975 to continue discussions begun a year earlier at Arden House, Harriman, New York, at the Forty-sixth American Assembly. The address printed below in a slightly revised form was given on the invitation of the chairman of the symposium, Sir John Pope-Hennessy.

I OWE the privilege of addressing this distinguished gathering to one of the oldest English traditions—the tradition of distrusting the expert. Its earliest manifestation must be the jury system, which makes sure that people are not judged by men learned in law. It is also rumoured that the diplomatic service is run on similar lines so that anyone who has made a reputation as a specialist in the language and lore of the Fiji islands is likely to be posted to the Eskimos where, as the saying goes, he has no axe to grind. Having spent my life in the university I have no first-hand acquaintance of the day-to-day problems which make the life of the museum man or woman so exhausting and frustrating today. But many of these major and minor issues have been fully ventilated in the volume which resulted from last year's symposium,[1] and if anything remained to be said it is sure to be found in the papers circulated this year.[2] The only voice which has not been heard yet is that of the consumer, the actual user of the museum. It is in this way that I shall interpret my brief. Without denying my background in art history I propose to speak as a person who goes to museums because he likes looking at works of art.

Nobody denies that this is one of the principal aims of the art museum. Admittedly one of them only, for without the activities going on behind the scenes in conservation, acquisition, research and cataloguing there might be no works of art for visitors to look at. But in defining the aim on which I wish to concentrate, I shall adapt the famous line from Horace's *Ars poetica* and suggest that *aut prodesse volunt, aut delectare custodes*. As museum people you want to offer us profit and delight. Or preferably both. Not that this is an obvious combination, for not everything that is good for us is also pleasant,

---

Address delivered at Ditchley Park, Oxfordshire, on 17 October 1975 to the European-American Assembly on Art Museums.

and notoriously not everything that is pleasant is also good for us. It is really wonderful that there are institutions which can reconcile these divergent purposes, but I shall argue that this reconciliation cannot be taken for granted but must be seen as a problem to which there is no easy solution. It is clear that social pressures in our time go very much in the direction of *prodesse*, the museum should be an improving institution, and though I shall not deny this function, I should like to restore the balance and stress the *delectare*, the delight which works of art can give us. I am prepared for the objection that delight may not be the *mot juste* for the rendering of suffering from the Laocoön to *Guernica*; the fact that all the arts are capable of transfiguring the tragic and the unpleasant has challenged philosophical aesthetics since the days of Aristotle, and I do not want to lose myself in this labyrinth. I am quite ready to change the word delight for another description of that special kind of thrill a great painting or work of sculpture can give us, but I still would not want to lose sight of *delectare*. I think, for example, of Vermeer's *View of Delft* (Fig. 6) as a paradigm because I happen to have experienced this wonderful delight a few weeks ago. Was it also an improving experience? It all depends what you mean by *prodesse*. I fear the well-meaning propaganda that art is good for you and will make you a better man or better citizen has been sadly disproved hundreds of times by tyrants and scoundrels who had an exquisite taste in art. Which need not be taken to mean that the enjoyment of art does not leave a permanent mark, that it is not an enriching experience. We treasure the memory of such encounters and we only wish we could fully evoke them at will. I have always envied an old civil servant, a refugee from Austria close to his hundredth birthday, who told me that during sleepless nights, he took a walk through the Louvre, as he remembered it from the beginning of the century, and could decide in front of which painting he wanted to stop this time so that he could look at it closely. I do not think he exaggerated much.

To most of us who lack such total recall, the fact that we know the moment to be irretrievable adds poignancy and urgency to the experience. True, this tension between *delectare* and *prodesse* is not peculiar to our enjoyment of art; that feeling of *Verweile doch, du bist so schön* which haunts and eludes Goethe's Faust may accompany any experience of happiness. I suppose it is one of the characteristics which sets us apart from the animal world, that for us human beings there is no presence without recollection of the past and anticipation of the future, but the emphasis we place on these dimensions will always shift and vary. I think it has also varied in the history of art appreciation and I should indeed like to redeem the promise of my title and attempt a kind of diagrammatic pedigree of the diverse traditions which, combined and sometimes entangled, determine the role the museum is asked to play today and will no doubt be asked to play in the future.

Among the remote ancestors of the museum of art I should like first to single out two contrasting types I propose to call the treasure and the shrine. The amassing and the display of treasures in temples, churches and palaces has always served to enhance the prestige of the owner and to overwhelm the visitor with these tokens of wealth and power. In such a collection, I would say, delight dominates over profit, for it is part of the intended effect that we could not possibly carry it all in our minds. What is intended to remain is the global memory of sheer endless riches, of an Aladdin's cave of gold, jewellery and exotic marvels. There are thrills after thrills, like in a display of fireworks which produces the proverbial 'ah' and 'oh' as the rockets burst and scatter the multicoloured stars over the scene. You may call this a childish delight, but it gives genuine pleasure. I suspect even that the very impossibility of taking it all in adds to our enjoyment. We do not have to learn anything. Nobody will ever cross-examine us about the individual items; we are here to relish the experience of being dazzled and overawed. I would guess that despite their more scientific pretensions even the curiosity cabinets, the *Kunst und Wunderkammern* of the Renaissance,[3] demanded little more of the visitor than the capacity to marvel and to gape. Stuffed sharks and pickled monsters, ostrich eggs and examples of intricate handiwork such as one can still see at Schloss Ambras in Tirol do not impose on the visitor a more exacting programme of learning than does the side-show at the fair. They are collections of the abnormal, of rarities, specimens of things you do not see every day, in other words of the sensational; but even where human skill is involved they are miracles of nature rather than of art.

The process by which the natural history museum parted company from the art museum is a long and interesting one which has lasted into our own day. After all, there are still museums which show stuffed birds on one floor and paintings on another, though which of these floors is more devoted to *prodesse* and which to *delectare* may be an open question. I think what marks the birth of the art museum is the awareness that there are things which are not simply rare but unique. This applies to famous landmarks and famous monuments, and these are what are called the sights, or as the expressive German word has it, *die Sehenswürdigkeiten*, the things worthy to be seen. I am sure I am not the first to regard the obligatory visit to such sights as a secularized form of pilgrimage. The transition is clear even in the lists of the *mirabilia* of Rome which included sacred and secular monuments.[4] I'd also like to remind you of the original meaning of the word *monumentum*, the memorial or reminder of a unique person or event, and close to it, of the *souvenir*, the token that

the pilgrim actually made it. It is into this context, then, that I should like
to place the origin of what I have called the conception of the museum as a
shrine. You made and you make your pilgrimage to Rome to see the *Apollo
Belvedere* in the same spirit in which you visit St. Peter's, and you go to
Athens, to Florence, to London or for that matter to the Mauritshuis with
similar expectations to see what used to be the works of art marked with one
or two stars in that admirable guide-book, the Baedeker.

In one of my recent publications I have defended what I called the canon
of excellence and its role in the fabric of civilization.[5] Whether we think of the
touchstones of greatness in literature, music or art, the sharing of some frame
of reference is a necessity for any culture. It would be an insult to the human
spirit to suggest that the encounter with the great masterpieces does not give
deep and lasting delight to many, but it would be unrealistic to seek for no
other motivation in what is after all one of the most influential social
phenomena of our age, the travel industry, the package tour. I believe no
social institution can endure unless it serves a variety of contradictory aims,
and like the pilgrimage and the grand tour, the sight-seeing trip presents a
compromise between entertainment, spiritual and social profit. Like the
pilgrim, the tourist knows that on his return he will be asked whether he
had visited the shrines his predecessors had seen. To reassure himself and to
prove it to his peers he drags himself on tired feet through the Louvre and
takes a snapshot of the *Mona Lisa*, or buys a souvenir, some hideous ashtray
with her distorted image.

It is easy enough to laugh at these consequences of artistic renown, but
there is surely a positive lesson to be learned. It is a lesson which should be
taken to heart by those who dismiss the treasure and the shrine as old-fashioned
élitist institutions. If anything, the opposite is the case. Granted that the profit
people seek will also include a gain in social status, granted, in other words,
that the visit to the shrine is not only undertaken for the sake of delight but
also in the hope of an initiation, this desire for status and for self-respect is
surely stronger rather than weaker among those who look over their shoulders
to find out whether they are still supposed to like the *Mona Lisa*. And in any
case, I still vastly prefer the *Mona Lisa* without a moustache to Duchamp's
version.

I am not blind, of course, to what might be called the sales resistance set
up nowadays by the Baedeker museum, and I would not deny for a moment
that there is also something valuable in this assertion of independence. I am
very fond of a little essay by the late Sir Herbert Read which every museum
man should read, all the more as its charm resists quotation. It is called 'The
Greatest Work of Art in the World'[6] and describes a visit to Florence in the

dark summer before the outbreak of the war, when Herbert Read found it impossible to respond to the famous works exhibited in the Uffizi and the Bargello. Never very fond of Renaissance art, he now felt as if imprisoned in some endless maze of meretricious junk and decided to revisit the Museo Archeologico to recapture the thrill which Etruscan art had given him. It did hold his attention a little better, but suddenly—and here I must quote—

> any impression the Etruscan bronzes had made on me was obliterated by a small object I had never seen before. It was not more than two or three inches high, and stood among a crowd of small objects, unlabelled and unhonoured, in one of those glass coffins with which museums are always furnished.
>
> It was also a bronze—the head of a negro boy, probably an African slave—and it seemed to shine there like a glow-worm in the darkness of my mood [Fig. 9]. It was vital: I almost felt, as it fused into my consciousness, that it was alive. What it was—what period and what style—I knew not, and have never troubled to find out. It obviously belongs to that category of vague outlines which we call Graeco-Roman.

It is characteristic of Herbert Read's integrity and honesty that the work which so revitalized his spirits was a piece which would have been treasured by any Renaissance collector rather than some primitive mask one might have expected to appeal to him. The bronze is shown on the frontispiece of his volume *A Coat of Many Colours*, and it is not hard to see how one can fall in love with this appealing work. For Read, it is true, it becomes the personal symbol of his anti-rhetorical bias, of his dislike of the Grand Manner and what he calls 'the *pompiers* of culture'—he always was on the side of the underdog, and this generous instinct surely also prompted him to proclaim his preference for that little bronze bust, two inches high, which, as he says, 'with some difficulty might be found in a case crowded with indifferent objects in the least frequented museum in Florence'.

There is a lesson to be learned here to which I should like to return in conclusion. At any rate Herbert Read's happy encounter introduces us to another type of museum, neither a treasure house nor a shrine, but a combination of the two further functions which shaped the museum in the last two centuries, I mean the functions of the depository and the didactic display. The depository or storehouse may be said to have grown out of the treasure house combined with the shrine. At the time when all relics of *sacrosancta antiquitas* were considered treasures, they were amassed in profusion simply because nothing could be thrown away. Rome still offers an example of these accumulations in which art is crowded out by archaeology, and with the growth of historical interest in early Christian, Etruscan and other antiquities, this need for a collecting point became paramount. What was to be done with all these relics and monuments? How could they be related to the canon? The answer was that they could serve as specimens to illustrate the rise of the arts as it was told by Pliny and Vasari. The archaeologists led the way; Winckelmann is often credited with this achievement of bringing order into the storehouses of Rome, but he was in fact anticipated by the great anti-quarian, the Count de Caylus, who fared so badly at the hands of the Germans.

Caylus opened his second *Recueil d'Antiquités* of 1756 with a remark pregnant with things to come:

> The arts partake of the character of the Nations that cultivated them; one can distinguish their beginnings, their infancy, their progress and the point of perfection to which they were brought among the nations. The works of sculpture and painting permit us no less to discern the genius of a nation, its customs, and the turn of their minds, if we may use that phrase, than do the books they have left us. A quick glance at one of the cabinets where these treasures are assembled encompasses in some way the picture of all the centuries—*le tableau de tous les siècles*.

Mark, however, that Caylus had no doubt about the canon as such: he knew at what point the arts had reached perfection. This same conception of a collection as an illustration of the road to perfection can be documented for eighteenth-century collections of Renaissance art. You find it in Winckel-mann's description of Cavaceppi's collection of drawings,[7] and in a similar passage from d'Hancarville's *Antiquités Etrusques* of 1785, which refers to the progress of ancient art and continues: 'And precisely as in arranging a gallery of paintings one tries there to assemble those of the masters who worked after Cimabue, such as Andrea Tassi, Gaddo Gaddi, Margaritone and Giotto, up to our own days, so one can put together in this collection the styles of all the ages of ancient art.'[8]

I think it can be demonstrated that the need for collecting points and the appeal of the didactic function interacted in the birth of the modern museum. The aftermath of the French Revolution with its spoliation of monasteries, most of all of course Napoleon's campaigns, led to an unprecedented accumulation of works of art in the Louvre, which also had its influence on the revision of the canon. It was in the Musée Napoléon that Friedrich von Schlegel discovered that he preferred Perugino to Domenichino. But the demotion of the Bolognese and the promotion of the so-called primitives, the masters of Vasari's *seconda maniera*, did not materially affect the structure and function of the didactic display. As late as 1857 the Margaritone of the National Gallery (Fig. 10) was notoriously recommended for purchase to show —as we read in the catalogue—'the barbarous state in which art had sunk even in Italy previous to its revival'.

This quotation illustrates what was happening to the earlier conceptions of the treasure house and the shrine. The Margaritone was neither seen as a treasure, nor as a work to be enjoyed. It was an instructive specimen which could help the visitor to learn and appreciate the canon of Vasari. At the same time the conception also collided somewhat with that of the depository or storehouse. For the storehouse as a collecting point is constantly made aware of the physical limitations to its function. Where should all these objects be housed? The didactic collection has a built-in need of expansion. There are always gaps in its displays which ought to be filled so as to illustrate the story more fully and more cogently.

This idea of the gap is inapplicable both to the treasure house and the shrine. The crown jewels in the Tower of London are no less enjoyable for lacking the treasures of other monarchs, nor would one say that the Ashmolean has a grievous gap because it does not own the *View of Delft*. But I remember an official document, admittedly many years ago, in which it was pointed out among other things that the London National Gallery possesses no Melozzo da Forli, a deficiency unlikely to be properly remedied until the Vatican decides to sell its treasures.

But why drag in Melozzo? There are many people today, much less sensitive and informed than Herbert Read, who dislike Renaissance art altogether and much prefer the crudest icon to Melozzo's beautiful angels in the Vatican. The twentieth-century rebellion against the canon has put a premium on anything that is unlike the masterpieces once housed in the shrine. André Malraux, who certainly knew a masterpiece when he saw one, wrote eloquently and persuasively about the situation and hailed the new catholicity of taste, the expansion of our horizon to encompass the whole of man's creative effort, as the museum without walls.[9] Maybe that impossible museum will yet accomplish what radical artists have demanded for so long—the destruction of the museum with walls.

Without some yardstick of values which the canon provided it is clearly impossible to predict which artefact anyone will find appealing or which image will give him that thrill which the shrine was once intended to provide. It takes the sensitivity and the self-confidence of a Herbert Read to pick out of the showcase the one little head he elevated into the greatest work of art. The second line of defence, the illustration of the rise of the arts, is also breached by the transvaluation of all values. Instead of teaching a complex

but finite story, the museum is now confronted with the impossible demand
that it should teach everything about everything. But if the demand is hard
on the museum, it is much harder still on the poor visitor who feels he is
expected to learn it all. No wonder also the charitable keeper will take pity
on him and reduce the number of exhibits. But to what purpose? Showcase
after showcase, room after room, wing after wing, floor after floor still offer
a sheer endless panorama of objects. Who can blame the hapless man if he
feels like the visitor to a restaurant who thinks he must eat through the
whole menu. To help him make up his mind the signposting and labelling is
improved, but it takes time to read an explanatory label, time which would
perhaps be more profitably used in looking. There is nobody who does not
realize this, and so other teaching devices are called in, and to make place
for them, more and more objects have to be removed from the display.

But what objects? Here of course is the rub. It is the essence of the work
of art in the shrine that it is unique and *sui generis*; it is expected of the treasure
that it must at any rate be rare; the didactic collection must be stocked with
suitable specimens, as is the case in the natural history museum and up to
a point in the archaeological museum, where we take what we see as a sample
of a class of things. The depository, finally, is neutral. Its capacious cellars
must accommodate anything that lands there unless it embarks on the slippery
path of shedding its duplicates—a term that notoriously covers a multitude of
sins. I know I have overdrawn the distinctions to explain my conviction that
the blurring of these categories lies at the root of many of our perplexities
and anxieties. How can we tell that the little bronze head that revitalized the
spirits of Herbert Read would not have been relegated to the storeroom as
a mere specimen that could at best have been seen on application? Archaeology must be neutral and egalitarian; the conception of art, I am sure, must
always be élitist in the original sense of selectivity. In the shrine I am always
ready to stand to attention in front of a great work of art; I am also eager
to wander through the labyrinthine splendours of a treasure house; but when
I am confronted with a row of didactic specimens nagging doubts begin to
arise in my mind, or rather in my feet. I have gloomy visions of a future
museum in which the contents of Aladdin's cave will have been removed to
the storeroom, and all that will be left will be an authentic lamp from the
period of the Arabian Nights with a large diagram beside, explaining how
oil lamps worked, where the wick was inserted and what was the average
burning time. I grant that oil lamps are after all human artefacts and tell us
more about the lives of ordinary people than the precious tinsel in Aladdin's
cave. But must I receive this improving instruction while standing on my tired
feet rather than sitting snugly in a chair and reading about the history of

domestic illumination? And should I learn about it in any case? The subjects in which I am ignorant are legion. Is all knowledge good for us? Television, radio, paperbacks and magazines bombard us with miscellaneous information to an extent which makes the ancient *Kunst und Wunderkammern* look like a specialized course.

It seems to me natural in this situation that the exhibition holds so much more attraction to the public than the museum and that this preference has led the museum as an institution to undergo yet another transformation. To some extent it has become an exhibition centre. The exhibition can avoid or evade the inherent problems to which the museum is prone. It is by its nature selective and the selection can concentrate on a particular theme, often one which is topical. There are sensible exhibitions such as the great one-man shows assembling the work of a particular master who had been neglected for one reason or another. There are the ceremonial tributes of centenaries and the like with which, I suppose, one has to reconcile oneself as a method of keeping the past before the public. But there are also many frivolous exhibitions, which teach us nothing we could not have learnt by looking at a few books. To move precious works of art across half the globe and to monopolize the time and energy of museum staff for a trivial purpose seems to me a misuse of slender resources. Why, then, is it done?

The answer must lie in the psychological motives which help to explain the tourist boom. We go to museums abroad because we want to make use of an opportunity which may never come back. At home the museum round the corner must wait till we have a free afternoon, which may never come; but the exhibition will close next week and so we must make time.

As with tourism, social pressure acts as a strong reinforcement. It is not usual in our circles to ask at a cocktail party: 'Have you been to Apsley House? Isn't the *Waterseller* by Velazquez wonderful?' But you can and do ask: 'Have you seen the exhibition of oil lamps from Saudi Arabia at the Hayward Gallery?' If enough people ask you, they will shame you into taking notice, and maybe you will even enjoy the show.

Many years ago, when I spent a term in Berlin, I took a seminar with Wilhelm Waetzoldt, then Bode's successor as the Director of Prussian Museums and Galleries. I remember him saying: 'Of course if you take our Rembrandts from the Kaiser Friedrich Museum and send them across the road, calling it a Rembrandt exhibition, they will all flock to look at them.' He certainly was not far out. When I visited the Corot exhibition in Paris— Corot being an artist who gives me special delight—I had to stand in line and to jostle my way through a crowd because I happened to arrive on a free day; what is remarkable in this gratifying interest is the fact that a very large percentage of the delightful paintings there exhibited really came from across the road, from the Louvre, where the upstairs galleries with the Corots are usually deserted, deserted, I hurry to confess, also by myself because the Louvre offers so many counter-attractions.

I have tried to account for the fact that even during my lifetime the exhibition has taken over an ever-increasing share of the attention and the energy of art lovers and of museum people. There are certainly many factors which pull in this direction. Ours is a publicity-loving age, and only novelty is news. Even if you prefer the Seven Wonders of the World to any Nine Days' Wonder, you cannot ignore the latter if you want to be noticed. Nobody looks at a rainbow, said Goethe, after it has been in the sky for half an hour. It is an observation familiar to any advertiser who will make his artificial rainbow blink, change colour and preferably whirl to make people look. The museum is now under pressure to prove by attendance figures that it merits the meagre support of society and fulfils its duty of *prodesse* and *delectare* to ever-increasing multitudes. I have expressed my doubt about the first; I confess that I am even more thoroughly perplexed about the second. Can one teach delight? To be sure, one can hope that visitors will discover a source of delight, but how can one best help them to make this all-important discovery?

In inviting me to give this talk, our chairman made it clear that he did not wish me to avoid controversial issues. I have followed this brief in discussing the past and the present and I shall not conceal my anxieties when I contemplate the future. I do not claim the gift of prophecy, but if present trends continue, public relations and education are likely to loom even larger in the future of our museums than they did in the past. It seems to me all the more urgent to examine the conventional wisdom on which their activities are so often based. I feel the need to question what I take to be widespread and unexamined assumptions about the psychology of the museum visitor. To question, not to answer. I am no more a psychologist than I am a museum man, and if I shall now mount my psychological hobby horse I do not want to claim the status of a professional. Nor do I want to suggest that in future professional psychologists should take over the running of our art museums. My plea is rather that those who do run the museums and organize their displays should also take cognizance in their difficult work of the critical tool offered by the psychology of perception and of memory.

After all it is obvious that what I have called the functions of *delectare* and *prodesse* are equally related to perception and to memory. It is a commonplace in art education that we must learn to see if we are to enjoy art, but having read a little psychology I have become much less sure of what is to be understood by this phrase than many well-meaning educators inside and outside the museums. Only recently, when on a visit to the United States, I was introduced to a charming young lady who told me she was teaching art appreciation at the local museum. On my inquiring what she had done that afternoon she told me she had scolded the children for their inability to see, because none of them could describe to her the houses and shops they had passed on their way to the gallery. I am afraid I sided with the children and found it unlikely that this economy of attention would interfere with their sensitivity to art. If you go to listen to Bach's B Minor mass you are under no obligation to pay attention to the traffic noise on your way to the concert hall. Looking is to seeing what listening is to hearing. The idea that we should feel guilty if we do not attend to all our sensations is a hangover of that nineteenth-century doctrine of the innocent eye which I belaboured in *Art and Illusion*. The very distinction between sensation and perception has become questionable. The eye is not a passive but an active instrument, serving a mind that must be selective if it is not to be swamped by a flood of indigestible messages. Seeing is always looking for something, comparing, interpreting, probing and disregarding. Consequently, we cannot learn to see in the abstract. Perception as a skill will always involve the whole person and the whole mind. What psychologists tell us about the acquisition of skills, both perceptual and motor skills, suggests they largely depend on what are called hierarchies. Just as in learning to play the piano certain movements and sequences must become so automatic that the mind is free to attend to other things, so the pilot in front of his complex instrument panel must learn to see the right dial at the right moment and ignore the rest, which he can take 'as read'. The mind may not be a computer but it is a marvellous sorting machine establishing categories or classes and subclasses which enable it to handle a vast amount of impressions in an incredibly flexible way. As far as looking is concerned, the flexibility is grounded in the mobility of the eye and of our focusing mechanism. The very achievement of learning to read should give us food for thought, for it is far from easy to describe the difference between looking at a page of an unknown script and reading a page in a familiar language. One thing is sure. The typographer may examine a page in his mother tongue without being conscious of its words while the average reader may put aside a book without remembering what fount it was printed in. You may deplore this selectivity of perception but it is a fact of life with which you must reckon. You must realize, to put the matter in the abstract, that logically any object can be regarded as belonging to a subclass of an infinite number of classes. Read's bronze head can be categorized with equal justification as a product of *cire perdue*, as Hellenistic art, as a representation of an African and so on, *ad infinitum*. For him it became a prized example of non-rhetorical art because he had found himself in the mood in which he rejected the whole large hierarchy of what he called the Grand Manner and the Gigantic Boredom. His response, fresh and unconventional as it was, was certainly not due to an innocent eye. Without knowing it himself, he had been scanning the objects and sorting them according to his own hierarchies.

I agree with the provocative paper by Werner Hofmann of the Hamburg Kunsthalle, circulated for this symposium, that there is something instructive and even exhilarating in any such process of reclassification which makes us attend to new aspects of our experience, but my point is and remains that you cannot do this from scratch. We all know the oversimplifications underlying the schema of progress adopted by Vasari from Pliny and accepted with little change by subsequent centuries. But the schema would not have survived so long if it had not brought the advantage of an ordered hierarchy into the teeming world of art. Those who had grasped this simple system knew on entering a museum where to glance, where to look, where to stand in admiration and where to turn away with disgust. In other words, the schema they had learned enabled them to scan, precisely because the hierarchies were comparatively rigid.

We cannot and we need not return to this conception, but I think we must face the fact that the activity of scanning is at least as important to the problem of the museum as the misleading problem of seeing. It has been shown that when we know what to look for we are astonishingly efficient in picking out a particular subclass from a vast array. Moreover there are indications that it does not take us much longer to scan a list of names for two or three particular names than it does for one.[10] We can sustain an alertness for a variety of categories though not, of course, for an infinite number. Without any categories at all we are helpless and confused. We tend to blame the mass of impressions, but it is our lack of preparedness. We all know for instance that a conversation in an unknown language sounds to us like a hopelessly rapid gabble because though we hear, we cannot listen. It is for this psychological reason that I am not convinced that the reduction of exhibits will help the casual museum visitor at all. It is not the number of objects that is responsible for the bewilderment and distress which overcomes him in a crowded gallery. The numbers of letters on a page do not worry the reader. The same people who claim that they feel distracted when several paintings are assembled in close proximity do not seem to experience any difficulty in looking at, say, four illustrations on a page or indeed in following a picture story or comic strip where any child can look at some sixteen frames on a page without his eye becoming confused by the

6. Jan Vermeer: *View of Delft*. The Hague, Mauritshuis

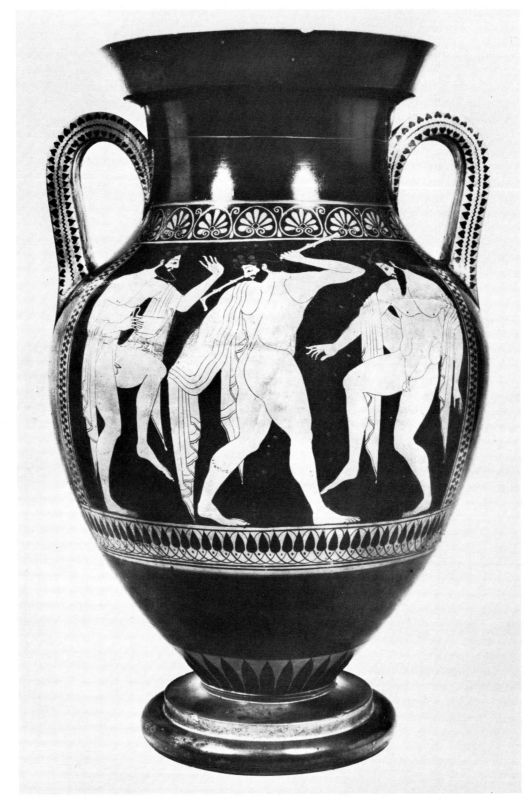

7. Euthymides: Amphora. Munich, Staatliche Antikensammlungen und Glyptothek

8. Euphronios: Calyx krater. West Berlin, Staatliche Museen Preussischer Kulturbesitz

9. Hellenistic bronze head. Florence,
Museo Archeologico

10. Margaritone d'Arezzo: *The Virgin and Child Enthroned and Narrative Scenes.*
London, National Gallery

neighbouring one. The magic which makes this feat possible goes under the commonplace name of interest and the result of interest is concentration.

Now, as every guide to a museum or country house knows, there are any number of ways of arousing interest; the problem is only that they are not all equally profitable in the long run. I dare say the most tired visitor will look with interest at an ordinary pencil if you tell him against all historical probability that it was Shakespeare's pencil or that it was the murder weapon in a monstrous crime. Using the persuasive rhetoric of the art educator you can also reclassify it as a masterpiece of contemporary sculpture, drawing attention to the way it achieves monumentality within a narrow compass by the uncompromising thrust into space of the crystalline shaft, the black lead setting up a tension with the smooth yellow facets, effectively contrasted with the raw wood of the pointed pyramid. Needless to say you could also decry the vile suburban taste of the vulgar yellow gloss as an example of cheap mass products or preach a sermon on the pencil which is blunted in writing as a symbol of man.

I hope you will agree, however, that the purpose of the museum should ultimately be to teach the difference between pencils and works of art. What I have called the shrine was set up and visited by people who thought that they knew this difference. You approached the exhibits with an almost religious awe, an awe which certainly was sometimes misplaced but which secured concentration. Our egalitarian age wants to take the awe out of the museum. It should be a friendly place, welcoming to everyone. Of course it should be. Nobody should feel afraid to enter it or, for that matter, be kept away by his inability to pay. But as far as I can see, the real psychological problem here is how to lift the burden of fear, which is the fear of the outsider who feels he does not belong, without also killing what for want of a better word I must still call respect. Such respect seems to me inseparable from the thrill of genuine admiration which belongs to our enjoyment of art. This admiration is a precious heritage which is in danger of being killed with kindness.

I remember a cheerful sight in an American museum where art education flourishes so much more than it does in our European institutions. A motley group of small children were sitting on the floor splashing ink on paper, touchingly cheered on by a warm-hearted teacher. She explained to me that the kids had just been to see the Chinese ink paintings up there and were now trying their hand at this delightful game. I certainly do not grudge them their pleasure. I only hope that the moment also came when the teacher explained to the children that what they did was the opposite of what the Chinese masters did and that it required years of concentration, industry and skill to master the rules and refinements of the Chinese tradition. To put the matter pedantically, Chinese Sung paintings can be categorized with any ink splashing but they are more usefully classed with the most refined evocations of nature achieved by human creativity. Once we approach them with this conviction we are also likely to attend to them differently.

Much as I myself love and enjoy this class of paintings I also know that my response is not as differentiated as that of a Chinese connoisseur. I have passed the stage where they would all look alike to me, but I certainly fail to see, or rather to notice, certain all-important nuances which distinguish the masterpiece from the copy or even the imitation. I hope and believe I am on somewhat safer ground with Vermeer's *View of Delft*. I need not be told why it is called an outstanding painting, for I can see that it stands out from the mass of fine townscapes painted in seventeenth-century Holland. It was the desire to induce such comparisons that inspired the didactic collections of the past, and those of the present. In his interesting paper circulated for this symposium, Mr. Michael Compton of the Tate Gallery reminds us that a director who admired Matisse would like to support Matisse with what he thinks are lesser works by Fauve artists and other contemporaries. I agree but I am anxious to stress that this is not only a didactic requirement but has also to do with that function of *delectare* which, to vary an old saw, is much too serious a matter to be left to art historians. We do not have to know the names and dates of other Dutch masters to enjoy the miraculous mastery of the *View of Delft*. What we need is a set of expectations, which can be modified and surpassed, a feel for what was common form and for what is unique—a feel which can no more be verbalized than can any other sensory discrimination, but which makes us sensitive to that fine calibration which underlies our experience of delight. Unless the visitor can at least get a first inkling of that experience, he really has no reason ever to come again. The colour print or picture postcard will do just as well.

I cannot help feeling that in some respects the old-fashioned museum had an edge here over many more recent experiments. By its very arrangement and emphasis it introduced the visitor to large classes of objects and to examples of special excellence. Far from interfering with each other, they produced a mutual enhancement, for there is also a joy in discovering in a fine Pieter de Hooch a quality one had previously associated only with Vermeer.

I have stressed that I am not speaking as an art historian, and yet I should like to buttress my advocacy of the full museum by an historical example. There is a vase by Euthymides in Munich, dating from around 500 B.C., showing the leave-taking of a warrior and a number of athletes at their exercises (Fig. 7). It bears the famous inscription: '*Hos oudepote Euphronios,*'

'Euphronios is nowhere like this.' The painter knew, or claimed, that he had surpassed a competitor of acknowledged excellence. The revolutionary innovation of drawing bodies in foreshortening produced a sense of rivalry and of advance which probably accounts for this expression of pride. Who can doubt that we would gain in our understanding of the vase by Euthymides if we could see it side by side with vases by Euphronios, if the collection is lucky enough to own them (Fig. 8)? But where should we stop? Would we not also learn to appreciate Euphronios better by seeing his work in the context of other productions, including the run-of-the-mill ware of his Athenian contemporaries? And why, again, stop here? Would it not also help to become aware of the distinctive features of Attic vase painting as compared with other centres? I will be told that this is a matter for the study collection and that the ordinary visitor will only be put off by so much crockery. I wonder if we do not underrate him. At any rate if he is so put off we have simply failed in our purpose.

Any window-dresser, if I may put it so bluntly, can place an isolated Greek vase under a spotlight in an empty room and force it on our attention. The problem of showing a large collection of superficially similar objects rather than hiding most of them from view is of a different order of complexity. Perceptually it arises from the very process of scanning and grouping which I have mentioned. Arrange a class of objects in some simple geometrical order and you will find that it is the similarities which tend to stand out and even fuse like images in a kaleidoscope. Somehow we must make the visitor see the similarities but notice the differences. We have to find suitable means of visual emphasis and articulation guiding the scanning eye to focus on the most rewarding points but allowing it to linger anywhere. It is a task which cannot be left to the designer unless he consults at every step with the keeper who knows every piece intimately and has a coherent picture of the whole field.[11] The result of this collaboration should be an arrangement which is intended to last at least as long as the vision of the past on which it is based. The displays devised according to the latest fashion in interior decoration remind me of the sand castles built for an afternoon till the next tide washes them away.

Werner Hofmann in the paper for this symposium to which I have already referred has voiced the opinion of many of his colleagues when stressing the thrill which every new juxtaposition of works of art can produce. I don't deny this altogether, but I happen to think that this comparatively superficial thrill is often too dearly bought. Instead of finding the delight for which we have come, we tend to be confronted on most museum visits by rooms which resemble a railway shunting yard; they are 'temporarily closed', they are 'in course of arrangement', they are accessible only on application. One cannot find what one has come to see and sometimes one does not want to see what one can find. Even if you discover a quiet corner still untouched by the whirl-wind of activities, the mood for contemplation and enjoyment will have evaporated.[12] What a blessing nobody has as yet thought of trying out the effect of swapping St. Peter's in Rome with the Colosseum!

I have mentioned the old gentleman who could walk through the Louvre in his mind as an example of *prodesse*, of the lasting profit we gain by remembering a collection. Those who have read *The Art of Memory* by Frances Yates[13] will know that the ability to hold an experience is rooted in our recollection of places and things. There is plenty of evidence that our topographical memory contributes decisively to our capacity of recall. I know full well that the veritable bugbear of the exhibition age is the so-called static collection where nothing is allowed to be changed or shifted. I don't want to overstate the case for this arrangement wherever we are sure that we can do better. But I should like to remind my enterprising colleagues in the museum world that among the many difficult skills which are demanded of them the one which calls for the most noble sacrifice is the great art of leaving well alone.

Reason and Feeling in the Study of Art

LEGEND has it, that at the moment of his triumph the victorious Roman general was accompanied by a slave who slapped his face to make him humble. I am grateful to your Royal Highness and your Board that, having given us so much reason for pride, you have not adopted this custom but have found a more subtle way to restore our humility. You have associated the prize with the name of Erasmus, whose lifework stands like an unscaled sunlit peak on the fringe of our horizon, a reminder of heights to which we cannot even dare to aspire. You have also made us search our hearts, because it has become tradition that the recipient of this great prize should respond with something like a profession of faith. It is a daunting task because, for reasons to which I shall have to return, we scholars are more used to speaking in public about our doubts than about our faith. It is part of our function to question accepted opinion and to probe arguments, in other words to exercise our rational faculty. But though I am a rationalist, I am not a sceptic, least of all a cynic. I have faith in the power of great art, great poetry and great music to embody human values which make life worth living. Only, I find the experience we can derive from these miracles of human creativity intensely personal and private. Is it not paradoxical therefore to embark on a rational study of art? Such a study, after all, must be intolerant of subjectivity, it must aim at objective results. How can we ever do justice to these rivalling claims and reconcile what I may call the demands of the heart with those of the head?

If the study of art has taught me anything it is that we not only can but must do this. I gained this conviction through the early contacts I was fortunate to make in my parents' house with the world of music. For the great musician it is a matter of moral as well as artistic duty to master any composition he studies with all the resources of wide-awake reason. At the same time he knows full well that no purely intellectual effort will suffice unless the performance derives its vital energies from the heart; but preferring reticence to gush he will rarely even mention this. I speak of music here because an unforced response to great music seems to me more widespread today than the enjoyment of other arts, and because I am sure that there can be few who

Speech on being awarded the Erasmus Prize in the Rijkmuseum Vincent van Gogh, Amsterdam, on 19 September 1975.

have not experienced the difference between music of which we cannot make head or tail, and music which we find easy to understand—which need not mean that we also like it. These reactions have nothing to do with a knowledge of technical terms or of the names and dates of musical history. Such intellectual competence may be enjoyable for its own sake but it has little bearing on our spontaneous understanding. Neither the analytic nor the enthusiastic programme note is likely to determine our experience. These may appeal to our intellect or work on our emotions. But what enables us to respond springs from a different kind of knowledge. From the intimate familiarity with a particular musical idiom, a set of expectations which the composer can fulfil, tease, disappoint or triumphantly surpass so as to make our heart beat faster or even miss a beat. Ideally, we should become alert to every nuance of his moves, much as a spectator of a familiar game will thrill to every stroke of the masterplayer.

Not that music or the other arts are games. I use the comparison merely to suggest that speaking about understanding a work of art does not commit us to a theory of art as communication. To understand a poem in this way we do not have to worry what the poet felt, which we shall never know anyhow. What concerns us is the exact significance of the words, images and rhythms he uses. Yet all this brain-work will not make the poem strike a chord in a heart that lacks that chord.

I have often urged that the study of the visual arts should include the kind of discipline that is traditional in the study of music and literature. In literature nobody would confuse linguistics with poetics. Linguistics is a scientific discipline and has gained much through contact with psychology, ethology and the theory of information. I am convinced that a similar analysis of the psychological and technical resources of the visual media is worthwhile and that it is in fact a subject that is at present struggling to emerge. Having tried to make my contribution to this development, I should express the hope that once the field is firmly established, its limits will also become clear.

I have indicated the lines of demarcation which have to be respected. Scientific studies of any medium can create interest, they cannot serve as substitutes for a personal response. They have little to do with the values of art except as safeguards against expansionist pressures from the other side. For wherever the frontiers are violated and the balance between head and heart is upset, intellectual disaster ensues. Emotional talk about styles seems to me as inappropriate as conceptual tabulations of visual delights. In other words, I am a rationalist but not an intellectualist. I have learned from my friend Sir Karl Popper that the strength of reason lies in its capacity to disprove a proposition. The rational study of art can do precisely this. It can dispose of popular misconceptions and thus clear the way towards an improved understanding, but it cannot tell us what to feel. It surely helps to know that the real van Gogh was not at all the frenzied madman of legend, but an adequate understanding of his œuvre can only come from long acquaintance. There are no short cuts to this feeling for the emotional and intellectual significance of his innumerable artistic decisions. Naturally therefore this will always remain an open quest. Every fresh encounter may reveal new facets and new depths. It is for that very reason that I have as little faith in the rhetoric of persuasion as I have in any scientific approach to the evaluative criticism of art, I have explained elsewhere (in 'Art History and the Social Sciences', see this volume pp. 131–66) that I see the function of criticism rather in the creation, maintenance and revision of cultural traditions. This emphasis on the crucial importance of tradition is not very fashionable today, but what is fashionable should always be submitted to the acid test of doubt. In any case I am not only a rationalist but I am also a realist, and I find it unlikely that either academic dogmatism or anarchic subjectivism could have shown us the way to this shrine of van Gogh. Discovering him for ourselves is a matter of the heart, but knowing of his existence is a matter of the head.

I hope you will not accuse me of vainglory if I remind you in conclusion that in his search for a faith that gives its due both to the head and the heart Erasmus arrived at a somewhat similar position, however different the issues were with which he had to contend. As a man of heartfelt piety he saw the mission of rational scholarship in the elimination of misunderstandings which clouded the meaning of the sacred texts. The tools of humanistic philology could thus help the faithful to read the letters of St. Jerome, the Psalms or the Gospels with more profound devotion. On the other hand Erasmus had little confidence in the logical subtleties that marked the theology of the schoolmen, precisely because, I believe, he regarded faith as a personal matter. Personal, but not entirely subjective. When it came to the crunch he sided with that tradition he had so frequently criticized.

But to recapture my humility I need only try to imagine what place Erasmus would have assigned to us art historians in his Praise of Folly, how he would have made fun of our relic cults, our snobbery and our jargon. Who would be so arrogant as to believe that he could have escaped this lash?

Notes

IN SEARCH OF CULTURAL HISTORY

1. See my *Aby Warburg, An Intellectual Biography* (London, 1970).
2. Karl J. Weintraub, *Visions of Culture* (Chicago and London, 1966).
3. Raymond Williams, *Culture and Society 1780–1950* (London, 1958).
4. See Raymond Williams, op. cit. note 3.
5. Thomas Mann, *Friedrich und die grosse Koalition* (Berlin, 1915).
6. Harry Levin, 'Semantics of Culture', *Science and Culture*, Daedalus, Winter 1965; G. M. Pflaum, *Geschichte des Wortes 'Zivilisation'*, Dissertation, University of Munich, 1961. (Copy at the Warburg Institute.)
7. A. L. Kroeber and Clyde Kluckhohn, *Culture, a Critical Review of Concepts and Definitions* (New York, 1963); and Milton Singer, 'Culture (Concept)', *International Encyclopedia of the Social Sciences* (New York, 1968).
8. T. S. Eliot, *Notes towards the Definition of Culture* (London, 1948).
9. L. Fox (ed.), *English Historical Scholarship in the 16th and 17th Centuries* (Oxford, 1956).
10. Arnaldo Momigliano, 'Ancient History and the Antiquarian', *Journal of the Warburg and Courtauld Institutes*, XIII (1950), pp. 285–315.
11. See my 'Art and Scholarship' (1957), *Meditations on a Hobby Horse* (London, 1963), pp. 106–19.
12. See my 'Renaissance and Golden Age' (1955), *Norm and Form* (London, 1966), pp. 29–34.
13. See now my 'The Leaven of Criticism in Renaissance Art' (1967), *The Heritage of Apelles* (London, 1976), pp. 111–31.
14. See G. M. Pflaum, op. cit. in note 6; and F. Rauhut, 'Die Herkunft der Worte und Begriffe "Kultur", "Zivilisation" und "Bildung"', *Germanisch-Romanische Monatsschrift*, Neue Folge, 1953, 3, 1, pp. 81–91.
15. See Karl J. Weintraub, op. cit. in note 2.
16. See now Isaiah Berlin, *Vico and Herder: Two Studies in the History of Ideas* (London, 1976).
17. I had an unexpected occasion to return to the problems here discussed from a different angle, when I was awarded the Hegel Prize of the City of Stuttgart for 1976, although I had referred those concerned to what I had written about the philosopher. My speech 'Hegel und die Kunstgeschichte' was published in *Die Neue Rundschau*, No. 2, 1977, pp. 202–19.
18. In *History of Western Philosophy* (London, 1946).
19. In 'What is Dialectic?' (1940) in *Conjectures and Refutations* (London, 1963), and *The Open Society and its Enemies* (London, 1946) with further comments in the 5th edition, 1966.
20. For example, J. N. Findlay, *Hegel: A Re-Examination* (London, 1958); and Bruce Mazlish, *The Riddle of History: The Great Speculators from Vico to Freud* (New York and London, 1966).
21. See Jacques Barzun, 'Cultural History as a Synthesis', *The Varieties of History*, ed. Fritz Stern (1956), pp. 387–402; R. L. Colie, 'Johan Huizinga and the Task of Cultural History', *American Historical Review*, LXIX (1964), pp. 607–30; Felix Gilbert, 'Cultural History and its Problems', *Comité International des Sciences Historiques*, Rapports (1960), Vol. I, pp. 40–58; Carlo Ginzburg, 'Da A. Warburg a E. H. Gombrich (Note su un Problema di Metodo)', *Studi Medievali*, S. III, 7 (1966); Gerhard Ritter, 'Zum Begriff der Kulturgeschichte', *Historische Zeitschrift* 171 (1951), pp. 293–302.
22. Georg Wilhelm Friedrich Hegel, 'Vorlesungen über die Philosophie der Geschichte', *Sämtliche Werke*, ed. H. Glockner, XI (Stuttgart, 1928), p. 508.
23. A. Funkenstein, *Heilsplan und natürliche Entwicklung, Formen der Gegenwartsbestimmung im Geschichtsdenken des hohen Mittelalters* (Munich, 1965); Ernest Lee

Tuveson, *Millennium and Utopia, a Study in the Background of the Idea of Progress* (Berkeley and Los Angeles, 1949).

24. Frank E. Manuel, *Shapes of Philosophical History* (Stanford, 1965).

25. Galvano della Volpe, *Hegel, Romantico e Mistico* (Florence, 1929); George Wilhelm Friedrich Hegel, 'Vom göttlichen Dreieck', *Dokumente zu Hegels Entwicklung*, ed. J. Hoffmeister (Stuttgart, 1936), pp. 303–6; and 'Vorlesungen über die Philosophie der Religion', II, *Sämtliche Werke*, XVI.

26. Hegel, op. cit. in note 22, p. 415.

27. Ibid., pp. 441–2.

28. Ibid., pp. 101–2.

29. Ibid., p. 515.

30. Carl Schnaase, *Geschichte der bildenden Künste*, I (Leipzig, 1843).

31. Jacob Burckhardt, *Briefe*, vollständige Ausgabe, ed. Max Burckhardt (Basel, 1949 et seq.), I, 206 f.

32. Arnaldo Momigliano, 'Introduzione alla Griechische Kulturgeschichte di Jacob Burckhardt', *Secondo Contributo alla Storia degli Studi Classici* (Rome, 1960), pp. 283–98. (With an important bibliographical appendix on Burckhardt up to 1959.)

33. Joachim Wach, *Das Verstehen* (Tübingen, 1926–33).

34. Jacob Burckhardt, *Briefe* (see note 31), III, p. 70.

35. Jacob Burckhardt, *Gesamtausgabe*, Berlin and Leipzig (1930 et seq.), V.

36. Ibid., IV, p. 186.

37. Jacob Burckhardt, *Briefe* (see note 31), IV, p. 30.

38. I did not wish to imply that Burckhardt's relation to Hegel has not been discussed before: see W. K. Fergusson, *The Renaissance in Historical Thought* (Cambridge, Mass., 1948); Werner Kaegi, *Jacob Burckhardt* (Basel/Stuttgart), Vol. III, 1956; Vol. VI, 1977, pp. 102–3; H. Schulte Nordholt, *Het Beeld der Renaissance, een historiografische Studie* (Amsterdam, 1948). But none of these has stated that Burckhardt's *Civilization of the Renaissance* is set in a Hegelian frame.

39. K. Löwith, *Jacob Burckhardt, der Mensch inmitten der Geschichte* (Luzern, 1936).

40. See for example, W. K. Fergusson, op. cit. in note 38; Leona Gabel *et al.* 'The Renaissance Reconsidered', A Symposium, *Smith College Studies in History*,

XLIV, 1964 (Northampton, Mass.); Tinsley Helton (ed.), *The Renaissance, a Reconsideration of the Theories and Interpretations of the Age* (Madison, 1961).

41. Arnaldo Momigliano, op. cit. note 32.

42. H. Wölfflin, *Renaissance und Barock* (Munich, 1888), p. 58.

43. See my *Art and Illusion* (New York and London, 1960); and now my *The Sense of Order* (Oxford, 1979), Chap. VIII.

44. See my review of A. Hauser in 'The Social History of Art' (1953), *Meditations on a Hobby Horse* (London, 1963); and 'Style', *International Encyclopedia of the Social Sciences*, New York, 1968.

45. See Karl J. Weintraub, op. cit. note 2.

46. Wilhelm Dilthey, *Der Aufbau der geschichtlichen Welt in der Geisteswissenschaft* (Plan und Fortsetzung). Gesammelte Schriften, VII (Leipzig und Berlin, 1927), p. 269.

47. See for example, Hans-Joachim Schoeps, *Was ist und was will die Geistesgeschichte? Über die Theorie und Praxis der Zeitgeistforschung* (Göttingen, 1959); and Edgar Wind, 'Kritik der Geistesgeschichte, Das Symbol als Genenstand kulturwissenschaftlicher Forschung', *Kulturwissenschaftliche Bibliographie zum Nachleben der Antike*, Einleitung, ed. Bibliothek Warburg I (Leipzig, Berlin, 1934).

48. Alois Riegl, *Die Spätrömische Kunstindustrie* (1901) (Vienna, 1927).

49. Ibid., p. 404.

50. Max Dvořák, *Kunstgeschichte als Geistesgeschichte* (Munich, 1924).

51. E. Panofsky, *Aufsätze zu Grundfragen der Kunstwissenschaft* (Berlin, 1964). See now my *The Sense of Order* (Oxford, 1979), Chap. VIII.

52. E. Panofsky, *Gothic Architecture and Scholasticism* (Latrobe, Pa., 1951).

53. E. Panofsky, *Renaissance and Renascences in Western Art* (Stockholm, 1960), p. 3.

54. R. L. Colie, op. cit. note 21; Karl J. Weintraub, op. cit. note 2. See now also my 'Huizinga's *Homo Ludens*', *Bijdragen en Mededelingen Betreffende de Geschiedenis der Nederlanden* 88/2, 1973, pp. 275–96; this issue has also been published separately as *Johan Huizinga, 1872–1972*, ed. W. R. H. Koops *et al.* (The Hague, 1973) and in my paper in *The Times Literary Supplement*, 4 October 1974.

55. J. Huizinga, *The Waning of the Middle Ages* (1919). London, 1924. Huizinga later regretted the choice of title for this reason, as I mentioned in 'Huizinga's *Homo Ludens*' (see note 54).

56. J. Huizinga, 'Renaissance and Realism' (1926), *Men and Ideas* (New York, 1959).

57. J. Huizinga, 'The Task of Cultural History: (1929), *Men and Ideas* (New York, 1959).

58. Morse Peckham, *Man's Rush for Chaos* (New York, 1966); Edgar Wind, op. cit. in note 47.

59. See my *Art and Illusion* (New York and London, 1960); and 'From the Revival of Letters to the Reform of the Arts: Niccolò Niccoli and Filippo Brunelleschi', *The Heritage of Apelles* (Oxford, 1976), pp. 93–111.

60. See my 'The Logic of Vanity Fair, Alternatives to Historicism in the Study of Fashions, Style and Taste' in this volume, pp. 60–92.

61. See my 'Art and Scholarship' (1957), *Meditations on a Hobby Horse* (London, 1963); and *Art and Illusion* (New York and London, 1960).

62. See Morse Peckham, op. cit. note 58.

63. A. O. Lovejoy, 'The Parallel between Deism and Classicism', *Essays in the History of Ideas* (Baltimore, 1948).

64. W. T. Jones, *The Romantic Syndrome* (The Hague, 1961).

65. See my 'From the Revival of Letters to the Reform of the Arts' (see note 59).

66. Eugene Marais, *The Soul of the White Ant* (1934) (London, 1937).

67. Colin G. Butler, *The World of the Honeybee* (London, 1954).

68. See now my 'The Renaissance—Period or Movement?' in *Background to the English Renaissance: Introductory Lectures*, ed. J. B. Trapp, London, 1974; pp. 9–30.

69. Francis Haskell, *Patrons and Painters* (London, 1963).

70. Edgar Wind, op. cit. in note 47.

71. K. R. Popper, 'Truth, Rationality and the Growth of Scientific Knowledge' (1960), *Conjectures and Refutations* (London, 1963).

72. N. Timasheff, *Sociological Theory* (New York, 1967).

73. K. R. Popper, *The Poverty of Historicism* (1944) (London, 1957); Evon Z. Vogt, 'Culture Change', *International Encyclopedia of the Social Sciences* (New York, 1968).

74. See my 'The Tradition of General Knowledge' in this volume, pp. 9–23.

75. W. K. Jordan, *Philanthropy in England, 1480–1660* (London, 1959).

THE LOGIC OF VANITY FAIR

1. K. R. Popper, *The Poverty of Historicism* (London, 1957).

2. Karl Mannheim, 'Beiträge zur Theorie der Weltanschauungs-Interpretation', *Jahrbuch für Kunstgeschichte* (Vienna, 1921/22), I, pp. 237–74.

3. Cf. my 'Art and Scholarship' in *Meditations on a Hobby Horse* (London, 1963), pp. 106–20.

4. For an informative survey of the situation see James S. Ackerman and Rhys Carpenter, *Art and Archaeology*, in *Princeton Studies in Humanistic Scholarship in America*, ed. R. Schlatter (Englewood Cliffs, N.J., 1963).

5. See my *Art and Illusion* (New York and London, 1960).

6. K. R. Popper, *The Poverty of Historicism*, p. 149.

7. K. R. Popper, *The Open Society and its Enemies*, 2nd ed. (London, 1952), Vol. II, p. 89.

8. Ibid., Vol. II, p. 96. See also (for a similar formulation) 'Theory of Tradition', in K. R. Popper, *Conjectures and Refutations: The Growth of Scientific Knowledge* (London, 1965), esp. p. 124.

9. I have dealt with some of these questions in an article on 'Style', *International Encyclopedia of Social Science* (New York, 1968), Vol. 15, pp. 352–61. The present contribution hopes to supplement rather than to duplicate that entry where, however, a fuller bibliography will be found.

10. For a discussion of this aspect see the last chapter of my book *The Story of Art*, eleventh (1965) and subsequent editions.

11. *The Poverty of Historicism*, p. 141.

12. See my review of Thomas Munro, 'Evolution in the Arts', *The British Journal of Aesthetics*, 4, No. 3 (July 1964).

13. Dwight E. Robinson, 'Fashion Theory

and Product Design', *Harvard Business Review*, 36, No. 6 (1958), 126–38.

14. Jean Gimpel, *The Cathedral Builders* (New York, 1961), p. 44.

15. Cf. my 'The Renaissance Conception of Artistic Progress and its Consequences' (1952), *Norm and Form* (London, 1966), pp. 1–11.

16. Adolf Göller, *Zur Ästhetik der Baukunst*, 1887, as summarized in Cornelius Gurlitt, *Die deutsche Kunst des neunzehnten Jahrhunderts* (Berlin, 1899), p. 491.

17. Karl Bühler, *Sprachtheorie* (Jena, 1934).

18. *Ars Poetica*, lines 48 ff. My translation is based on that by H. Rushton Fairclough in the Loeb Classical Library (London, 1947), pp. 455–7.

19. Cf. my paper, 'Ritualized Gesture and Expression in Art', *Philosophical Transactions of the Royal Society in London*, Series B, *Biological Sciences*, 251, No. 772 (1966), 393–401.

20. *The Open Society and its Enemies*, Vol. II, pp. 307–8, 357; and 'Theory of Tradition', in *Conjectures and Refutations*, esp. p. 135.

21. Cf. my *Art and Illusion*, Chapter XI.

22. *Institutio Oratoria*, VIII, vi, 51. My translation here and in the subsequent quotations is based on that by H. E. Butler in the Loeb Classical Library (London, 1959).

23. J. F. d'Alton, *Roman Literary Theory and Criticism* (New York, 1931). I have discussed some of the influences of this quarrel in 'Mannerism: The Historiographic Background', *Norm and Form* (London, 1966), pp. 99–107.

24. *Institutio*, VIII, v, 34.

25. *Institutio*, XII, x, 47.

26. Cf. my *Meditations on a Hobby Horse*, Index s.v. 'Avoidance' and 'Expectancies'.

27. The term is applied to the followers of Caravaggio by G. B. Bellori in his *Idea*, 1672, translated in Elizabeth Holt, *A Documentary History of Art* (New York, 1958), Vol. II, p. 103. This seems to be the first application of an 'ism' term to a movement in art.

28. Vincenzio Carducho, *Dialogos de la pintura* (Madrid, 1633). The passage is also translated in Elizabeth Holt, *A Documentary History of Art*, Vol. II, p. 209.

29. As I was told by my mother, who witnessed this incident.

30. Frank Rutter, *Evolution in Modern Art* (London, 1926), pp. 82–4.

31. Cf. my 'Psycho-Analysis and the History of Art', in *Meditations on a Hobby Horse*, pp. 30–44.

32. *The Poverty of Historicism*, p. 149.

33. Jonathan Swift, *A Voyage to Lilliput* (1727), Chap. IV.

34. Cf. my review of Arnold Hauser, 'The Social History of Art', in *Meditations on a Hobby Horse*, pp. 86–94.

35. Francis Haskell, *Patrons and Painters* (London, 1963), Chap. 3.

36. Cf. my review of T. Munro, 'Evolution in the Arts' (see note 12).

37. *The Poverty of Historicism*, Chap. 32.

38. R. P. Dore, 'The Special Problem of Agriculture', *The Listener* (London, 9 September, 1965), 367.

39. Geraldine Pelles, *Art, Artists and Society*, Englewood Cliffs, 1963.

40. *The Open Society and its Enemies*, Chap. 10.

41. *Art and Illusion*, Chap. 4.

42. Cf.. my lecture 'Visual Discovery through Art', *Arts Magazine*, December 1965. Now reprinted in *Psychology and the Visual Arts*, ed. J. Hogg (Harmondsworth, Middlesex, 1969).

43. Cf. my 'Norm and Form', in *Norm and Form*, pp. 81–98.

44. Gurlitt, op. cit. note 16, p. 466.

45. *The Poverty of Historicism*, p. 70.

46. Thomas Munro, *Evolution in the Arts* (The Cleveland Museum of Art, 1963), Chap. XX.

47. 'On the Sources of Knowledge and of Ignorance', in *Conjectures and Refutations*, esp. pp. 22 ff.

48. Cf. my paper, 'The Vogue of Abstract Art', in *Meditations on a Hobby Horse*, pp. 143–50.

49. I believe I read this story in a feuilleton by the Viennese critic, A. F. Seligmann, who was presumably present.

50. The line from Schiller's prologue to *Wallenstein* is as untranslatable as all such epigrams; its meaning lies somewhere between 'Life is serious, art is gay' and 'Life is business, art is play'.

51. For Popper's response see pp. 1174–1180 of the original publication (cited in full on p. 218).

MYTH AND REALITY IN GERMAN WARTIME BROADCASTS

1. The principal documents produced by the Monitoring Service of the British Broadcasting Corporation were the two-part *Daily Digest of Foreign Broadcasts*, a bulky duplicated publication, and the *Monitoring Report* containing a concise analysis of the day's broadcasts. From 1941 onward the daily *Deutschlandspiegel* offered an anthology of verbatim transcripts. These important documents are now not easily accessible even in the British Library. University Microfilms Ltd. have announced a microfilm version of the *Digest* and the *Report* to be published shortly.

   The historian who proposes to use these truly invaluable sources should perhaps know of the situation under which they were produced. Reception was often poor and the task confronting us monitors, whose English was sometimes inadequate, to translate or summarize under pressure was not easy. Even more difficult was the problem confronting the sub-editors and editors of the *Digest* who were originally expected to 'boil down' this sytematically repetitive material on the lines of a newspaper only to find us monitors accusing them of having emasculated a significant utterance. But if mishaps did occur in hearing, translating and editing, the total record of the ether war preserved in the nearly 2,000 numbers of these publications is still unique.

   In what follows I have relied mainly on memoranda compiled by a team of monitors at the time. One of these, 'The German Wireless at War', was made available to some of the early students of the subject; a much-expanded version for which I had collected material on news, commentaries, and other topics was never circulated.

2. Willi A. Boelcke, *Kriegspropaganda 1939–41, Geheime Ministerkonferenzen im Reichspropagandaministerium* (Stuttgart, 1966). Subsequently quoted as Boelcke, 1966.

3. Willi A. Boelcke, *Wollt ihr den Totalen Krieg? Die geheimen Goebbels-Konferenzen, 1939–1943* (Stuttgart, 1967). Subsequently quoted as Boelcke, 1967.

   [An English translation by Ewald Osers was subsequently published.]

4. 9 June 1940, Boelcke, 1966 and 1967.

5. 12 April 1941, Boelcke, 1966.

6. Werner Maser, *Hitlers Mein Kampf* (Munich, 1966), pp. 83 ff.

7. A. Hitler, *Mein Kampf* (Munich, 1933), Chap. 6, p. 203.

8. D. Sington and A. Weidenfeld, *The Goebbels Experiment* (London, 1942), and E. Kris and H. Speier, *German Radio Propaganda* (Oxford, 1944).

9. op. cit., pp. 347–53.

10. *Das Reich*, 26 May 1940. Quoted in Boelcke, 1966, p. 364.

11. 'Sie wollten das Reich uns verderben, doch der Westwall der eherne hält, wir kommen und schlagen zu Scherben, ihre alte verrottete Welt.' Quoted in Boelcke, 1966, p. 364.

12. Boelcke, 1966, p. 129 n.

13. Heinz Laubenthal, *Mit dem Mikrophon am Feind* (Dresden, 1942), p. 9. For a shortened version cf. Kris and Speier, op. cit., p. 156.

14. Laubenthal, op. cit., p. 49.

15. Unless otherwise stated the quotations here given are from the German Home Service.

16. 9 September 1940, Boelcke, 1966.

17. Boelcke, ibid.

18. Boelcke, ibid., 19 September 1940.

19. Henry Picker, *Hitlers Tischgespräche, 1941/42* (Bonn, 1951), pp. 273–4.

20. 12 November 1942, Boelcke, 1967.

21. 14 November 1942, Boelcke, ibid.

22. K. R. Popper, *The Open Society and its Enemies* (London, 1966), II, p. 267.

23. New York and London, 1960.

24. For this and the following see also my lecture 'The Cartoonist's Armoury' in *Meditations on a Hobby Horse* (London, 1963), pp. 127–43.

25. Peter Aldag, *Worüber berichten wir heute? Aus dem Zeitgeschehen des grossdeutschen Rundfunks* (Berlin, 1941).

26. Norman Cohn, *Warrant for Genocide, The Myth of the Jewish World Conspiracy and the Protocols of the Elders of Zion* (London, 1967).

27. Quoted in Boelcke, 1967, p. 235.

28. The infamous announcement of the High Command Communiqué of 12

April 1945 that General Lasch had been condemned to be hanged for surrendering Königsberg and that his family was 'being held liable' came close to the end of the war.

29. 16 December 1942, Boelcke, 1967.
30. op. cit., p. 199.
31. 24 January 1943, Boelcke, 1967.
32. 3 February 1943, Boelcke, 1967.
33. Kris and Speier, op. cit., pp. 431 ff.
34. It is characteristic that the emphasis of the propaganda effort shifted from the radio to the written word. To his chagrin Goebbels had no complete power over the press, but he used the weekly leader he wrote for *Das Reich*, and which was regularly read out over the German Home Service, not only to exhort and incite, but also to provide a safety valve for complaints nobody else could have voiced.
35. 4 January 1943, Boelcke, 1967.
36. Kris and Speier, op. cit., pp. 176–7, 419, 431.
37. Popper, op. cit., II, pp. 61–80.
38. Friedrich Gundolf, *Caesar, Geschichte seines Ruhms* (Berlin, 1924). 'The historian . . . cannot be a good politician, he cannot take fruitful decisions from hour to hour as destiny unfolds. But he can help to stir the air in which visionary deeds may thrive and he can recruit the minds of men for coming heroes. In this sense he summons the forces of history, and their embodiments, the peoples and the leaders' (p. 7). In discussing the veracity of Caesar's writings Gundolf says that 'no great man practices small swindles'; even where Caesar 'forces the facts' he must be acquitted of utilitarian

rationality (p. 9). The implied racialism, the tone of the references to the Germanic 'Reich' and the abject worship of Napoleon make all the more melancholic reading today as the author, who thus helped to 'stir the air', would himself have reaped the whirlwind, had he not died in 1931.

39. London, 1965.
40. I should like to thank my friend Dr. Lux Furtmüller of the Monitoring Service for helping me to locate the speech in *Deutschlandspiegel*. It is mentioned (but not quoted) in Bramsted, op. cit., p. 488. For the full text, see *Der Völkische Beobachter* (Munich edition), 2 March 1945.
41. Never fully, for the myth could always be saved by claiming that it was the people rather than History who had failed in the end. According to Hans Fritzsche, Goebbels did in fact take that line at his last conference on 21 April 1945, blaming first the officers and then railing at the German people at large: Nobody had forced them when they voted to leave the League of Nations. Why, indeed, had his collaborators worked with him? Now they should not be surprised if their throats were cut. The remark, which has often been quoted, may well have been made, but the whole account should be treated with some caution since it served Fritzsche's purpose to claim that only at this last meeting had Goebbels shown himself in his true colours. He had always taken him to be a true patriot. (*Es sprach Hans Fritzsche*, ed. Hildegard Springer (Stuttgart, 1949), p. 28.)

RESEARCH IN THE HUMANITIES: IDEALS AND IDOLS

1. For this view of science and its indebtedness to K. R. Popper see the paper by John C. Eccles, 'The Discipline of Science with Special Reference to the Neurosciences', *Daedalus*, Vol. 102, No. 2, Spring 1973, pp. 85–101.
2. See my essay, 'The Tradition of General Knowledge', in this volume, pp. 9–23.
3. There is a vivid description of the good and bad sides of the system in Richard B. Goldschmidt, *The Golden Age of Zoology* (Seattle, 1956), Chap. 1.

4. There is little consolation in the fact that the authorities on the spot are partly responsible. The small band of scholars who try to stem this tide find little support either East or West. Even the holdings of Indian material in famous European libraries are largely uncatalogued.
5. K. R. Popper 'On the Sources of Knowledge and of Ignorance', in *Conjectures and Refutations* (London, 1963), pp. 3–30.

6. Professor Karl W. Deutsch pointed out to me that collections of data are still important for testing theories. I certainly accept this *caveat* particularly in relation to the social sciences.

7. Richard F. Gombrich, *Precept and Practice, Traditional Buddhism in the Rural Highlands of Ceylon* (Oxford, 1971).

8. In this volume, p. 57.

ART AND SELF-TRANSCENDENCE

1. Todd, J. M. (ed.), *The Arts, Artists and Thinkers. An Inquiry into the Place of the Arts in Human Life* (London, 1958).

2. 'Ver' è che come forma non s'accorda
   molte fiate alla intenzion dell'arte,
   perch'a risponder la materia è sorda.'
   ('True is it, that (as) the form often accordeth not with the intention of the art, because that the material is dull to answer.') *Paradiso* I, 127–9, English translation by the Rev. Philip H. Wicksteed in The Temple Classics, 1889.

3. 'Ma la natura la dà sempre scema,
   similemente operando all'artista
   ch'ha l'abito dell'arte e man che trema.'
   ('But nature ever furnisheth it faulty, doing as doth the artist who hath the knack of the art and a trembling hand.') *Paradiso* XIII, 76–8, trans. as above in note 2.

4. '... come all'ultimo suo ciascuno artista.'
   ('as at his utmost reach must every artist'). *Paradiso* XXX, 33, trans. as above in note 2.

5. Panofsky, E., 'Idea. Ein Beitrag zur Begriffsgeschichte der älteren Kunsttheorie', *Studien der Bibliothek Warburg*, ed. F. Saxl (Hamburg, 1924). English translation by J. J. S. Peake (Columbia, 1968).

6. Mengs, A. R., *Gedanken über die Schönheit und den Geschmack in der Malerei* (Zurich, 1762). (Slightly paraphrased in the interest of readability.)

7. Courthion, P., *Courbet raconté par lui-même* II (Geneva, 1950), pp. 78–9.

8. Ringbom, S., 'Art in the Epoch of the Great Spiritual. Occult Elements in the Early Theory of Abstract Painting', *Journal of the Warburg and Courtauld Institutes* (1966), Vol. 29.

9. Popper, K. R., 'Epistemology without a knowing Subject' (1968) and 'On the Theory of the Objective Mind' (1968), both in *Objective Knowledge, an Evolutionary Approach* (Oxford, 1972), pp. 106–52 and 153–90.

10. van Gogh-Bonger, J. (ed.), *Verzamelde Brieven*, III (Vincent van Gogh) (Amsterdam, 1953). Letter 507, summer 1888.

11. Popper, K. R., 'Of Clouds and Clocks', in *Objective Knowledge* (see note 9), pp. 206–50, my *The Story of Art* (1950), with examples of the emergence of fresh artistic problems, and now also my *The Sense of Order* (Oxford, 1979), Chapter III.

12. See my 'The Use of Art for the Study of Symbols', *The American Psychologist*, XX (1965). Reprinted in J. Hogg (ed.), *Psychology and the Visual Arts* (Harmondsworth, Middlesex, 1969).

13. Tovey, D. F., *The Integrity of Music*, Lecture I (London, 1941).

14. See my 'Visual Discovery through Art', *Arts Magazine* (November 1965). Reprinted in J. Hogg (ed.), *Psychology and the Visual Arts* (Harmondsworth, Middlesex, 1969).

15. See my 'Freud's Aesthetics', *Encounter* (January 1966). (In this paper I have tried to show that Freud's theory of art was not predominantly expressionist.) Tillyard, E. M. W. and Lewis, C. S., *The Personal Heresy* (Oxford, 1939). (The second author's contribution presents a forceful case against current ideas of art as self-expression.)

ART HISTORY AND THE SOCIAL SCIENCES

1. For this and the following see also my 'In Search of Cultural History', and 'A Plea for Pluralism', in this volume, pp. 24–59 and 184–88.

2. Karl R. Popper, *The Poverty of Historicism* (London, 1957), pp. 143–7; and 'On the Theory of the Objective Mind', in *Objective Knowledge, An Evolutionary Approach* (Oxford, 1972), pp. 179–90.

3. Christopher and Stephen Wren, *Parentalia* (London, 1750), p. 335.

4. *Parentalia*, p. 340.

5. The official description of the ceiling is reprinted in H. M. Colvin's pamphlet, referred to above, from Dr. Plot's *Natural History of Oxfordshire*. It was also printed separately under the title *A Description of the Painting of the Theatre in Oxford*; the first edition known to me (in the Bodleian Library) dates from 1673. There are many later reprintings.

6. Thomas Sprat, *The History of the Royal Society of London* (London, 1667), pp. 53–4. Reprinted in the author's *The Decorative Arts of Europe and the Islamic East* (London, 1977).

7. Otto Kurz, 'Lion Masks with Rings in the West and in the East', *Scripta Hierosolymitana*, XXIV (Jerusalem, 1972), pp. 22–41.

8. As yet unpublished; see also his 'On the Theory of the Objective Mind', cited note 2.

9. 'Grundrisse der Kritik der politischen Oekonomie, 1857/8', in Karl Marx, *Texte zu Methode und Praxis*, III, ed. Gunther Hillmann, Rowohlts Klassiker (1967), p. 35 (the translation in the text is my own).

10. *Urania* (Oxford, 1669) (Madan 2818).

11. *Le Vite* etc., ed. G. Milanesi (Florence, 1881), pp. 214–15.

12. I have discussed the relevance of this philosophy for the problem of values in 'Art and Self-Transcendence' (see this volume, pp. 123–30); and from a historical point of view in 'Icones Symbolicae', *Symbolic Images* (London, 1972), pp. 123–91.

13. Quoted in *The Listener*, 24 January 1974.

14. I have discussed this important book in the essay quoted above, p. 210, note 54.

15. Roger de Piles, *Cours de peinture par principes avec une balance des peintres* (Paris, 1708). The attempt is discussed in Jakob Rosenberg, *On Quality in Art* (Princeton, 1967), Chap. 2.

16. 'In Search of Cultural History', see this volume, pp. 24–59.

17. See my 'The Leaven of Criticism in Renaissance Art', in *The Heritage of Apelles* (Oxford, 1976), pp. 111–132.

18. For a criticism of this view see D. E. Hirsch, *Validity in Interpretation* (New Haven, 1967).

19. Chiang Yee, *Chinese Calligraphy* (London, 1938), p. 107.

20. Op. cit., p. 203.

21. Arthur O. Lovejoy, 'The Parallel of Deism and Classicism', *Essays in the History of Ideas* (Baltimore, 1948); paperback edn., 1960, pp. 78–98.

22. See my 'Expression and Communication', in *Meditations on a Hobby Horse* (London, 1963), pp. 56–69; and 'Freud's Aesthetics', *Encounter*, XXVI, No. 1 (January 1966), pp. 30–40.

23. I have discussed this matter in 'The Use of Art for the Study of Symbols', *American Psychologist*, XX (1965), pp. 34–50; reprinted in J. Hogg (ed.), *Psychology and the Visual Arts* (Harmondsworth, Middlesex, 1969).

24. For the implications of this gradualism see my 'André Malraux and the Crisis of Expressionism', *Meditations on a Hobby Horse*, pp. 78–85.

25. This is the answer I would now give to the question I raised in 'The Logic of Vanity Fair: Alternatives to Historicism in the Study of Fashions, Style and Taste', see this volume, pp. 60–69.

26. For a recent searching discussion of this vital issue see Allen Wheelis, *The Moralist* (New York, 1973).

27. I have talked about the value of these rumours in my address to the London School of Economics, 'The Tradition of General Knowledge', see this volume, pp. 9–23.

28. Reprinted in R. Hinden (ed.), *The Radical Tradition* (Harmondsworth, Middlesex, 1966), pp. 191–219.

29. The nearest translation might be 'To the University of Oxford and to Humane Letters'. To spell out the full meaning of *bonae literae* (good letters) would require another lecture.

CANONS AND VALUES IN THE VISUAL ARTS: A CORRESPONDENCE WITH QUENTIN BELL

1. See Quentin Bell, 'The Art Critic and the Art Historian', *Critical Inquiry* 1 (1975), pp. 497–519.
2. Michael Levey's address 'Putting the Art back into Art History' was published in *Leonardo*, Vol. 9, 1976, pp. 63–5. On reading (rather than hearing) this salutory challenge to academic art historians I should now like to qualify the critical remarks in my letter.
3. Angela Ravà and Biancamaria Bianco, *Incontri di Bimbi con i Capolavori di Brera* (Milan, 1959).
4. Now included in this volume, pp. 60–92.

A PLEA FOR PLURALISM

1. Thomas S. Kuhn, *The Structure of Scientific Revolutions* (The University of Chicago Press, 1962).
2. Imre Lakatos and Allen Musgrave (Editors), *Criticism and the Growth of Knowledge* (Cambridge University Press, 1970). I refer in particular to the paper by K. R. Popper, 'Normal Science and its Dangers'.
3. I am indebted to my friend Prof. Otto Kurz, who convinced me in conversation that with the co-operation of a major art school such a systematic test of attributions and chronology would be quite feasible. Meanwhile I have also indulged in the kind of exercise foreshadowed in the preceding paragraph in 'Rhétorique de l'attribution: *Reductio ad absurdum*', *Revue de l'Art*, 42, 1978, pp. 23–5.
4. The demand is sometimes raised that the art historian should go to school with the literary critic, whose standards of value and whose procedures rest on a more developed tradition, but much as I sympathize with the sentiments underlying this demand, I am not entirely convinced that our colleagues in Eng. Lit. have all the answers.
5. Particularly in 'Art and Scholarship', now reprinted in *Meditations on a Hobby Horse* (London, 1963), pp. 106–20, and in my 'Deneke Lecture' *In Search of Cultural History*, see this volume, pp. 24–59.
6. In *Norm and Form* (London, 1966), p. 92.
7. *Jahrbuch der kunsthistorischen Sammlungen in Wien*, N.F. 8, 9 (1934, 1935).
8. *Journal of the Warburg and Courtauld Institutes*, VIII, 1945; I have included this controversial paper with a discussion on the methodological issues which it raises in *Symbolic Images: Studies in the Art of the Renaissance* (London, 1972).
9. 'A Pluralistic Approach to the Philosophy of History', in *Roads to Freedom*, Essays in honor of Friedrich A. von Hayek (ed. Erich Streissler) (London, 1969).
10. For literature see the astringent book by Donald E. Hirsch Jr., *Validity in Interpretation* (New Haven, 1967).
11. *Art and Illusion, a Study in the Psychology of Pictorial Representation* (New York, 1960) (now Princeton University Press and Phaidon Press), 'Visual Discovery through Art' and 'The Use of Art for the Study of Symbols', in *Psychology and the Visual Arts* (ed. James Hogg) (Penguin Books, Harmondsworth, Middlesex, 1969) and 'The Evidence of Images', in *Interpretation Theory and Practice* (ed. C. S. Singleton) (Baltimore, 1969). And now also in 'Illusion and Art' in *Illusion in Nature and Art* (ed. jointly with R. L. Gregory) (London, 1973) (with further bibliography) and *The Sense of Order* (Oxford, 1979).
12. 'Three Decades of Art History in the United States', in *Meaning in the Visual Arts* (New York, 1955).

THE MUSEUM: PAST, PRESENT AND FUTURE

1. *On Understanding Art Museums*, ed. Sherman F. Lee (Englewood Cliffs, N.J., 1975).
2. *Art Museums: The European Experience*, ed. Christopher White. This collection of papers by Michael Jaffé, Hubert Lan-

deis, Wend von Kalnein, Michael Compton, Erik Fischer, Pierre Rosenberg, Werner Hofmann, Maria Fossi Todorow and the editor has not, so far, been published.

3. Julius von Schlosser's *Kunst und Wunderkammern der Spätrenaissance* (Leipzig, 1908) is still the most informative study of this subject.

4. Julius von Schlosser, *La Letteratura Artistica* (Florence, 1956), pp. 56–7, provides a bibliography of the earlier editions of these guide-books for pilgrims to Rome.

5. 'Art History and the Social Sciences', see this volume, pp. 131–66. See also my correspondence with Quentin Bell, pp. 167–83.

6. In *A Coat of Many Colours: Occasional Essays* (London, 1945), pp. 1–5.

7. J. J. Winckelmann, *Anmerkungen über die Geschichte der Kunst* (Dresden, 1767), p. 31. I have discussed the implications of this reference in *Ideas of Progress and their Impact on Art*, The Mary Duke Biddle Lectures, New York, 1971, privately circulated by the Cooper Union.

8. Vol. I, p. 76.

9. See my chapter 'André Malraux's Philosophy of Art in Historical Perspective', in Martine de Courcel's *Malraux: Life and Work* (London, 1976).

10. Ulric Neisser, *Cognition and Reality* (San Francisco, 1976), where many of the author's experiments are also quoted.

11. In his lecture, 'Design in Museums', *Journal of the Royal Society of Arts*, 123 (October 1975), 717 ff., Sir John Pope-Hennessy advocates 'long term collaboration between designers and academic staffs, based on real mutual understanding'.

12. In an article, 'Should a Museum Be Active?', *Museum*, 21 (1968), pp. 79–86, I made use of the ancient distinction between the active and the contemplative life.

13. London, 1966.

Bibliographical Note

Details of the previous publications of the papers in this volume are as follows:

THE TRADITION OF GENERAL KNOWLEDGE. Oration delivered at the London School of Economics and Political Science on Friday, 8 December 1961. Published by the London School of Economics and Political Science 1962, and in M. Bunge (ed.), *The Critical Approach to Science and Philosophy*, New York, by the Free Press of Glencoe, 1964.

IN SEARCH OF CULTURAL HISTORY. The Philip Maurice Deneke Lecture delivered at Lady Margaret Hall, Oxford, on 19 November 1967. Oxford University Press, 1969.

THE LOGIC OF VANITY FAIR: ALTERNATIVES TO HISTORI-CISM IN THE STUDY OF FASHIONS, STYLE AND TASTE. *The Philosophy of Karl Popper*, ed. Paul A. Schilpp, Open Court Publishing Company, La Salle, Ill., pp. 925–57. © 1974 by The Library of Living Philosophers, Inc.

MYTH AND REALITY IN GERMAN WARTIME BROADCASTS. The Creighton Lecture in History 1969. The Athlone Press, University of London, 1970.

RESEARCH IN THE HUMANITIES: IDEALS AND IDOLS. Re-printed by permission of *Daedalus: Journal of the American Academy of Arts and Sciences*, Boston, Massachusetts, Spring 1973, *The Search for Knowledge*, pp. 1–10.

ART AND SELF-TRANSCENDENCE. Address to the 14th Nobel Symposium in Stockholm on 16 September 1969. Published in *Nobel Symposium 14: The Place of Value in a World of Facts*, ed. Arne Tiselius and Sam Nilsson, Almqvist and Wiksell, Stockholm, Wiley Interscience Division, John Wiley & Sons, Inc., 1970, pp. 125–33.

ART HISTORY AND THE SOCIAL SCIENCES. The Romanes Lecture for 1973 delivered at the Sheldonian Theatre, Oxford, on 22 November 1973. Oxford University Press, 1975.

CANONS AND VALUES IN THE VISUAL ARTS: A CORRESPON-DENCE WITH QUENTIN BELL. *Critical Inquiry*, Volume 2, No. 3, Spring 1976, The University of Chicago Press, 1976, pp. 395–410. © 1976 by The University of Chicago.

A PLEA FOR PLURALISM. *The American Art Journal*, III, I, Spring 1971, pp. 83–7, as part of a series *The State of Art History*.

THE MUSEUM: PAST, PRESENT AND FUTURE. Address delivered at Ditchley Park, Oxfordshire, on 17 October 1975, to the European-American Assembly on Art Museums. *Critical Inquiry*, Volume 3, No. 3, Spring 1977, The University of Chicago Press 1977, pp. 449–70. © 1977 by The University of Chicago.

REASON AND FEELING IN THE STUDY OF ART. Speech on being awarded the Erasmus Prize on 19 September 1975 in the Rijksmuseum Vincent Van Gogh, Amsterdam. Printed with kind permission of the Praemium Erasmianum Foundation in *Simiolus; Netherlands Quarterly for the History of Art*, Vol. 8, No. 2, 1976, pp. 47–8.

Sources of Photographs

Thomas Photos, Oxford: Figs. 1–5
Mauritshuis, The Hague: Fig. 6
Alinari, Florence: Fig. 9
National Gallery, London: Fig. 10
Hirmer Fotoarchiv, Munich: Figs. 7, 8

Index

BY ANNE GASKELL

Abstract art, 75–6, 92
Abstract expressionism, 125
Academic disciplines, 17–18, 20–1,
  56–9, 119–20, 132, 140, 184, 188;
  see also Art History, History, Social
  Sciences
Academic doctrines in art, 67, 124,
  145, 146, 148, 156, 172, 177, 178,
  179, 180, 207
'Academic industry', 18–19, 58, 115,
  117, 118–19, 120–1, 187–8
Advertisements, 16, 66–7, 109, 149,
  198
Aeschines, 156
Aesop, 11
Aesthetic movement, 49, 128
Aesthetic values, 83, 85–6, 88, 126,
  128, 144, 149, 150, 158, 177, 178,
  179; see also Academic doctrines in
  art, Values
Aesthetics, 33, 88, 123, 126, 190
Aldag, Peter, 106
Alice in Wonderland, 11
Amadis of Gaul, 71, 86
Angelico, Fra, 48, 84
Anglo-Irish art, 154
Animals, 14, 32, 50, 142, 151
Anthropology, 10, 25, 48, 58, 105,
  118, 152–3, 188
Antiquarianism, 26, 54, 87, 134, 193–
  4
Anti-Semitism, 106, 108
Apelles, 168, 171, 173, 180, 182
Archaeology, 150–1, 193–4, 196
Architecture, 33, 45, 53, 64, 77, 81–
  3, 119, 132, 136–7, 138, 150, 152,
  159, 160–1, 169, 171, 187; see also
  Sheldonian Theatre
Aristotle, 71, 123, 190
Arnold, Matthew, 25
Art: term, 149–52, 171
Art and Illusion, 61, 104–5, 151, 175,
  199
'Art appreciation', 84, 86, 164, 179,
  190, 199
Art History, 7–8, 16, 20, 26, 33–4, 36–
  7, 43–6, 60, 71, 112–13, 123, 127,
  131–4, 141, 146–8, 149, 150–2, 155,
  159–60, 165, 167, 171, 177, 179,
  184–8: see also 'Art appreciation',
  'Canon', 'Formal Analysis', Icono-
  graphy, Iconology
Arts, Liberal, 13
Astrology, 88, 119, 183
Attention, 26, 62–6, 74, 76, 125, 133,
  199, 203
Attributions, 123, 133–4, 184–5
Austen, Jane, 11
Austrian culture, 59, 71, 90, 114, 161,
  187
Authoritarianism, 67, 114, 164

Bach, Johann Sebastian, 58, 91, 129,
  199
Bacon, Francis, 7, 116
Bandinelli, Baccio, 155
Baroque, 48, 50, 51, 65, 146, 147, 156,
  160, 161
Beaufort, Lady Margaret, 59
Beauty, 16, 37, 71, 123–4, 126

Beethoven, Ludwig van, 16, 19, 56,
  89, 91, 157
Behaviour, 50, 51, 62, 85, 118, 142,
  151; see also 'Rationality principle'
Bell, Quentin, 8, 167–83
Berenson, Bernard, 182
Biography, 52, 55
Bisseker, E. G., 104
Bluecher, sinking of, 97
Boas, George, 45, 182
Bode, Wilhelm, 197
Bodin, Jean, 26
Boeckh, A., 36
Bolsheviks, 101–2, 106, 108, 109
Botticelli, Sandro, 187
Brahms, Johannes, 71, 88
Bramstedt, Ernest K., 110–11
Bühler, Karl, 66
Bullfights, 152, 162
Burckhardt, Jacob, 25, 34–42, 45, 48,
  52, 54–5, 113–14
Burne-Jones, Sir Edward, 49
Burnett Tylor, Sir Edward, 25
Butterfield, Herbert, 27
Byrd, William, 133
Byzantine art, 47, 146

Caesar, Julius, 110, 173
Calligraphy, Chinese, 157–9
'Canon', 8, 155–7, 161, 163, 164, 165,
  167, 168, 169, 171, 172, 173, 176,
  177–82, 192, 194, 195
Caravaggio, Michelangelo Merisi da,
  71
Caricature, 105, 106, 165
Carlyle, Thomas, 110
Catalyst, 11, 17, 20
Catherine the Great of Russia, 110
Cato, 68
Cavaceppi, Bartolommeo, 194
Caylus, Anne Claude Count de, 194
Cellini, Benvenuto, 37, 155
Ceramics, 177–8, 202–3
Ceremonies, 78, 96, 133
Cervantes, Miguel de, 11, 17, 71, 85–
  6
Cézanne, Paul, 16, 72, 79, 180
Chardin, J. B. S., 169
Chinese arts, 12, 14, 22, 76, 81, 84, 127,
  146, 157–8, 169, 177–8, 201–2
Christie, Agatha, 9
Churchill, Sir Winston, 98–9, 100,
  105, 106, 108, 109
Cicero, 15, 52, 55, 68, 69, 156
Cimabue, 194
Civilization: term, 27, 163
Čižek, F., 175
Classical tradition, 9–10, 12–13, 14–
  15, 21, 33, 40, 47, 49, 53, 112–13,
  115, 123, 132, 136, 139, 140–1, 156,
  185
Classicism, 47, 49, 67, 71, 87, 124
Classics, 9–10, 14–15, 18, 52, 58, 112–
  13, 115
Cleer, Richard, 133
Colie, R. L., 11
Colvin, H. M., 131–2
Communications, 11, 13, 50, 55, 67,
  206
Communism, 76, 108

Competition, 27, 62–3, 64–5, 68, 155,
  178, 203
Compton, Michael, 202
Concentration, 201, 203
Connoisseurs, 81, 149, 152, 153, 158,
  184–5, 202
Conspicuousness, 63–4, 69
Constable, John, 151, 182
Constantine the Great, 36
Continuity, historical, 52, 55, 59, 142;
  see also Tradition
Conventions, 10, 20, 80, 87, 89; musi-
  cal, 89; artistic, 159, 160, 161, 171;
  see also 'Rules', Style, Tradition
Corot, J. B. C., 197–8
Correggio, Antonio, 139
Counter-Reformation, 51; see also
  'Jesuit style' of art
Courbet, Gustave, 124
Crafts, 79, 125, 128, 149, 152, 162,
  171, 175, 182, 191
Creativity, 129, 165, 172, 202, 205
Croft Murray, Edward, 147, 149, 156
Cromwell, Oliver, 160
Crowther, Sir Geoffrey, 13
Cubism, 73
Cultural history, see History
Cultural psychology, 25, 43–5, 48, 50–
  3, 56, 61, 76, 186; see also 'National
  Spirit', 'Spirit of the Age'
Cultural relativism, see Relativism
Culture: term, 25–6, 27–8, 29, 37, 47,
  55, 58; 'morphology of', 45, 47
'Culture clash', 79

Daedalus, 112, 153
Dante, 11, 120, 123–4, 128
Darlan, Admiral J. F., 100–1
Decoration, see Ornament
Decoration, military, 65, 66
Decorum, 150, 162
Degas, Edgar, 79
Deism, 47
Demosthenes, 68, 156
Deneke, Philip Maurice, 59
Determinism: social, 60, 141–4, 168;
  see also Exegetic method, Hegel,
  Historicism, Holism, Marxism
Deutsch, Karl W., 215 note 6
Dialectic, Marxist, 29, 44, 61, 142
Dickens, Charles, 58
Dilthey, Wilhelm, 43, 44
Diodorus Siculus, 182
Domenichino, 194
Donatello, 182
Drawing, 176–7, 182
Duchamp, Marcel, 117, 192
Dvořak, Max, 44, 187
Dyck, Sir Anthony van, 168–9, 171,
  180

Economics, 18, 43, 55, 61, 62, 132,
  164–5, 186, 188
Education, 9, 12–15, 61, 113, 127,
  134, 163, 172–4, 179, 186, 188, 193–
  8, 199, 201–2; university, 17–20,
  56–9, 70, 113–15, 118–22
Egyptian arts, 32, 33, 44, 47, 80, 135,
  138, 142, 168, 169, 171–2, 175–6,
  182

Elite, 10, 14, 157, 161, 169, 179, 192, 196
Empiricism, 145
Engineering, 81–2, 137, 185
Enlightenment, the, 27, 52, 79, 141
Epicurus, 15
Erasmus, Desiderius, 205, 207
Escapism, 56, 130
Ethics, 88, 138, 162
Etruscan art, 193, 194
Euphronios, 202–3; fig. 10
Euripides, 143–4
Euthymides, 202–3; fig. 9
Evolution, 129, 142; cultural, 35, 40, 44, 89–90, 110, 129, 143; *see also* Progress
Examinations, 18–19, 20, 57, 58, 118–20, 152, 163, 187
Excellence, scale of, 28, 149, 168; *see also* 'Canon'
Exegetic method, 31–2, 42, 43, 46, 47–8, 57
Exhibitions, 197–8, 204
Expectation, 65, 70, 86–7, 89, 154, 160, 161, 202, 206
Eyck, Jan van, 45–7, 48, 49

Fashion, 51, 60, 61–6, 68–9, 75, 81, 92, 117–18, 133, 177, 178, 184, 186–7
Feeling in art, 84–5, 126, 158, 169, 205–7
Fehl, Philipp, 24
'First Eleven' in art, 155–6, 161
'Formal analysis', 120, 186, 187
Frederick the Great of Prussia, 110
French Revolution, 48, 76, 79, 194
Fresenius, Karl, 35, 54–5
Freud, Sigmund, 171
Friedländer, Max J., 44
Fritzsche, Hans, 95, 105
Functionalism, 78, 92, 149–50, 152, 160
Furtmüller, Lux, 214 note 40

Gaddi, Gaddo, 194
Gainsborough, Thomas, 179
Games, 11, 12, 80–1, 84, 126, 127, 128, 152, 153–4, 155, 161, 206
Geistesgeschichte: term, 43–5, 57, 60, 134, 187
General Knowledge, 8, 9–23, 58, 112–13, 119, 142, 186
German: arts, 14–15, 25, 30, 48–9, 65, 67; war propaganda, 7, 25, 93–111
Gibbons, Grinling, 154
Giotto, 80, 194
Giovanni da Bologna, 179
Goebbels, J., 93–5, 96, 98–102, 104, 108, 109–11
Goethe, J. W. von, 15, 87, 120, 190, 198
Gogh, Vincent van, 16, 126, 207
Gombrich, Richard, 24, 215 note 7
Gothic, 22, 28, 44–5, 49, 50, 51, 64, 65, 79, 126, 138, 148
Gracchi, 68
Grace, W. G., 12
Greek arts, 10, 27, 33, 42, 44, 80, 143–4, 148, 156, 162, 171, 173, 175, 182–3, 186, 193, 202–3
Gundolf, Friedrich, 110

Hadamovsky, Eugen, 98
d'Hancarville, P. F., 194
Handel, George Frederick, 89
Haskell, Francis, 51
Hayek, A. von, 60
Hegel, Georg Wilhelm Friedrich, 7, 28–34, 35–47 *passim*, 48, 49, 50, 52,

54–6, 57, 60, 61, 76–7, 89, 90, 91, 186; *see also* Holism, 'National Spirit', 'Spirit of the Age'
Herbarthian associationism, 43
Herder, Johann Gottfried von, 28, 32
Herodotus, 26
Hesse, Hermann, 128
Heydrich, Reinhard, 108
Hierarchies, 10, 33, 53, 82, 151, 154, 178, 199–200
Hillman, Sidney, 106
Himmler, H., 96
Historicism, 8, 60–2, 68, 79, 81, 82–3, 89–92; *see also* Hegel
History, 20, 27, 41–2, 95–6, 101, 103, 110–11, 133, 134, 135–6, 138, 141, 181; cultural, 7, 25–8, 29–41 *passim*, 42–3, 44–9 *passim*, 50–9; economic, 42–3, 56–7, 134; political, 25, 26, 42–3, 56; providential, 28–32, 41, 57, 110–11; social, 53, 134; of the spirit, *see Geistesgeschichte*, Hegel, 'National Spirit', 'Spirit of the Age'
Hitler, Adolf, 65, 94–5, 96, 99, 100, 101, 106–11
Hofmann, Werner, 200, 203
Holism, 28–34, 35–56 *passim*, 60, 78, 82–3; *see also* Hegel, Historicism
Homer, 87, 162
Hooch, Pieter de, 202
Horace, 66, 189
Huizinga, Johan, 45–6, 47, 49, 52, 152
Humanists, 58, 112, 113, 115, 117, 118; Renaissance, 37, 112, 207
Humanities, 7–8, 15, 18, 57–8, 112, 114, 116, 117–21, 127, 132, 165, 181
Hyperides, 156
Hypothesis, 54, 57–8, 86–7, 116, 151, 165–6, 185

Iconography, 113, 159
Iconology, 119, 187
Ideals, 7, 116; *see also* Beauty, Perfection, Platonism, Values
'Idols', 7, 116–22; *see also* Inductivism, Innovation
Illusionism, 80, 139, 147, 149, 151, 162
Images, 150–1; *see also* Visual Media
Impressionism, 10, 72
Indian arts, 11, 22, 56, 84, 115–16
'Individualistic model', 61, 73
Individuals in history, 38–40, 50–1, 55, 57, 62–3, 135, 177
Inductivism, 116–17
Industrial Revolution, 22–3, 138
Inflation, 62, 64, 65, 66–7, 68, 70–1, 81
'Innocent eye', 199–200
Innovation, 67–9, 71, 77–8, 79, 80–1, 117, 153, 161; *see also* Fashion, Progress
'Interdisciplinary studies', 57, 119
Isidore of Seville, 21
Islamic arts, 11, 22, 47, 154
Isocrates, 156

James I, King of England, 139
Jargon, 14, 59, 62, 115, 118, 132, 207
Jerome, Saint, 207
'Jesuit style' of art, 49, 51, 77
Joachim of Fiore, 29–30
Johnson, Dr. Samuel, 168
Jones, W. T., 48
Judaism, 29, 47, 94, 106, 108
Judgement of Paris, 9–10, 12, 20
Juvenal, 186

Kandinsky, V., 125
Kant, I., 28, 86

Kepler, Johannes, 31
Kinkel, G., 36
Klee, Paul, 125
Koehler, Wolfgang, 130
Kris, Ernst, 96, 165
Kuhn, Thomas, 184–5, 187, 188
Kurz, Otto, 217 note 3

Lamprecht, Karl, 25, 43, 52
Language, 11, 12–13, 14, 15, 18, 20, 26, 53–4, 68–9, 77, 81, 107, 112, 113, 115, 135, 136, 160–1, 166, 181, 199, 200, 206, 207; Corruption of, 65–7
Laubenthal, Heinz, 97
Leach, Bernard, 177
Le Bon, Gustave, 94, 107
Leonardo da Vinci, 80, 171
Lessing, G. E., 30
Levey, Michael, 170
Literature, 12, 14–15, 26, 45, 47, 54, 71, 162, 164, 173, 206
'Logic of Situations', 61–6, 68–70, 73–5, 79, 81, 88, 91–2, 137, 148, 155, 159, 164
Longinus, 26–7
Lorrain, Claude, 156
Lovejoy, Arthur, 28, 47
Lysias, 156

Macaulay, Thomas Babington, Lord 27, 40
Machiavelli, Niccolò, 40
Magic, 44, 79, 85, 117, 157, 187–8
Malevich, Kasimir, 76
Malraux, André, 195
Mannerism, 51, 155, 187
Mannheim, Karl, 60, 82–3
Marais, Eugene, 50
Maratti, Carlo, 180
Margaritone d'Arezzo, 194, 195; fig. 8
Martini, Simone, 174
Marx, Karl, 61, 143–4, 162
Marxism, 43, 60, 76–7, 103, 118, 142
Masterpieces, 'Old Masters', 87, 128, 130, 152, 153, 154–8, 161–3, 164, 165, 168, 171, 173, 177, 185, 192, 195, 202; *see also* 'Canon'
Mastery, 80–1, 87, 127, 152–6, 161, 162, 164, 165, 167, 171, 202, 206
Matisse, Henri, 202
Medici, Lorenzo de', 27, 41, 155
Melozzo da Forli, 195
Mengs, Anton Raphael, 124, 183
Metaphor, *see* Symbol
Metaphor, sources of, 11–15, 16–17
Metaphysics, 28–42, 48, 123–5, 145
Method, academic, 7, 16, 42–3, 47, 54–5, 57, 60–1, 83, 132, 133–4, 148, 187, *see also* 'Logic of Situations', Scientific method, 'Zero method'
Michelangelo, 15–16, 19, 58, 112–13, 144–6, 148, 151, 153, 154–5, 163, 164, 167, 168, 171, 178, 179, 181, 185, 187
Michelet, Jules, 40
Middle Ages, 22–3, 32–3, 36–7, 38–9, 41, 45, 48–9, 59, 68, 71, 82, 114, 118, 146, 162, 171; *see also* Gothic, Scholasticism
Millar, Sir Oliver, 146–7
Miltiades, 171, 173
Momigliano, Arnaldo, 36
Mona Lisa, 11, 14, 117, 192
Mondrian, Piet, 125
Montesquieu, Charles, Baron de, 26
Montgolfier, J. M., 185
Moore, Henry, 145

More, Thomas, 26
Morgan, William de, 177
Morris, William, 79
Motifs, *see* Ornament
Movement, historical, 49, 50–2, 61, 62, 68
Mozart, Wolfgang Amadeus, 16, 19, 84, 91
Museum, 8, 133–4, 185, 189–204
Music, 16–17, 20, 33, 56, 57, 67, 71, 84, 88, 89–91, 93–4, 96, 109, 119, 128, 130, 157, 158–9, 161, 199, 205–6
Myth, Nazi, 93–4, 96–7, 99, 101, 105–11
Mythology, 10, 11–12, 14, 15–16, 20, 93, 105–6, 107, 112–13, 153, 154, 156, 186, 187; *see also* Daedalus, *Judgement of Paris*

Nadel, George H., 24
Napoleon, 29, 194
'National Spirit', 30–4, 36, 39, 40, 42, 47, 50, 54; *see also Geistesgeschichte*, Hegel, 'Spirit of the Age'
Naturalism, *see* Realism
Naturalisti, 71
Nazism, 93–111, 130
Neoclassicism, 71, 76
Newton, Isaac, 136, 148
Nicaea, Council of, 21–2
Nicholas of Verdun, 171
Norm, departure from, 26, 62, 63, 69–71, 160

Objectivity, 16, 38–9, 40, 82, 84–5, 92, 125, 129–30, 138, 143, 144, 148, 150, 152, 157–8, 164, 169, 205; *see also* 'Problem Solutions'
Oratory, *see* Rhetoric
Ornament, 44, 49, 65, 77, 79, 116–17, 125, 127, 132, 135, 142–3, 147, 150, 154, 160–1, 175, 178
'Ossian', 87, 173

Painting, 10, 33, 36–7, 45–9, 72–3, 75–6, 79–81, 92, 124–6, 128, 130, 132, 139–40, 141, 144–9, 150–2, 156, 158–60, 161–2, 163, 167, 168–9, 173–5, 177, 183, 190, 194, 198, 200, 201–3; figs. 3, 4, 6, 8, 9, 10
Palissy, Bernard, 177
Panofsky, Erwin, 44–5, 188
'Paradigm', 184–5, 186, 187, 188, 190
Paranoia, 102, 106–7, 109, 110
Pastoral, 56
Patronage, 20, 27, 46, 134, 165
Pepys, Samuel, 144, 153
Perception, *see* Psychology, of perception
Perfection, 123–4, 125, 128, 145, 194
Periods, historical, 50–1, 61; *see also* Hegel
Personification, 105, 107, 111, 140, 143, 159–60; fig. 4
Perspective, 80, 147
Perugino, Pietro, 27, 155, 194
Petrarch, 119
Pevsner, Nikolaus, 132–3
Phillips, Claude, 174
Photography, 118, 121, 149–50
Picasso, Pablo, 78
Piero della Francesca, 180
Pietro da Cortona, 156
Piles, Roger de, 153, 171, 180
Plato, 15, 33, 67, 123
Platonism, 41, 54, 123–4, 125, 128, 143, 145, 182, 187
Plekhanov, Georgy Valentinovich, 178

Pliny, 194, 200
Plotinus, 44
Plutarch, 15
Poetry, 10, 11–12, 20, 33, 43, 48, 87, 119, 120, 128, 130, 143, 156, 158–9, 161, 205, 206
Polarizing issues, 69, 71–7, 79, 80–1, 87–8, 89–91
Polo, Marco, 26
Pompadour, Mme de, 169
Pope-Hennessy, John, 189
Popper, Sir Karl, 8, 15, 28, 54, 60–3, 67–8, 73, 77–8, 79, 82–3, 84–5, 89, 90–1, 92, 125, 135, 137, 143, 148, 183, 187, 206; *see also* Historicism, 'Logic of Situations', 'Problem Solutions'
Poussin, Nicolas, 84, 87
Precedents, 70–1, 135–6, 139, 153, 165; *see also* Tradition
Pre-Raphaelites, 16, 49, 172, 179
'Primitive' societies, 63, 69, 77–8, 79, 105
'Problem Solutions', 82, 112, 125–7, 128–30, 137, 138, 139, 141, 143, 148, 153, 186
Progress: 77–82; idea of, 27, 28–30, 33–4, 35, 39–41, 44, 79, 89–90, 185–6, 200
Propaganda, 7, 94–111
Proust, Marcel, 15
Psychedelic art, 56
Psychoanalysis, 13, 84, 88, 91, 103, 118, 165
Psychological warfare, 94, 103, 109
'Psychologism': term, 61
Psychology, 48, 55, 56, 64, 65, 70, 73–4, 77, 94, 103, 107, 118, 124, 132, 158, 165, 171, 188, 197, 206; of memory, 198, 204; of perception, 198–203; *see also* Cultural Psychology, Psychoanalysis
Pugin, Augustus Welby, 49
'Puritan style' of art, 77, 150, 153

Quaratesi, Andrea, 171
Quintilian, 68–9, 75, 91

Racine, Jean, 87
Radio, 14, 16, 93–111
Raphael, 16, 19, 44, 139, 172, 174, 179, 184
'Rarity game', 63–4
'Rationality principle', 62–3, 77–8, 79–80, 85, 92, 137, 159, 165, 186, 206–7; *see also* 'Logic of Situations'
Read, Sir Herbert, 192–3, 195, 196, 199–200
Realism, artistic, 40, 45, 46, 48, 49, 72, 76, 80, 81
Reformation, 17, 22, 30, 33, 40–1
'Regression', 107
Relativism, 7, 28, 32, 34, 82, 141, 145–9, 154, 156–8, 161–2, 164, 168, 172, 174, 178, 182
'Relevance', 7, 13, 16, 42, 43, 53, 74, 127, 132, 179
Religion, 11–12, 14, 16, 20, 21–2, 28, 29–34, 36–41, 43, 46, 48–9, 51, 52, 54, 70, 73, 77, 78, 79, 85, 96, 124, 127, 128, 130, 139, 140, 141, 153, 155, 162–3, 171, 174, 176, 194; *see also* Scriptures, Theology
Rembrandt van Rijn, 16, 44, 84, 87, 126–7, 156, 162, 173, 176, 197
Renaissance, 22, 27, 32–3, 36–42, 45, 51, 54, 55, 65, 71, 80, 112, 124, 137, 138, 155, 162, 177, 191, 193, 194, 195
Reni, Guido, 180

Repetition, 65, 70, 94, 99, 101
Research, 15, 53–5, 57–8, 61, 103, 112–16, 119–22, 133–4, 187–8
Resonances, cultural, 25–6, 55–6, 141, 163
Reynolds, Sir Joshua, 145, 179
Rhetoric, 12–13, 16, 26–7, 68–9, 156
Richard, Cliff, 14
Riegl, Alois, 43–4
Ripa, Cesare, 140
Ritual, 62–3, 78–9, 81, 85, 154, 157
Robbia, Luca della, 182
Rococo, 65, 71, 76
Roman arts, 17, 39, 44, 82, 137, 142–3, 162, 193, 205
Romanes, George, 142
Romano, Giulio, 187
Romanticism, 36, 39, 48, 71–2, 84, 90, 110, 146, 148, 182
Roosevelt, Franklin D., 95, 100, 101, 105, 108
Rosa, Salvator, 156
Roscoe, William, 27
Rosenberg, Alfred, 96
Rousseau, Jean-Jacques, 27, 87
Royal Society, 138–9, 140–1
Rubens, Sir Peter Paul, 10, 16, 84, 139, 144, 153, 154, 161, 168–9, 171, 180, 181, 182
'Rules' in art, 80–1, 125, 128, 153–4, 158, 171, 176, 202; *see also* Convention
Ruskin, John, 49, 138, 162, 182
Russell, Bertrand, 28

Scamozzi, Vincenzo, 136
Scanning, 102, 105, 199–200, 203
Schiller, F., 144, 164
Schlegel, Friedrich von, 194
Schlosser, Julius von, 114
Schnaase, Carl, 34
Schoenberg, Arnold, 90–1
Scholastics, 33, 44–5, 136, 186, 207
Schopenhauer, A., 28
Science, 13, 18, 20, 22, 56, 72, 77–8, 80, 83, 126, 148, 151, 165–6, 184–5, 188
Scientific method, 16, 54, 57–8, 83, 84–5, 112, 116–17, 126, 135, 141, 151, 171, 181, 184, 187, 188, 206–7
Scriptures, 30, 31–2, 47, 112, 163, 207
Sculpture, 33, 37, 44, 79–80, 145–6, 150, 152, 154, 156, 176–7, 182, 193, 194, 195–6, 199–200, 201; fig. 7
'Self-expression', 124–5, 129, 174–5
'Self-reinforcement', 84, 88, 89, 90, 161
'Self-transcendence', 125–30
Shakespeare, William, 14–15, 58, 71, 87, 118, 119, 120, 151, 201
Shaw, Bernard, 49, 128, 163–4
Sheldon, Archbishop Gilbert, 133, 134, 140, 166
Sheldonian Theatre, 131–7, 139–51, 154, 156, 159–60, 162, 163, 166, 167, 169; figs. 1, 2, 3, 4, 5
Sherman, General William T., 173
'Signs of the Times', 29, 37, 44–6
Skill, 26, 118–19, 123, 125, 127–8, 133, 139, 146–7, 149, 153, 154, 155, 158, 161, 162, 175–6, 182, 185–6, 191, 199, 201–2
Slogans, 72, 94–5, 96, 99, 107
Snow, C. P., 25
Social Sciences, 7, 25, 55, 57, 58, 60, 61, 73, 118, 131–2, 135, 138, 142, 149, 151, 152, 154–5, 159, 162, 164–5, 167, 186
'Social testing', 85–6, 88, 90

Sociology, *see* Social Sciences
Specialization, academic, 17–18, 20–1, 52, 57, 117, 134
Speech, *see* Language, Rhetoric
Speier, Hans, 96
Spengler, Oswald, 50
'Spirit of the Age', 28–34, 35–42, 42–51 *passim*, 54, 56, 60, 61, 62, 129, 194; see also *Geistesgeschichte*, Hegel, 'National Spirit'
Sprat, Thomas, 140–1
Staël, Mme de, 173
Stalin, Joseph, 103
'Standards', 65, 69, 79, 84–6, 88, 92, 127, 141, 143–9, 152–4, 157, 163, 168, 203; *see also* Beauty, 'Canon'
'Starting Point', 54, 86–7, 129, 135–6, 153, 165, 170–1, 180, 181, 200
Statistics, 53, 57, 116–17, 151, 155, 167, 186
Status Symbols, 10, 16, 178, 191, 192
Stein, Gertrude, 29
Sterne, Laurence, 26
Stoics, 15
Story of Art, 17, 151–2, 168, 171
Stradivarius, 182
Streeter, Robert, 139, 141, 144, 145–8, 149, 153, 154, 156, 159–60, 163, 167, 168, 178; figs. 3, 4
Stukeley, William, 136
Style, 42, 45–6, 48–51, 55, 56, 60–2, 69, 71–2, 76–7, 80, 92, 114, 123, 127, 133, 135, 136, 138, 143, 146–9, 153–5, 160, 164, 169, 186, 194, 206; *see also* Baroque, Gothic, Mannerism, Rococo, 'Jesuit style', 'Puritan style'
Stylistic relativism, 146–9, 154; *see also* Relativism
Subjectivity, 16, 20, 38, 39, 84–5, 103, 124–5, 126, 130, 143, 149, 152, 157, 161, 164, 171, 182, 205–7
Summerson, Sir John, 131, 132, 137, 138, 148, 156, 161
Surrealism, 186
Swift, Jonathan, 26, 73–5
Symbolism, 46, 134, 149, 186
Symbols, 10, 11, 12, 14–15, 19, 32, 47, 54, 55, 66, 77, 79, 97, 102, 110, 111, 113, 143, 159–60; *see also* Personification
'Syndrome', 47–9

Taborda, 100
Tacitus, 26–7
Taine, Hippolyte, 26
Tassi, Andrea, 194
Taste, artistic, 60, 61–2, 82–3, 85–6, 92, 133, 150, 161, 162, 165, 178, 186, 190
Tawney, R. H., 164–5
Technological approach to art, 146–7
Technology, 77–8, 79, 80, 81–3, 138, 146–7, 148, 153, 165–6
Theology, 21, 28, 41, 47, 118, 129, 140, 207
Thucydides, 15, 143
Tiepolo, Giovanni Battista, 156, 176
Titian, 112–13
'Top Ten' in art, 155–6, 157, 161
Totalitarianism, 50, 60
Tour, Quentin de la, 169
Tourism, 151, 154, 163, 164, 191–2, 197
Tradition: artistic, 65, 71, 79, 82, 125, 138, 139, 147, 153, 155, 176, 202; *see also* Convention, Style; cultural, 12, 18–19, 54, 55, 59, 86–7, 128–30, 135, 140, 142, 148, 149, 154, 156, 160, 164, 181, 187, 190–1, 207; *see also* 'Canon'; social, 65, 69–70, 77, 85, 154, 189; *see also* Precedents; of General Knowledge, *see* General Knowledge
Turner, Father Vincent, 123

Uccello, Paolo, 150

Value Judgements, 25–6, 29, 137–8, 144, 154, 163, 168–9; *see also* 'Canon'
Values, 7–8, 27, 29, 34, 58–9, 62, 65, 82, 88, 92, 113, 123–30, 138, 141, 143–4, 146, 155–7, 162, 163, 164, 165–6, 167, 169, 170–1, 178–9, 180, 182–3, 185–6, 205–6; financial, 16, 62, 144, 169, 178, 185, 191; *see also* Aesthetic Values, 'Canon', Objectivity, Relativism, Subjectivity, Value Judgements

Vasari, Giorgio, 26–7, 34, 37, 145, 155, 182, 194, 195, 200
Veblen, Thorstein, 178
Velazquez, Diego, 72, 197
Vermeer, Jan, 190, 195, 202; fig. 6
Vespasiano da Bisticci, 37
Vico, Giambattista, 26, 27
Virgil, 87
Visual Media, 206
Vitruvius, 136, 148
Voltaire, François Arouet de, 27

Waetzoldt, Wilhelm 197
Wagner, Richard, 16, 71, 89–91
Waley, Arthur, 158
Warburg, Aby, 20, 25, 43, 53, 119, 121
Warburg Institute, 9, 20–1, 25, 38, 53, 93, 121–2, 187
Waterhouse, Ellis, 146
Watson, Thomas, 12
Watteau, J.-A., 127
Weltanschauung, 41, 43–4, 46, 48–9, 134
Weltgeschichte: term, 40, 95–6
Whinney, Margaret, 146–7
Whistler, James McNeill, 169
Whitehall, Robert, 144, 153, 159–60, 163
Wilde, Oscar, 128, 182
Wilhelmina, Duchess of Luxembourg, 99–100
Wilkins, John, 140
Winckelmann, J. J., 27, 34, 71, 124, 183, 194
Wisden's Almanack, 12
Wittkower, Rudolf, 119
Wölfflin, Heinrich, 42, 114, 186, 187
Wolf, Hugo, 71, 88
Wren, Christopher, 131, 133, 134, 136–7, 138–40, 143, 144, 148, 149, 150, 151, 153, 154, 156, 161, 162, 167
Wright, Orville and Wilbur, 185

Yates, Dame Frances, 204
Yee, Chiang, 158

'Zero Method': term, 62, 68, 78, 79; *see also* 'Rationality principle'
Zeuxis, 173